A JUST FUTURE

A JUST FUTURE

GETTING FROM DIVERSITY AND INCLUSION TO EQUITY AND JUSTICE IN HIGHER EDUCATION

NIMISHA BARTON

CORNELL UNIVERSITY PRESS
Ithaca and London

First published 2024 by Cornell University Press

Library of Congress Cataloging-in-Publication Data

Names: Barton, Nimisha, author.
Title: A just future : getting from diversity and inclusion to equity and justice in higher education / Nimisha Barton.
Description: Ithaca [New York] : Cornell University Press, 2024. | Includes bibliographical references and index.
Identifiers: LCCN 2023055032 (print) | LCCN 2023055033 (ebook) | ISBN 9781501775390 (hardcover) | ISBN 9781501775406 (paperback) | ISBN 9781501775413 (epub) | ISBN 9781501775420 (pdf)
Subjects: LCSH: Racism in higher education—United States. | White supremacy (Social structure)—United States. | Social justice and education—United States. | Universities and colleges—United States—Sociological aspects. | Racial justice in education—United States.
Classification: LCC LC212.42 .B37 2024 (print) | LCC LC212.42 (ebook) | DDC 378.008—dc23/eng/20231229
LC record available at https://lccn.loc.gov/2023055032
LC ebook record available at https://lccn.loc.gov/2023055033

For my dad,

who taught me that standing up for what you believe in always pisses people off,

but sometimes you've just got to do it anyway

History is instructive, not because it offers us a blueprint for how to act in the present, but because it can help us ask better questions for the future.

—Mariame Kaba

Contents

ACKNOWLEDGMENTS

First and foremost, I owe a great debt of gratitude to Emily Andrew, my first editor at Cornell University Press. It was Emily who gave me the courage to take this project on and, even when she moved on to another press, continued to support me. I must also thank Bethany Wasik, my CUP editor who inherited the project, who cheered me on, and who managed to get this book past the finish line. My deepest thanks to you both.

I am so grateful to all those who volunteered their time and energy to describe their experiences doing movement work as college students in the sixties and seventies, and all those who discussed what it's been like pursuing equity in higher-education institutions over the last fifty years. Thank you not only for sharing your insights with me but also for showing up every day committed to fighting for students and communities.

I want to thank the following friends and colleagues for agreeing to read—and reread!—what were surely insufferable early drafts of various chapters: Michael Aranda, Jean Beaman, Ian Coller, Gen Creedon, Bridget Draxler, Regan Galvan, Sarah Horowitz, Andrea Lepage, Zitsi Mirakhur, Chandani Patel, Leslie Ribovich, Shelley Tochluk, Taylor Walle, Shannon Winston, and most especially Ronny Regev.

Thanks also to Cate Denial, Shelley Tochluk, and Trudi Wright, who were generous enough to make their book manuscripts available to me prior to publication.

A special shout-out to mentors and friend-tors near and far who have rooted for me along the way: Lourdes Andrade, LaTanya Buck, Rochelle Calhoun, Judith De Groat, Rachel Jean-Baptiste, Kerstin Larsen, Michelle Minter, Christy Pichichero, Trina Moore-Southall, Keith Shaw, Stephanie Tuccio-Reyes, Jeff Williams, Aaron Willis, and Pamela Wright.

Many others offered me love and support during difficult pandemic years: Catherine A-N., Danna A., Michael A., Jean B., Alexis C., Muriel C.,

Efthymia D., JP, Emmy and Tom G., Regan G., PPG, Randi G., Marina G., Matt G., Sarah H., Katie J., Nithya J., Tala K., Minayo N., Sarah R., Jackie S., Andrea and Patrick T., Katie W., and Ronny (again).

Mom, Dad, Anjali—thank you for believing in me when so often I can't.

Same goes for you, Matt. I'd tell you that nothing would be possible without you, but you already know that, don't you.

A JUST FUTURE

Introduction

The year 2020 exposed just how much trouble higher education is in—and diversity and inclusion efforts along with it. Certainly, the pandemic tested university leadership unlike ever before, but it also revealed with painful clarity the impact of wider structural inequalities on students from historically marginalized backgrounds. Many low-income students of color struggled to make the shift to online learning. Some had no privacy at home. Others had no Wi-Fi. Still others suffered from food insecurity and housing precarity.[1] While COVID-19 offered yet another reminder that our existing political and social systems fail to meet many people's basic needs, a savage series of high-profile murders of Black Americans in early 2020 cruelly demonstrated that some aren't even entitled to a life free of violence in this country. The public police lynching of George Floyd in May 2020 was the final straw, igniting waves of protest against the corrosive force of anti-Blackness in the United States. The historical conjuncture between a global public health crisis that took a disproportionate toll on historically marginalized communities and a national reckoning with the impact of systemic racism on people of color galvanized many college students and faculty on a scale not seen since the 1960s and 1970s. As they had decades before, students and faculty joined forces against a common foe. Above all, they demanded that higher-education leaders acknowledge how histories of white supremacy and systemic racism continue to shape higher education and academia more widely. In so doing, they laid bare the unfinished business of the civil rights era on college campuses and the limits of diversity and inclusion reform efforts to date.

In response to these joint crises, college presidents across the nation scrambled to meet the moment. Across the United States, higher education leaders crafted heartfelt messages of solidarity with communities of color. They convened DEI committees and task forces, drafted endless DEI strategic plans, and churned out hundreds of new diversity staff positions. But these most recent DEI efforts will founder without a better sense of the fraught history of higher education, the common obstacles we share, and the will to reimagine a new way forward.

I join a chorus of higher-education leaders, scholars, educators, and students in my call to return to the original social justice imperative of what has become known in today's colleges and universities as DEI. To do so, we must bravely confront a single unnerving truth: historically white colleges and universities (HWCUs)—that is, higher-education institutions created exclusively for wealthy white men by wealthy white men—were forged in the crucible of white supremacy, an ideology that justified the conquest, enslavement, and oppression of nonwhite peoples whom white Europeans deemed intellectually and culturally inferior.[2] Over time, HWCUs accumulated centuries of exclusivist traditions, structures, and practices. Consequently, they are suffused with what many sociologists of education have termed "institutional whiteness," meaning that their policies, practices, and cultures are deeply influenced by histories of race-based exclusion and oppression.[3] Until we can name white supremacy and until we are ready to combat institutional whiteness, HWCUs will remain utterly incapable of the kind of transformation they so badly need.

Higher-education professionals have more tools at their disposal to tackle systems of institutional oppression than ever before. In the first place, we enjoy a vast scholarship in fields such as education, history, sociology, and psychology, which gives us the analytic language necessary to describe the origins, operations, and impact of structural racism and institutional whiteness in HWCUs. Second, we've had decades to develop, experiment with, and even fine-tune different solutions to address obstacles to college access and success for historically marginalized students. Third, there is arguably more faculty interest in disruptive pedagogies, and thus greater commitment to ensuring equity in college classrooms, than ever before. Most significantly, though, we have the all-too-recent memory of summer 2020, which demonstrated just how quickly universities can act in the face of serious crisis. Our joint challenge, then, is to remember those lessons, to maintain momentum, and to hold steady in the face of the predictable backlash that always follows great bursts of social progress in this country.[4]

I wrote this book because I have a unique perspective that allows me to see clear continuities that run through the past, present, and future of higher education. Trained as a historian, I can't help but view our world as a product of what those who came before us have built and, at times, destroyed. I also believe that for better or worse, we are inheritors of those legacies and are responsible for confronting them. As a college educator, I've seen firsthand how students from first-generation, lower-income backgrounds, most of whom are students of color, struggle academically and socially at today's HWCUs. Finally, as an equity practitioner who has worked both inside and outside educational institutions, I know that most higher-education leaders, staff, and faculty truly crave both analytical and practical tools to help them navigate our tumultuous era. And they want these things because they care about their students. Writing as a scholar, an educator, and a practitioner allows me to marry research with reality, and in so doing to imagine ways we can get closer to a more truly democratic and even liberatory vision of higher education.

In this book, I focus on selective HWCUs. White supremacy runs deep in HWCUs, so, naturally, institutional whiteness appears there in its most concentrated form. Selective HWCUs, then, are where histories of white supremacy and cultures of institutional whiteness collide with the compositional diversity of today's multiracial student body, creating a perfect storm for campus unrest. And while I focus on selective HWCUs, these analyses are broadly applicable to higher ed because, with the exception of tribal colleges and historically Black colleges and universities (HBCUs), the policies and procedures, recruitment and retention practices, and course structures and curricula of most four-year colleges and universities in this country were patterned off of those institutions that preceded them.

Though this book is informed by recent scholarship, my intention is not to produce a scholarly tome. Rather, I aim to offer college educators, diversity practitioners, and higher-education leaders a resource, a cipher, and a new set of frameworks that will help us chart a path through a situation of the utmost urgency. Certainly, I synthesize a wealth of existing scholarship. I do so because I often wished for a resource like this when I first began my career in the field of DEI. To get a sense of how institutional equity work has evolved, I've also conducted interviews with participants in the Black campus movement who went on to lead multicultural centers, affirmative action offices, and minority affairs offices in the 1960s, 1970s, and 1980s. I spoke, too, with practitioners from the 1990s, 2000s, and 2010s who occupied, and who in some cases continue to occupy, a variety of DEI roles, from student-facing program administrators and director-level program managers to executive-level leaders responsible for broader institutional equity efforts. Speaking with different generations of diversity officers allowed me to trace the arc of antioppression work in institutions, to see what has and hasn't changed, and to suggest what we need to do to get back on track. Altogether, then, this book reflects my own professional experiences as a researcher, educator, and equity practitioner.

Without a doubt, as you read, you'll see that I'm influenced by multiple, overlapping, sometimes conflicting ways of thinking pervasive in twenty-first-century social justice worlds.[5] Abolitionist thinking in particular guides my analysis. At base, abolitionists focus on the structural conditions in our society that cause harm and that incentivize people to commit harm. To be sure, abolitionism as dreamed into existence by activists of color, community organizers, and public intellectuals past and present has a very distinct set of goals: an end to policing, mass incarceration, and other forms of state violence, to name just a few. I have no desire to co-opt an ideology with such a specific intellectual lineage, genealogy, and meaning. That said, I am deeply influenced by abolitionist modes of analysis because of the focus on relationship building that contributes to community, justice, and transformation; the commitment to creating a world that values everyone's dignity; the dedication to creative experimentation; and the willingness to stumble, learn from our mistakes, and try again. Indeed, there's a common misconception that abolitionism is a destructive project, but nothing could be further from the truth. Rather, abolitionism is constructive, generative, creative, and imaginative.[6] And it is in that spirit that I offer up this book.

Transformation on the scale that I'm interested in requires fundamental shifts in mindset. First we must understand that equity and justice work is not the responsibility of the few but of the many. Any college or university that proclaims solidarity with antiracist movements and support for marginalized students, staff, and faculty in institutional mission statements, brochures, and other university-wide messages implicitly acknowledges that everyone in its employ is a diversity practitioner. In other words, every college president and administrator, every faculty member and student leader belonging to a higher-education institution with a clearly articulated commitment to the value of diversity is, by virtue of their affiliation with the university, responsible for DEI work on campus. It's time to start seeing DEI as everyone's work, not just because it should be but because it is.

Second, we must free ourselves from the old narratives that limit and constrain us. Indeed, when it comes to DEI work, we're often reminded that change takes time. But the pandemic put paid to that myth. COVID-19 showed us that even the most traditional HWCUs could shift on a dime. Resource-rich selective colleges and universities, in particular, managed to adapt quickly and weather the storm. As such, COVID-19 provides a useful, if brutal, example of how fast institutional change can take place. It's a reference point that we've never had before, and it serves as a reminder that, as underresourced colleges that serve the vast majority of first-generation and low-income students struggle, resource-rich HWCUs have a greater responsibility to educate all. As we'll see, they also have an inarguable obligation to help eliminate the societal inequalities in this country that they've had a hand in creating over the centuries.

This book starts by acknowledging how deep white supremacy runs in HWCUs. Like the United States itself, HWCUs were built on stolen Indigenous land and on the backs of the enslaved. They were funded through the profits made from the illegal sale of appropriated lands and the trade in enslaved persons (chapter 1). HWCUs were centers of knowledge production whose scholars churned out pseudoscientific drivel about the cultural, intellectual, and biological inferiority of women, Jews, and nonwhite peoples. And they were sites where elite white Christian men learned their place in society, as masters of the earth and inheritors of a world made in their image (chapter 2).

It wasn't until the 1960s and 1970s that students of color were numerous enough on predominantly white campuses to mount a challenge to the white-supremacist status quo. With the support of a multiracial coalition, students of color, and Black students especially, forced HWCUs to engage in rapid radical change. They demanded the racial and ethnic diversification of the student body through targeted outreach and recruitment efforts. They demanded that HWCUs hire more faculty of color and dismiss openly racist white faculty. They demanded alternatives to a wholly Eurocentric curriculum. In short, they made it abundantly clear that they would no longer tolerate white-supremacist institutions that condoned the racist mistreatment of people of color

In spite of significant gains, the progressive moment turned out to be just that—a moment. Reagan-era whitelash reared its ugly head in the 1980s. In response to the rightward shift in US culture, diversity officers, too, shifted gears. They learned to speak less about dismantling institutional racism and oppression. In keeping with the times, they instead learned to celebrate multicultural difference of all varieties, divorced from a wider sociopolitical framework. They learned to speak "happy talk," inflected by the "feel-good" accents of diversity to make their once-revolutionary work more palatable to folks who were tired of hearing about it.[7] In so doing, HWCUs returned to what Angelina Castagno terms "power-blind" analyses that again obscured the very white supremacy and institutional whiteness that the civil rights era had only so recently dragged into the light. This was the dawn of what James Thomas calls the diversity regime, an ideological framework that fetishizes "difference" rather than attending to how systems of power impact communities in distinct ways, affording more advantages to some over others (chapter 3).[8]

These are the legacies that today's diversity practitioners inherit. Under a power-blind diversity-and-inclusion framework that's more interested in celebrating difference than in fighting structural oppression, diversity practitioners often find themselves reduced to minority managers: that is, staff who manage identity-based crises on behalf of predominantly white institutions. That's particularly the case for student-facing diversity staff who work closely with undergraduates. Chief diversity officers feel the pressure too, but in different ways. Not only are senior DEI leaders highly visible institutional representatives and thus subject to increased scrutiny like any other senior administrator, but in moments of campus crisis they must mobilize their moral legitimacy and political credibility with students in order to shield the institution from the consequences of its own inaction. Regardless of where exactly they're placed in the university hierarchy, then, all diversity practitioners functionally bridge gaps between historically marginalized students and predominantly white institutions in ways that relieve HWCUs of the responsibility to engage in much-needed institutional change (chapter 4).

Institutional whiteness poses a formidable obstacle to diversity officers, but so, too, do other factors. As we'll see throughout, diversity practitioners are limited in terms of what they can accomplish when they are located exclusively in student affairs divisions. Nowadays, administrators frame DEI as a student life issue, but the college classroom is the beating heart of the university, and that makes faculty critical to institutional transformation. For a number of reasons, there was an unfortunate parting of ways between diversity practitioners and faculty that started around the 1990s. Consequently, two parallel DEI paths emerged, one focused strictly on what happens inside the classroom and another focused on everything that happens outside the classroom. Over time, diversity practitioners and faculty stopped speaking the same language and started fighting different struggles separately from one another. Part of the work ahead, then, is to reestablish those relationships, because history tells us that faculty can—and do—serve as diversity officers' most powerful allies.

In order to serve as effective partners, faculty need new frameworks to help them navigate today's culture wars. I argue that we must adopt a historical lens that centers structural oppression and systemic inequality to help us see how seemingly "neutral" concepts like quality, merit, rigor, freedom of speech, safe spaces, trigger warnings, and so on are anything but. Once we reframe student failure as institutional failure, more faculty might be willing to examine what they teach and how they teach it. They may even be open to experimenting with liberatory pedagogies that get us closer to equity in the college classroom than current iterations of inclusive teaching ever could (chapter 5).

This book uses a particular set of analytic frameworks to reexamine and make sense of the current DEI landscape in higher education. But it also points to concrete models that already exist and have a proven track record of supporting the college success of historically marginalized students. For instance, for more than half a century, officers of scholars programs have developed effective blueprints for curricular and cocurricular support infrastructure for first-generation, low-income students that resource-rich institutions can and should emulate (chapter 6). And in many ways, scholars programs are just the tip of the iceberg. There are endless possibilities for experimentation and transformation at the institutional level when we allow reparative frameworks rooted in abolitionist thought to guide us in institutional equity efforts (chapter 7).

No doubt, it is a daunting task I set before us. But there is value in thinking big, imaginatively, and free of constraints. At best, it fires the imagination, it encourages creative experimentation, and it illuminates a path forward. It's my hope to provide higher-education leaders, diversity practitioners, and college educators with the ideas, resources, and inspiration necessary to work together toward a shared vision. The past can never be undone. But it can be faced with humility, courage, and resolve in the here and now.

CHAPTER 1

Origins

In 1823, Chief Justice John Marshall breathed new life into a medieval European principle that had already radically changed the face of the North American continent. Writing for the majority opinion of the US Supreme Court, he declared that the doctrine of discovery, a papal bull issued in 1455, would serve as law of the land in the United States. The doctrine of discovery intellectually and religiously justified European colonial endeavors from the fifteenth century onward. It "permitted" the Portuguese monarchy to seize West Africa. It was among the first principles of international law that Christian monarchs of Europe adopted with the express aim of laying claim to lands and peoples beyond Europe.[1] Nearly four hundred years after a Catholic edict provided cover for European kings and queens who sought to consume a world they could barely even imagine, the US Supreme Court invoked that very same doctrine to expand its dominance over a continent it had acquired through force and deception. Though few of us can imagine it, colleges and universities played an enormous role in this process.

To tell the story of modern colleges and universities is to shed light on the darkest corners of our nation's past. It is to tell the story of white settler colonialism and Atlantic slavery. Colleges and universities—like this very nation itself—stand on stolen land, acquired through deceit, predation, violence, and warfare.[2] They also have shockingly deep ties to the institution of slavery: nurturing it, maintaining it, and manufacturing knowledge to sustain it. In the words of Craig Steven Wilder, the first five colleges in the British American colonies—Harvard (established 1636), the College of William and Mary (1693), Yale (1701), Codrington in Barbados (1745), and the College of New Jersey (1746)—"were instruments of Christian expansionism, weapons for the conquest of Indigenous peoples, and major beneficiaries of the African slave trade and slavery."[3] This chapter, then, is not merely a prehistory to the story of exclusion and marginalization that will be recounted throughout the rest of the book. It is a grappling with the very grounds on which our entire higher-education structure—and this nation—were founded.

Colonial Colleges: The Third Pillar of Conquest

Although American national mythology holds that Europeans conquered a vast and "savage" wilderness, many found instead what they recalled as a "disease-free paradise." Scholars such as Roxanne Dunbar-Ortiz have reconstructed the continent as it once was under the stewardship of Indigenous peoples. The portrait she paints is one of a Northern American landscape replete with well-maintained gardens, wide grazing lands, and sophisticated trade routes.[4] In 1804, the ethnologist Dale Lott, who accompanied Lewis and Clark on their western expedition, observed with wonder the world he saw before him, remarking that it was "not a wilderness but a vast pasture managed by and for Native Americans."[5] Disembarking on the shores of this "virgin" continent, Europeans did not, in other words, find a world in ruin, as I myself was taught. Rather, European explorers, merchants, soldiers, and priests found complex Indigenous societies with advanced agricultural and political systems, societies that had created what, in their minds, approximated a veritable Garden of Eden. In due time, however, Indigenous societies in this so-called New World would succumb to disease, violence, and devastation brought on by European invasion and settler colonialism.

Settler colonialism is a system of imposed power that defines who land belongs to, that extracts from the land, and that dispossesses any others from said land in the process.[6] In the famous words of Patrick Wolfe, it is a structure, not an event, an ongoing reality, not a bygone relic of the past.[7] Settler colonialism defines the early history of the

United States, but it did not arise in a vacuum. For some time, European elites had set their sights on the peasantry in their own lands, seeking to bring them under the control of landed masters. England, in particular, had a wealth of experience with dispossession and colonization projects at home that it later exported abroad. As the English conquered Ireland throughout the seventeenth century, they forced the "opening" of newly acquired northern territories to resettlement by western Scots. Though England had previously conquered and assimilated Scotland and Wales, never before had they attempted to remove Indigenous inhabitants and resettle new populations as brazenly as they did in Ireland. In many ways, as Dunbar-Ortiz has written, "although the Irish were as 'white' as the English, transforming them into alien others to be exterminated previewed what came to be perceived as racialist when applied to Indigenous peoples of North America and to Africans."[8] Europeans brought their signature land lust to the so-called New World. And while they were supported by religious and military authorities, education soon came to serve as an auxiliary tool in their endeavors.

In these early days, churches and forts announced the European military and spiritual presence in the Americas. But colleges, universities, and institutes came fast on their heels. As early as the 1500s, Spain began raising universities in the Americas—Dominican, Franciscan, and Augustinian seminaries in Mexico and Christian order universities in Lima, Santo Domingo, and Medellín—modeled on Spanish universities. They offered faculties, featured academic divisions with full courses of study, and conferred degrees. A century later, seventeenth-century English colonists also sought to establish centers of learning, which stretched from Virginia to Massachusetts. Patterning colonial higher education on the Oxford and Cambridge academic model, British settlers established residential colleges including Harvard and William and Mary. These institutions appeared within the first decades of settlers' arrival in the British colonies of North America. Thus, while it is not always apparent to us today, the founding of institutions of higher education in the Americas served a critical imperial purpose: to manufacture knowledge about the Americas and its peoples that justified their conquest.

College leaders dabbled in early efforts to educate Native Americans. Centuries before, the English had used the establishment of colleges to exert a political and cultural influence in newly conquered Scotland and Ireland. In the British Americas, the English church and state drew heavily on this legacy to facilitate colonial campaigns. In the 1670s, two Indian graduates of Harvard served as translators and emissaries to Chief Metacomet of the Wampanoag and Narraganset peoples in his communication with the English.[9] Educating Indians served as a way to facilitate English imperial expansion in the Americas. The English also raised colleges among the colonists to ensure that the growing confederacy did not get too carried away with ideas of self-government, which, as we know, it eventually did.[10]

Perhaps even more important than political considerations, religious motivations drove seventeenth- and eighteenth-century Europeans to conquest. In the early 1600s, King James I was reminded of his divine mission to spread Christianity far and wide. He subsequently ordered that a "College be erected in Virginia for the conversion of the Infidels."[11] He was not alone in his missionary zeal. An English education was to aid in the expansion of European influence on the North American continent through the spread of the Christian faith.[12] Wealthy British elites were very excited about the opportunity to tame "native savages." The prospect of Christianizing "exotic" Indians inspired colonists and English donors alike to matriculate the sons of Native American chiefs in "Indian schools" at Dartmouth, Harvard, Princeton, and William and Mary, among others.[13]

Indian schools became a standard feature of many early colonial colleges.[14] In 1655, the first Indian College appeared in Harvard Yard. In fact, it was the first building constructed on campus. Located in the historic epicenter of what has become Harvard University, the Indian College was a two-story building equipped with study chambers, halls, and boarding rooms for twenty students.[15] Before the American Revolution, three of nine colonial colleges sought to educate Natives, an effort that featured even in the mission statements of Harvard, the College of William and Mary, and Dartmouth. Indeed, Dartmouth's founding charter boasted that the university was founded "for the education and instruction of youth of the Indian Tribes in this Land in reading, writing and all parts of Learning which shall appear necessary and expedient for civilizing and Christianizing Children of Pagans well as in all Liberal Arts and sciences and also of English Youth and any others."[16] Together, early colonial colleges enrolled approximately forty-seven Native students in the course of the seventeenth and eighteenth centuries. Just four graduated.[17]

In addition to land lust and religious zeal, cultural arrogance fueled European conquest. As Europeans enrolled Natives in their colonial colleges, they necessarily devalued and disregarded Indian forms of education. Native communities had developed education traditions that were incomprehensible to white settlers. There were no schools per se, which is to say that formal schooling did not take place in designated buildings. Instead Indigenous peoples taught lessons to their youth adapted to their specific way of life. Naturally, these lessons varied from tribe to tribe. We often obscure the extent to which early settlers relied on Indian knowledge of agriculture, medicine, and other areas in those first encounters. But Indigenous knowledge existed and even saved European settlers from famine, starvation, and disease. How else did early settlers learn to till this unfamiliar soil? From whom did they learn the potent medicinal effects of certain herbs and plants?[18]

For Native students, the "opportunity" to receive a Christian education came at a significant cost. Students had to dress like young Englishmen, eschewing their native dress if they left their rooms. Their "grooming and comportment," according to Craig Steven Wilder, had to reflect standard norms for English gentlemen. They were "required to think and speak in the language of imperial Europe," and as a result, "the hegemonic language of the Europeans displaced native languages and their attendant values and ideas." Many felt a gnawing sense of dislocation, preferring never to return home to their communities now that they no longer shared the same culture, traditions, and values. In truth, it was a two-way street. Indian fathers scarcely recognized these English gentlemen who returned home.[19] Native access to a European education cannot, then, be severed from the expectation that they would forfeit their culture, their way of life, and perhaps their communities altogether.

Many tribal elders were understandably reluctant to send their sons to colonial colleges. Benjamin Franklin recorded a reply from a Six Nations chief to an offer made by Virginia representatives to educate their young men. This was the chief's cheeky response:

> Several of our young people were formerly brought up at the colleges of the Northern Provinces; they were instructed in all your science; but when they came back to us, they were bad runners; ignorant of every means of living in the woods; unable to bear either cold or hunger; knew neither how to build a cabin, take a deer, or kill an enemy; spoke our language imperfectly; were therefore neither fit for hunters, warriors, or counselors; they were totally good for nothing. We are however not the less obliged by your kind offer though we decline accepting it: And to show

our greatful sense of it, if the gentlemen of Virginia will send us a dozen of their sons, we will take great care of their education, instruct them in all we know, and make men of them.[20]

In documenting the defects of English-educated young Native men, this chief suggested the overall deficiencies of both an English education and its products: young white men. These were the sort of deficiencies that, he claimed, only a *Native* education could address.

In the end, Indian schools didn't actually last very long. Within a few years of their establishment, the ongoing violent clashes between European settlers and Indians suggested to college leaders that Natives were not yet ready to be "civilized." In 1693, Harvard administrators decided that the Indian College could simply be put to better use, as Natives were a lost civilizational cause. The building was soon razed and the bricks of the erstwhile college sold for twenty pounds.[21] Still, the brief life of the Indian College is revealing. Its construction coincided with an early belief in the European imperial civilizing mission; its demise indicated a general move away from seeing Natives as having the potential to be civilized.

Indeed, colonial institutions of higher education functioned as part of a wider strategy of colonial domination, furnishing both the soldiers and the ideology for these campaigns of destruction and then profiting from ill-gotten gains. Colleges churned out soldiers who participated in early colonial wars against Indigenous societies. Harvard students participated in the Pequot War (1636–38), helping fellow New Englanders burn Pequot food supplies. Harvard College even acquired two thousand acres of land after the Pequot War, demonstrating the multiple ways that colonial colleges stood to gain from these violent wars of conquest.[22]

Colonial colleges also produced increasingly racialized discourse about degraded Natives that drove its leaders and alumni to wage war against them. During the French and Indian War, for example, the Reverend Samuel Finley, later the president of the College of New Jersey (now Princeton University), encouraged parishioners to join in the holy Protestant struggle against so-called heathens. The Reverend Samuel Davies, who would follow Finley as president of the College of New Jersey, raised an army in Virginia to thwart "the savage Tyranny of a mongrel Race of French and Indian Conquerors."[23]

By 1750, going to college signified prestige and high social status among the settlers of the British colonies. As John Thelin has written, "The purpose of colleges was to identify and ratify a colonial elite" and "[transmit] a relatively fixed social order."[24] As Thelin puts it succinctly, colleges were "neither egalitarian nor democratic."[25] Colonial colleges were very much founded with the express intent of educating the white race, and wealthy white men at that. Colonial colleges served as one means by which early white American men became socialized into the new racial order that placed Natives at the bottom of a civilizational hierarchy.

As they contributed to the new world order and took their place as victors in it, colleges proudly displayed the vestiges of what colonial settlers hoped would become a vanishing race. Faculty, students, and administrators decorated their campuses with Indian bones and artifacts. Dartmouth, for example, eagerly solicited donations to expand its collection of Indian remains. This was a far cry from the Dartmouth that had once sponsored an Indian College, though both efforts relied on a fundamental belief in the inferiority of Native peoples. In the nineteenth century, colleges continued to display Native remains and other "human curios," as Amherst leaders called them.[26] Many would later expand their collections to include the body parts of enslaved African and African-descended men and women.[27]

While wars of conquest provided land for colleges and universities during the colonial period, after the American Revolution, treaties became another effective tool of Indian dispossession.[28] By 1871, the US government had concluded 371 such treaties with various Indigenous nations, ceding approximately two hundred million square miles of land to the United States. While some of these land cessions were effected through treaties, much land was amassed through explicit breach of contract. After 1871, as part of the Indian Appropriation Act, Congress refused to even negotiate such contracts anymore. Rather, the United States unilaterally asserted that Indigenous groups held no sovereignty and, as such, that the US government could make laws with or without their participation or consent.[29] By appealing to manifest destiny—that is, the God-given right to push westward and populate the continent with white Christian settlers—the government relied on a manufactured "need" to displace and eliminate Native Americans, a displacement and elimination carried out through coercive and fraudulent treaties.[30]

It was against this background that we see the appearance of the Morrill Act in 1862. Often referred to as the Agricultural College Act, the Morrill Act established land-grant universities on appropriated Native land.[31] Sponsored by Representative Justin Morrill from Vermont and signed by Abraham Lincoln, the Morrill Act aimed to stimulate economic development by expanding access to higher education to white men of lesser means, particularly the sons of the rising agricultural and industrial classes.

The sale of lands provided seed money for many HWCUs, raising the endowment principal for fifty-two institutions. As Robert Lee and Tristan Ahtone have reported, "The money provided interest income, inspired gifts and boosted local economies," making the Morrill Act the kind of "gift that keeps on giving." Today those endowments would total up to nearly half a billion dollars.[32] Lee and Ahtone have further pointed out that "according to the Morrill Act, all money made from land sales must be used in perpetuity, meaning those funds still remain on university ledgers to this day," adding, "at least twelve states are still in possession of unsold Morrill acres as well as associated mineral rights, which continue to produce revenue for their designated institutions."[33] In other words, land-grant colleges continue to benefit from the money made off of the dispossession and sale of Indian lands and all the advantages the land provides. Thus, whether through seizure or treaty, land-grant universities dispossessed Indigenous groups of millions of acres of land and turned a profit along the way. This profit continues to provide enduring funds for many of today's most prestigious colleges and universities.

FIGURE 1.   Painting commemorating the Morrill Act. This college building in Kansas was one of the first created under the 1862 Morrill Act.
Source: Architect of the Capitol, 1993–1994, Westward Expansion Corridor, Cox Corridors.

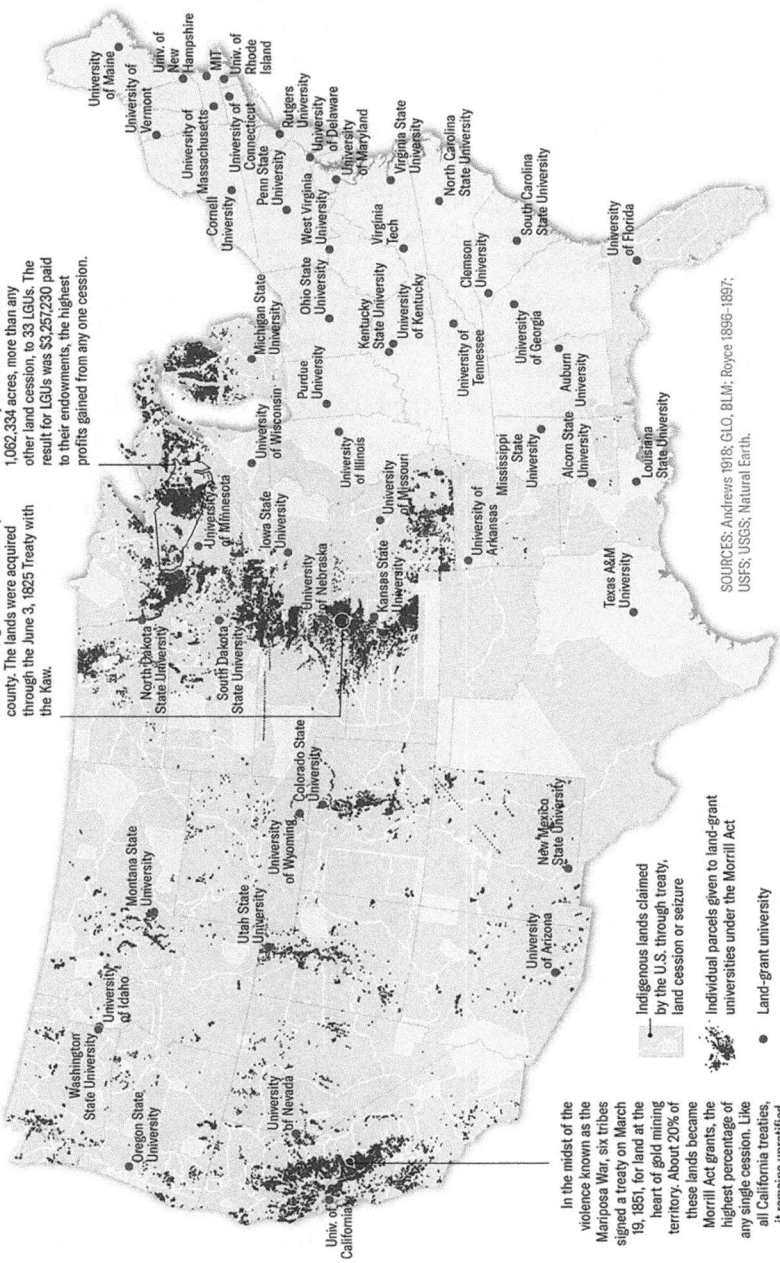

In Gage County, Neb., 40% of the land was given to Morrill Act parcels, the second highest amount of any county. The lands were acquired through the June 3, 1825 Treaty with the Kaw.

The Treaty of 1837 contributed 1,062,334 acres, more than any other land cession, to 33 LGUs. The result for LGUs was $3,257,230 paid to their endowments, the highest profits gained from any one cession.

In the midst of the violence known as the Mariposa War, six tribes signed a treaty on March 19, 1851, for land at the heart of gold mining territory. About 20% of these lands became Morrill Act grants, the highest percentage of any single cession. Like all California treaties, it remains unratified.

University of Maine
Univ. of New Hampshire
University of Vermont
MIT
Univ. of Rhode Island
University of Massachusetts
University of Connecticut
Rutgers University
University of Delaware
Cornell University
Penn State University
University of Maryland
West Virginia University
Virginia State University
Michigan State University
Ohio State University
Virginia Tech
North Carolina State University
Kentucky State University
University of Kentucky
Clemson University
South Carolina State University
University of Wisconsin
Purdue University
University of Tennessee
University of Georgia
Auburn University
University of Florida
University of Illinois
University of Missouri
Mississippi State University
Alcorn State University
Louisiana State University
University of Minnesota
Iowa State University
University of Arkansas
Texas A&M University
North Dakota State University
University of Nebraska
Kansas State University
South Dakota State University
Colorado State University
New Mexico State University
Montana State University
University of Wyoming
Utah State University
University of Arizona
University of Idaho
University of Nevada
Washington State University
Oregon State University
Univ. of California

Indigenous lands claimed by the U.S. through treaty, land cession or seizure

Individual parcels given to land-grant universities under the Morrill Act

Land-grant university

SOURCES: Andrews 1918; GLO, BLM; Royce 1896-1897; USFS; USGS; Natural Earth.

FIGURE 2. Land-grant universities funded by the Morrill Act. The Morrill Act gave 79,461 parcels of Indigenous lands, totaling about 10,700,000 acres, to fifty-two land-grant universities to fund their endowments.

Source: Map by Margaret Pearce for *High Country News.* https://www.hcn.org/issues/52.4/indigenous-affairs-education-land-grab-universities.

Of course, even before the passage of the Morrill Act, many land-grant colleges and universities had existed. Among the private colleges, these included Brown, Cornell, Rutgers, and MIT. State colleges included today's universities of Georgia, Tennessee, Delaware, Michigan, Missouri, Wisconsin, Minnesota, Florida, Louisiana, and Vermont.[34] But the Morrill Act vastly expanded their numbers. After 1862, the Morrill Act permitted the establishment of state universities in Massachusetts, Kentucky, Maine, New Hampshire, Illinois, California, West Virginia, Nebraska, Arkansas, Ohio, and Nevada, as well as new agricultural and mechanical arts colleges in Colorado, Mississippi, Kansas, Oregon, Indiana (Purdue), Texas, Alabama, and Virginia.[35] Moreover, eastern states benefited from this westward expansion too, making a tidy profit off of Indian land dispossession.[36]

What were the consequences of the Morrill Act? In the end, it redistributed eleven million acres of Indigenous land across twenty-four Western states.[37] And there is enough evidence to suggest that white settlement increased in the West as a result.[38] As Lee and Ahtone have

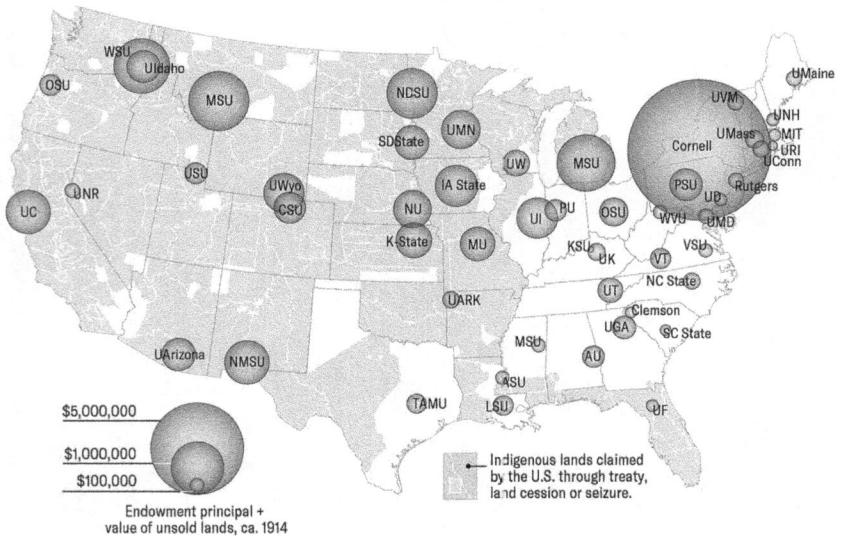

SOURCES: U.S. Office of Education 1906; Andrews 1918; GLO, BLM; Royce 1896–1897; USFS; USGS; Natural Earth.

FIGURE 3.   University endowments funded by land grants. Land-grant university endowments benefited when their acreages were sold and the proceeds invested.
Source: Map by Margaret Pearce for *High Country News*. https://www.hcn.org/issues/52.4/indigenous-affairs-education-land-grab-universities.

Cornell University	977,909
Pennsylvania State University	776,514
Ohio State University	614,325
University of Illinois	477,710
Purdue University	380,600
University of Tennessee	301,243
University of Kentucky	281,123
University of Missouri	270,613
North Carolina State University	269,977
University of Georgia	269,651

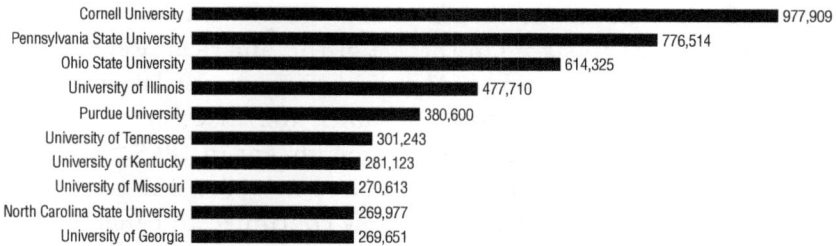

FIGURE 4.   Top ten land-grant university recipients of Indigenous land by acreage.
Source: Chart by Margaret Pearce for *High Country News*. https://www.hcn.org/issues/52.4/indigenous-affairs-education-land-grab-universities.

argued, "There would be no higher education as we know it in the United States without the original and ongoing colonization of Indigenous peoples and lands, just like there would be no United States. . . . There is no moment or time or place or institution that is not deeply entangled with the violence of colonialism."[39]

Hallowed Halls, Poisoned Roots

In North America, colleges and universities were built on Indigenous land, and they were built on the backs of the enslaved. Higher education expanded at the same time as the African slave trade reached its peak (the 1780s). While there had been but a handful colleges in the colonies in the 1750s, by 1800, there were twenty-five degree-granting colleges in the United States. By 1820, that number had more than doubled. What that meant was that by the 1800s, there were more people of African descent in the United States than Indigenous populations throughout all of North America, a grisly testament to both the scale of devastation suffered by Native communities and the magnitude of the trade in enslaved persons.[40]

Although much of our national mythology casts the institution of slavery and attendant anti-Black racism as a singularly Southern sin, it was not in fact restricted to the South. Throughout the eighteenth century, the trade in human beings remained vibrant in the North. It led to demographic shifts in northeastern college towns such as New Haven, Connecticut; New Brunswick, New Jersey; and Cambridge, Massachusetts, where the number of African and African-descended people increased. Wealthy white families in Princeton and New Brunswick owned enslaved persons. By the 1780s, one in five residents of New Brunswick was enslaved; in Princeton, one in six.[41] On the eve of the American Revolution, 20 percent of the population of New York City were enslaved people. Abolition did not come to New York until 1827. New Jersey waited until the passage of the Thirteenth Amendment in 1865.[42] In Massachusetts, the institution was abolished in 1783. But even after its abolition, the local Boston economy continued to benefit from Caribbean trade networks. Banks considered the enslaved property, an indication of enslavers' personal wealth, and treated them as collateral when it came to loans.[43] In spite of what we may have been led to believe, slavery, as an institution, was alive and well in the North in the eighteenth and early nineteenth centuries.

College and university trustees and presidents were intimately involved in the burgeoning slave economy of the colonial Americas. In 1782 the trustees of Liberty Hall in Virginia leased Black workers to supplement their budgets, thereby enriching the university's endowment through the trafficking of enslaved people.[44] In 1784, the new board of trustees for King's College (now Columbia University) were all slaveholders and included some of this nation's founders, such as Alexander Hamilton.[45] The first president of Rutgers University once owned Sojourner Truth.[46] The first eight presidents of the College of New Jersey (now Princeton University) were all slaveholders.[47]

University presidents, faculty, and especially students at Harvard, Yale, and Princeton often brought their slaves with them to their colleges. There, the enslaved lived in kitchens, in president's houses, or in "slave quarters" throughout campus.[48] They were responsible for keeping the colleges running smoothly.[49] They built classrooms, cooked, tended to the campus grounds, cleaned the latrines, and even staffed the brothels of our nation's most "venerable" institutions.[50] The enslaved toiled away on these campuses in life, and some were laid there to rest in death. The University of New Hampshire, once one of the largest slaveholding colleges in the colony and in the state, buried both enslaved and free Black laborers in its college cemetery.[51]

University coffers swelled thanks to the profit turned from the sale of human beings. Slave labor funded William and Mary from its very founding in 1693.[52] The enslaved constructed the University of Virginia and Rutgers University.[53] At Yale, money earned from slave trading funded fellowships, professorships, and library endowments.[54] Indeed, early chroniclers of colonial colleges remarked on the "conspicuous presence of bound people."[55]

Over the next century, universities would continue to accumulate wealth both directly and indirectly through the trade in enslaved persons. In 1826, "Jocky" John Robinson entrusted 73 enslaved men, women, and children to the university that would become Washington and Lee, stipulating that the college could hire out the laborers in order to raise funds (see photos below).[56] In the 1830s, Georgetown sold 272 enslaved men, women, and children to Southern plantation owners in Louisiana in order to keep the institution's doors open.[57]

As more schools cropped up, competition for money generated by the slave economy grew. While initially supported by British donors and colonial elites, colleges were soon on the lookout for additional sources of income. In the second half of the eighteenth century, US colleges set their sights on Southern donors. Over time, they increasingly depended on these wealthy plantation owners, enslavers, merchants, and financiers for support.[58] When King's College (Columbia) first opened its doors in 1754, it enrolled "more children of Atlantic traders

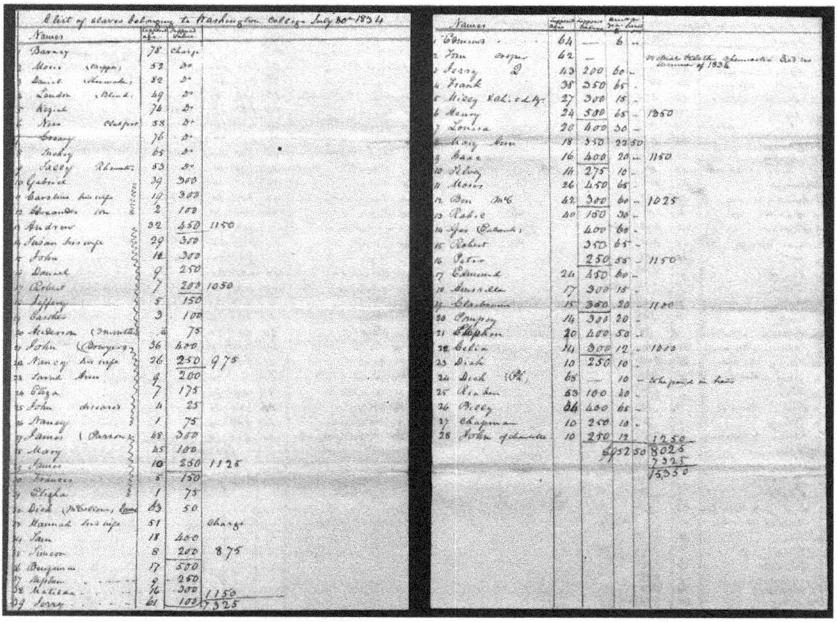

FIGURE 5. "A list of negroes belonging to the Estate of John Robinson recd at death time," 1827. List of names, ages, appraised values, and other details of the eighty-four enslaved men, women, and children hired out to the townspeople of Lexington, Virginia, by what was then known as Washington College. The document also indicates how much each enslaved person was hired out for.
Source: Historical marker on the Washington and Lee University campus. Photo by the author.

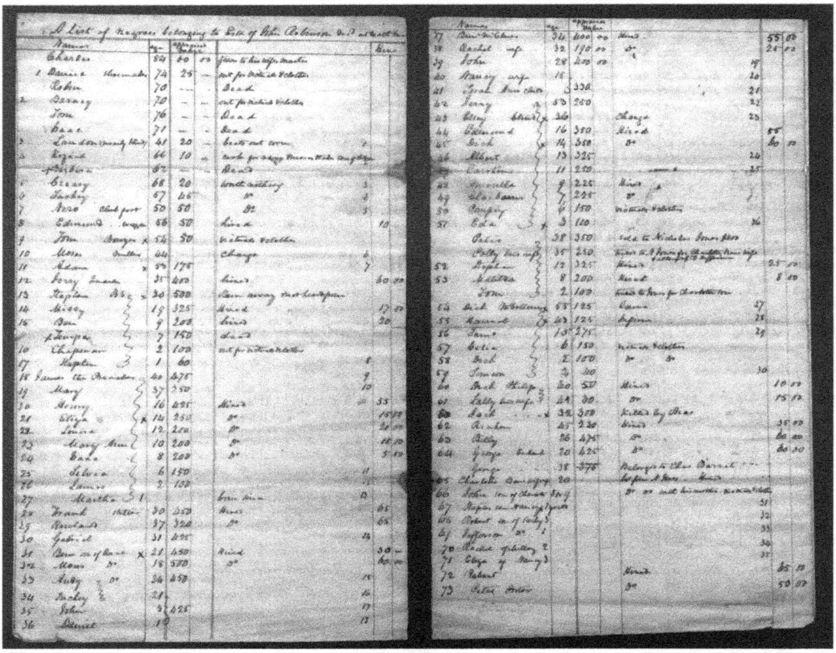

FIGURE 6. "A list of slaves belonging to Washington College," 1834. While the first page of this document lists the names, ages, and values of enslaved persons belonging to Washington College, the second page is a list of twenty-eight enslaved persons hired out and the annual income they produced for the college.
Source: Historical marker on the Washington and Lee University campus. Photo by the author.

than any other college in British North America," according to Wilder.[59] Forty percent of undergraduates at Princeton (famously described as the nation's "most pleasant country club") came from slave states during the early Republic. In due time, Harvard, William and Mary, Yale, Philadelphia, King's College, Queen's College, Rhode Island, and Dartmouth found themselves in a veritable bidding war for the sons of wealthy slave-owning families.[60] They sought to enroll these white sons of privilege in order to build relationships with wealthy Southern slave-owning families. As colonial colleges reoriented away from British donors, they came to depend increasingly on wealthy plantation families and the Southern merchant class. In the process, colleges extended the social and cultural influence of enslavers into the North and into the realm of higher education.[61]

Until the twentieth century, higher education functioned as a sort of finishing school for white Christian slave-owning gentlemen. As John

Thelin observes, they were, after all, meant "to inherit grave responsibilities as leaders and men of influence in a new world."[62] Throughout the eighteenth and nineteenth centuries, they developed their own distinctive culture characterized by "elite dress, argot, symbols, and affiliations," a general "collegiate code" to which young white men who attended these schools adhered.[63] As a result, these Southern sons brought their own notions of mastery and domination to the unfree—and free—Black communities they found in the North.

Acculturated into the violent and dehumanizing world of slavery, many white male college students created a hostile climate for enslaved persons in colleges and universities. The hostility was rooted in their perceptions of Southern white masculinity, which asserted "honor" as central to maintaining their racially superior masculine identities. They protected their fragile egos by bullying those whom they considered inferior, especially the enslaved.[64] Though it was frequently presidents, staff, and faculty who had brought their enslaved to college campuses in the North, white male students expected these slaves to do *their* bidding. The issue of "too many masters" soon emerged. William and Mary, for instance, had to expressly define for students what they were and were not allowed to ask enslaved persons to do for them, suggesting the liberties that students must have taken with enslaved persons on college campuses.[65]

Young college men used the unfree for their amusement, forcing them to satisfy their desire for entertainment through boxing, singing, dancing, and fiddling. At Williams College, white students paid an enslaved man to repeatedly bash his head into wooden barrels. Sometimes the purpose of this abuse was explicitly to sow terror. In 1772, a Columbia student attacked a slave; the attacker later became a trustee.[66] In 1811, at the University of North Carolina, drunk white students rioted, firing guns at an enslaved child and assaulting for sport other slaves they came across. To protect themselves, the enslaved developed expert conciliation skills, using any means at their disposal to avoid violence, harassment, and abuse.[67] These episodes serve as a reminder that elite white male socialization in the colonial and antebellum United States centered on Black dehumanization. And these colleges and their cultures served as training grounds for the powerful positions "too many masters" would later come to hold.

Following graduation, alumni played a major role in every major institution in colonial society—from the church to commerce to lawmaking and nation-state building. During the colonial period, for example, graduates went on to participate directly in the Atlantic slave trade. This was the case for many Harvard graduates who pursued careers as slave traders in the Caribbean slave trade.[68] Early colleges and universities also graduated many clergy members who would play influential roles in pushing theological racism in the moral life of the colonial United States. In 1701, Harvard graduated twenty alumni who became slave-owning religious leaders in the Northeast. As spiritual leaders in New England, they led by example, normalizing the institution of slavery among their congregants. Their influence grew as they ministered to the spiritual needs of burgeoning populations in large colonial cities such as Boston, Charlestown, and Cambridge.[69] Alumni of these colleges served as the ruling colonial elite in British America. They were politicians, lawmakers, and judges. They brought the values and lessons in which they had been schooled into their future professions. And as alumni returned to the South or moved out west, they brought those lessons in racist brutality along with them.

Faculty played an enormous role in these students' socialization, teaching them the principles of race science that many alumni would implement in their chosen professions. Notions of race that had reigned in the colonial period were soon supplanted by a certainty in African primitivism and an unshakeable belief in Africans' racial inferiority.[70] In the 1850s, a Harvard faculty member took daguerreotypes of enslaved men and women to provide photographic evidence of the inherent inferiority of people of African descent and the superiority of the white European race.[71] These acts and others demonstrate the extent to which faculty members participated in the advent and promulgation of the new race science.

Nowhere was the marriage between scientific racism and the right to access the bodies of the enslaved more evident than in the origin story of this nation's medical colleges. After the French and Indian War (1754–63), medical colleges multiplied. With Western medical science ascendant, physicians, surgeons, and doctors sought to expand their empire of knowledge about the workings of the human body. Medical colleges thus required corpses on which they might practice their surgical arts. Early on, they experimented on the cadavers of poor whites, but such forensic forays soon stirred controversy within a republican nation that increasingly imagined white bodies as inviolable, even those of vagrants and criminals. Black bodies were another story.

In the first medical college in the British colonies, faculty acquired the body of an enslaved man who had committed suicide.[72] The

Philadelphia medical school set a grisly precedent. Colleges' hunger for corpses only grew, leading their faculty to increasingly experiment on the bodies of the unfree. King's College (Columbia) acquired Black bodies directly from "Negro burial grounds" in Manhattan. Other colleges employed grave robbers to snatch up corpses from burial grounds for poor Blacks.[73] Anatomical dissections of Black enslaved bodies became the norm. Some medical college faculty even displayed a sick fascination with dehumanized Black bodies. A Dartmouth physician peeled the skin off a cadaver, boiling the flesh in order to access the skeleton. He later tanned the skin of this man, using it to dress his instrument case.[74]

These macabre assaults on the corpses of the unfree brought prestige to universities that competed for dominance in the sciences. Such competition led to a horrifically impressive accumulation and cataloguing of human remains in the new sciences of craniometry (the measurement of human skulls) and phrenology (assessments of character and mental ability based on skull shape and size). At the University of Pennsylvania, the anthropologist Samuel Morton assembled some 867 human craniums over the course of his lifetime, many belonging to enslaved persons from the United States and Cuba.[75] Based on his studies in craniology, Morton advanced a theory that ancient Egyptians were "Caucasoid," whereas their slaves were "Negroid." He thus argued that white enslavement of Black people had ancient roots, propping up the institution of chattel slavery during his lifetime. In memory of the acclaimed scientist, the *Charleston Medical Journal* wrote of him in 1851, "We can only say that we of the South should consider him as our benefactor, for aiding most materially in giving to the negro his true position as an inferior race."[76]

Critically, slave owners, planters, land speculators, and Atlantic merchants sponsored scientific research at colleges and universities, making colleges veritable "distribution points" of proslavery ideas and, in the decades prior to the Civil War, a hotbed of proslavery activity.[77] At the University of Virginia, faculty generated slave tracts filled with proslavery theory and philosophy. They taught these ideas to their students.[78] Southern academics, embedded as they were in local slave society, were at the forefront of intellectual production that sought to prove the moral rightness of slavery. Many produced histories of slavery that focused on its economic benefits. They found justifications for slavery in constitutional and political theory, demonstrating its basis in religion and the emerging race science.[79] At Emory, these texts formed part of the curriculum for students. There, faculty framed slavery as a benign paternalistic institution.[80]

As race science went mainstream, faculty took on increasingly public roles in the dissemination of proslavery ideas. They held public discussions and debates, bringing their proslavery facts and fictions into the public sphere. Agents of law and justice gradually came to rely on their so-called expertise on matters of race.[81] They fashioned themselves into what Wilder calls "the racial guardians of the United States."[82] At a time when race science was on the rise, faculty participated in the reimagining of US citizenship and belonging on decidedly racial—and downright racist—terms. These white supremacist ideas were not confined to the ivory tower. Through graduates, alumni, and public intellectuals, these notions spread far and wide, undermining the basic humanity of nonwhites throughout the nation along the way.

Unsurprisingly, colleges and universities emerged as the epicenter of secessionist debates in the Civil War years. Many academics, especially in the South, argued in favor of secession. As before, they took their academic claims to the public to demonstrate the rightness of the institution and its centrality to Southern life. They also proposed new arguments. In the eighteenth and early nineteenth centuries, most Americans had argued that slavery was good for republican governments; by the 1840s and 1850s, Alfred F. Brophy demonstrates, arguments shifted to the notion that "slavery is good for the enslaved."[83] According to the new scientific racism, natural hierarchies among peoples made some more "fit for freedom" than others.[34] The emerging science could thus mollify the conscientious and provide talking points to counter abolitionist arguments.

By the mid-nineteenth century, colleges served as a conservative force, maintaining the racialized political and social order in the antebellum United States. Nowhere was this more evident than in their role in thwarting abolitionism. While the period did witness a decline in slaveholding among faculty and administrators, overall colleges emerged as antiabolitionist spaces.[85] Students and graduates of these universities who dared to voice abolitionist ideas became outcasts and pariahs on college campuses.[86] Though some may have managed to form antislavery societies on campus, doing so insulted the Southern gentry who bankrolled these institutions, making college leaders nervous about their future financial prospects.[87]

Rather than support the growing abolitionist movement, students, faculty, and university administrators were more likely to throw their lot in with the American Colonization Society (ACS), an organization founded in 1816 by white religious leaders, politicians, educators, and so-called antislavery advocates. Members advocated for the resettlement of African-descended peoples in Liberia in order to avoid the prospect of a multiracial American future. Seven out of eight Ivy League institutions endorsed African resettlement schemes.[88] Furthermore, the ACS engaged in activities that would prevent the establishment of free Black colleges, part of a larger tendency to hinder the development and advancement of African and African-descended peoples in the United States.[89]

There were a tiny handful of exceptions. Oberlin, for example, stood out as one of very few abolitionist college communities during the antebellum period that welcomed students who opposed slavery. But Oberlin was the exception that proved the rule. Princeton was, by contrast, more representative of nineteenth-century colleges. According to Craig Hollander and Martha Sandweiss, by 1840, "the Princeton gentleman" increasingly saw abolitionism as a "greater threat than slavery to the survival of their beloved republic." Princeton administrators supported this view, making Princeton "an increasingly conservative institution" throughout the 1830s, 1840s, and 1850s. After the Civil War, university leaders continued to try to appease both abolitionists and slaveholders among their student body. They did so mainly by avoiding the topic of slavery altogether. Much later, they would continue to seek a middle ground on the subject so as not to offend the families of their wealthy white, Southern, male student body. In the early 1920s, Princeton erected a monument inscribed with the names of all students who fought in the Civil War. The university president, however, refused to clarify which side they fought for.[90]

The Past Is Never Past

It's easy to write all this off as unpleasant stories of a bygone past, one that bears little resemblance to our present. But to this day, colleges and universities continue to grapple with centuries-long legacies of dispossessing Indigenous groups, extracting the labor of enslaved persons, and manufacturing the intellectual underpinnings of scientific racism. Every few months, we learn that some university or another is holding on to the remains of Indigenous peoples. In 2022 alone, these reports surfaced at Harvard, the University of North Dakota, the University of Kansas, the University of Alabama, and others.[91] In January 2023,

ProPublica launched a searchable database of federally funded institutions that still hold Native remains. UC Berkeley topped the list with nearly ten thousand bones and bodies of Indigenous peoples that have yet to be returned to their tribes.[92]

And it's not just relics from the "distant" past that HWCUs hoard. In 1985, local police in Philadelphia bombed a neighborhood occupied by MOVE, a Black liberation group. Over a dozen people were burned alive, including children. In April 2021, it came to light that the remains of two of those children had been housed for decades in a cardboard box on some dusty shelf of the Penn Museum of Archaeology and Anthropology. Their parents were never informed and certainly never consented. At some point at the turn of the century, the bones of these two children were used by Princeton faculty as instructional material in an online forensic anthropology class. This took place as recently as 2019.[93]

If you're anything like me, you may find it hard—intellectually and also emotionally—to wrap your mind around the idea that higher education promoted racism and settler colonialism. This is certainly not what I learned in high school. Looking at this nation's past through the perspective of those who were willfully silenced and, worse yet, exterminated forces us to confront ugly truths. But we must acknowledge how our institutions came to be in order to understand the legacies they've left behind. Settler colonialism and anti-Blackness run deep in today's colleges and universities and have given rise to racist institutional traditions, practices, and cultures that endure still. As we'll see next, early violence against Natives and African and African-descended persons laid the foundation for ongoing exclusions on the basis of race, gender, religion, and ethnicity in the centuries to come.

CHAPTER 2

Whitelash

In the centuries before and after this nation's founding, higher education was the exclusive right of elite, white Protestant men. From the late nineteenth century on, however, that began to change. Wealthy white women increasingly attended women-only colleges and coeducational institutions. Similarly, with the early twentieth-century immigration wave to the United States, Jewish students of eastern European origin gained more access to selective colleges and universities. Yet, as they entered these higher-education spaces, they elicited significant backlash. In this, we see the beginnings of a pattern that would repeat itself throughout the twentieth and twenty-first centuries—namely, that new *inclusions* provoke broad-based backlash leading to new *exclusions*.

Nowhere was this dynamic of inclusions and exclusions more obvious than in the efforts to deprive Black and Native Americans of a college education. Legally denied an education since the founding of this country, many Black Americans hungered for higher learning after emancipation. Some circumvented white-supremacist institutions entirely by establishing their own colleges and universities after the Civil War. Others tried their luck at segregated HWCUs in the North. But for both Black men and the small handful of Black women in HWCUs, education came at a serious psychosocial cost, not to mention constant threats of physical violence and harassment. To some extent, Native Americans were "spared" such a fate, but only because federally funded and government-run schools had so thoroughly failed to meet the most basic educational needs that few ever made it to college to begin with. Those that did were expected to assimilate to white Christian American culture, an echo of what Native students had experienced in colonial colleges hundreds of years earlier.

World War II should have been a massive turning point. Certainly, the 1940s and 1950s witnessed an enormous expansion in college going, but it was primarily white working-class men who benefited. Some Native and Black veterans attended college, but institutions began to take measures to keep them out, for instance implementing quotas that had first been developed in the early twentieth century to limit the enrollment of Jewish students of eastern European origin. As a result, the undergraduate body expanded monumentally in the decades after World War II but without diversifying appreciably. It was not until federally mandated desegregation efforts in the late 1950s that this situation began to change.

This chapter traces how new inclusions over the course of the twentieth century led to backlash in the United States, thus inscribing new exclusions in higher education.[1] While we start with the educational journeys of white women and Jews of immigrant origin, we must pay special attention to the trajectories of Native and Black Americans, as they experienced the greatest systematic, state-sanctioned exclusion from education in the history of this country. Importantly, it was African American men and women who bore the brunt of what Carol Anderson has called white rage—the white American response to Black achievement and progress in this country. The backlash they experienced, then, was motivated by anti-Black racism and white supremacy. It was, in a word, whitelash.[2]

Backlash

Even as the nineteenth century gave way to the twentieth, the majority of college students remained wealthy white Protestant men, the American aristocracy. But elite white women had made solid gains. Since the 1700s, many wealthy white women could count on receiving a thorough European education abroad.[3] Others attended women-only institutions in the British colonies that were, like Indian colleges, short lived.[4] Although some wealthy white women had been able to pursue college-level work in antebellum colleges and seminaries, few, if any, actually received degrees.[5] But by 1840, the tide had turned. White upper-class and middle-class women enjoyed increasing access to formal higher education. By 1860, some forty-five collegiate institutions had allowed white women into their establishments. In 1870, eleven thousand white women were enrolled in colleges; by 1880, forty thousand; and by 1900, eighty-five thousand.[6]

What accounts for this rapid expansion in access to higher education for monied white women? Throughout the nineteenth century, the white middle class had begun to use higher education to distinguish themselves from the middling and working-class poor. As had been the case for white American men, attending college thus became a status symbol that signaled their wealth, position, and readiness for the womanly duties of republican citizenship, defined as white wifehood, motherhood, and other domestic concerns (indeed, gendered ideas of Black womanhood and their "femininity" were understood by white America very differently than those for white women).[7] As a result, women-only colleges proliferated between 1880 and 1920.

Women's colleges, or "the Seven Sisters," as they were known, were exclusively for wealthy and middle-class white Protestant women whom these colleges, according to John Thelin, were to make "confident, affluent, poised young women who brought to the women's college all the advantages of wealth, academic preparation, and social graces."[8] Wellesley, Radcliffe, Mount Holyoke, Smith, Vassar, Barnard, and Bryn Mawr would eventually inspire the founding of Mills College in Oakland, Sophie Newcomb College in New Orleans, and Agnes Scott College in Georgia. While in some ways we might consider these institutions wealthy white women's finishing schools, they did nevertheless represent significant gains for white women in the realm of education. Though coeducation offered possibilities, in reality coed institutions remained few and far between in the nineteenth century. Indeed, it was not until the 1960s that the longest holdouts finally went coed, and even then it was to better appeal to their traditionally all-male, mostly white student body.[9]

Always at the vanguard of higher education, Oberlin distinguished itself as the first coeducational college. There, white women received a classical education like their male peers, but they also received what J. Brent Morris calls "instruction on etiquette and refinement." They were subject to a curriculum that placed a strong emphasis on moral and religious education, training in domestic science and economy, and preparation for careers in teaching.[10] Essentially, coeducational institutions sought to prepare women to take on roles as angels of the hearth who would train the next generation of virtuous US citizens.[11] In other words, the late nineteenth-century swing toward coeducation, despite drastically increasing women enrollees, was less radical than it may at first seem.

Even limited progress in the domain of white women's education was met with backlash. As white women's enrollment in colleges and universities soared between 1880 and 1920, male onlookers began to voice moral anxieties. They worried that a collegiate education would "unsex" white women, rendering them unfeminine and unfit for marriage. And they grew distraught at the idea that, worse yet, women's colleges might promote lesbian relationships. Other critics bemoaned the "invasion" of white women on college campuses, which they compared to the so-called Yellow Peril—a racist construct of the white imagination that construed East Asian, and especially Chinese, immigrants as a threat to the white racial purity of the United States.

In the wake of a late nineteenth-century crisis of American masculinity, new fears about coeducation came to the fore. Some worried that women distracted their male counterparts from serious study.[12] By contrast, others fretted about the possibility that proximity between the sexes might feminize American men. As women began to academically outpace their male peers at colleges such as Berkeley, Cornell, and Michigan, many took umbrage at the implicit challenge to male intellectual supremacy that white women represented.

To counter these dreadful outcomes, college faculty and administrators introduced certain measures. They segregated classes by sex, prevented white women from enrolling in certain men's classes, and implemented ratio restrictions to ensure that white men predominated in academic settings. Some even founded separate female campuses to sequester white women from white men before they could exert their feminizing influence on them. This is, for example, the origin story for Barnard College, the "sister" school to Columbia University, as well as Radcliffe at Harvard, Jackson at Tufts, and Sophie Newcomb at Tulane.[13]

White women on coed campuses had their fair share of difficulties—a reminder that the right to higher education has long been understood as limited to white men. At coed schools, women reported that they experienced gender- and sex-based harassment, segregation, tracking, and exclusion from extracurricular organizations.[14] Though women's colleges and coeducation certainly chipped away at the notion of womanly intellectual inferiority, that didn't mean women were ready for the full rights of citizenship enjoyed by white men—in universities or beyond their gates. Again, white women were afforded an education only because they had a critical role to play as moral influencers, winsome wives, and republican mothers in the United States. Access to a full curriculum was thus deemed unnecessary for them.

We often speak of the nineteenth- and twentieth-century expansion of higher education for "women" writ large. But, as I've sought to make clear above, this so-called expansion was limited to elite and middle-class *white* women. In the main, poor and working-class white women and most women of color, especially Black women, were unaffected. As a result, the story of their entry into US higher education differs substantially from that of white women.

In addition to class, race posed a nearly insurmountable obstacle to a college education for Black women. Before the Civil War, just a few universities admitted Black women: Oberlin (founded in 1833), Antioch (1853), Wilberforce (1856), all in Ohio; Hillsdale (1844) in Michigan; Cheyney (1837) and Lincoln (1854) in Pennsylvania; and Berea (1855) in Kentucky. Still, the very notion of Black women's education incited white violence throughout the United States. In 1833, Prudence Crandall opened a school for Black girls that was subsequently destroyed by white mob violence.[15]

Even on those campuses where Black women were admitted, they could expect to be housed in separate campus dormitories and dining halls, to be forbidden to pursue campus leadership positions, and to be tracked into so-called "appropriate majors." On the one hand, that they were pushed into less academically challenging courses paralleled what white women experienced in college.[16] On the other hand, because of the long history of sexualized racism in this country, Black women were forced to contend with other curricular challenges.

While women's education overall emphasized the importance of middle-class respectability, the curriculum for Black women underscored the virtues of chastity and purity that were rooted in slavery-era stereotypes. Black women in higher education were responsible for countering the cliché of the jezebel, an image conjured up during slavery to naturalize the sexual predation of Black women by white slave-holding men. This curricular emphasis reversed the historical truth, blaming Black women for inciting the passions of white men when it was really white men who subjected Black women to extreme sexual violence. Lessons in respectability for Black women were thus rooted in deeply racist ideology.[17]

Racism haunted Black female students on white college campuses. Edmonia Lewis, of African American and Chippewa ancestry, started at Oberlin in 1859. White students accused her of poisoning two classmates and stealing art supplies—both false accusations. In response, they physically attacked Lewis. Her white peers viciously beat her and were never called to account for their behavior. Even in spite of Lewis's eventual exoneration, Oberlin refused to confer a degree on her.[18] To avoid provoking the fury of white students as Lewis did, most Black women learned to keep their heads down and their noses in books. In other words, they learned to silence parts of their humanity in return for a postsecondary education.

Women-only colleges were hardly much better. The Seven Sisters were unforgivably slow to admit Black women. In the 1930s, Barnard imposed a quota of two Black girls per year.[19] Where Black women were refused admission, racist ideology thrived. The founding president of Bryn Mawr, for one, was not shy about voicing her belief in Anglo-Saxon superiority, and she withheld admission from Black women during her tenure. Bryn Mawr would not grant Black women degrees until 1930.[20] When Black women did manage to attend these colleges, it was often on account of their racial ambiguity: for instance, being so light-skinned that they could inadvertently "pass" as white. Among the Seven Sisters, the first avowedly Black woman graduated from Vassar only in 1940.[21] For the most part, then, Black women would have to find other ways to achieve an education.

The combination of racism and sexism that Black women have endured in this country, both then and now, should never be underestimated. One devastating statistic captures this historical truism. Between 1882 and 1898, fifty Black women were lynched in the United States, at least three of whom were clearly pregnant. In the words of Stephanie Evans, "Statistically, for every five black women who had graduated with a college degree by the turn of the twentieth century, one black woman had been lynched."[22] Thus, while it is true that wealthy white women faced obstacles to a college education, they faced nothing on the order of what Black women endured every day.

In considering the expansion of education for white American women and an extremely limited number of Black women, we see the cycle of inclusion, backlash, and exclusion. We also cannot ignore that white women occasionally played a part in that vicious cycle. Though many white women experienced barriers to entry in higher education, Black women's experience of exclusion was compounded by their race. Certainly, white women aroused the ire of their male peers for daring to challenge male supremacy.[23] But many white women visited precisely the same violence on their Black female peers for daring to challenge white supremacy.

In the early twentieth century, the US public school system expanded dramatically. Consequently, elite colleges admitted increasing numbers of public school students for the first time. Although colleges and universities had long relied on what we would now recognize as "feeder schools" (Exeter, Lawrenceville, Philips Academy, and so on), the doors to higher education were slowly opening to other prospective students. Because this period also coincided with a substantial rise in immigration to the United States, Jews of eastern European origin especially were the unexpected beneficiaries of increasing access to higher education.

More and more students from immigrant backgrounds attended these schools, reflecting their greater presence in the US. The number of Jewish students of eastern European origin swelled on college campuses in the early twentieth century. Jews accounted for 7 percent of incoming students to Harvard in 1900, 15 percent in 1909, and 21.5 percent in 1915.[24] But once again, their growing numbers provoked a backlash that fundamentally reconfigured our modern admissions system in ways that persist to this day.

Growth in the matriculation of Jewish college students took place against a rising tide of political and cultural conservatism in the United States. Years of anti-immigrant sentiment, the prominence of scientific racism, and the thriving eugenics movement culminated in the Immigration Act of 1924, which prevented the migration of Asians, southern Europeans, and eastern European Jews to the United States. The intensification of nativism coincided, too, with the resurgence of the Ku Klux Klan, members of which renewed their emphasis on white Anglo-Saxon national identity. In this context, all immigrants, especially non-white immigrants, suffered.

In an era when the racial category of "whiteness" was still being consolidated, eastern European Jews were widely considered racial and social "undesirables." As their numbers multiplied, college and university administrators began to worry that so many Jewish students would upset their chief constituents and primary donor base—namely, white Anglo-Saxon Protestant (WASP) families. In a sense, admissions to elite institutions abided by a market logic: by keeping higher education exclusive to the WASP sons and daughters of elite and middle-class white families, colleges were assured a steady income. To offend these stakeholders was to risk grave financial consequences. In this, we hear an echo of how college presidents and administrators wooed Southern sons to keep their colleges afloat in the antebellum years, as well as how they sought to maintain a campus atmosphere conducive to these young white men so as not to displease their wealthy slaveholding families.

At the start of the twentieth century, college admissions depended on one's academic performance on a standardized test, but admissions criteria shifted sharply with the rise of a high-performing Jewish student body. Colleges and universities introduced applicant intake forms asking would-be students to identify their race, mother's maiden name, and religion—demographic data that served as a blunt instrument for weeding out so-called racial undesirables and Jews especially. Admissions criteria also began to de-emphasize straightforward academic performance in favor of hard-to-pin-down perceptions of "character" and "leadership."

As they introduced these new sociocultural admissions criteria to keep Jews out, colleges substantially lowered their academic standards, creating what Jerome Karabel has described as "a student culture largely hostile to academic exertion."[25] Twentieth-century institutions of higher education focused instead on recreating the atmosphere of pomp and privilege to which their students were so accustomed. They emphasized social status and hierarchy through eating clubs, extracurricular activities, and sports, many of which excluded Jewish students.

Soon, college admissions criteria ensured quite pointedly that the wealthy sons of alumni (now called "legacies") had the opportunity to attend the same elite schools as their fathers and grandfathers.[26] And of course, as descendants of recent immigrants, few Jewish students could claim such a thing. Overall, then, in order to exclude Jewish students, the college admissions process, as well as the wider campus culture, devalued academic achievement and instead placed greater emphasis on what Karabel calls an "all around" man of "sturdy [Christian] character, sound body, and proper social background" with the racial qualifications to match.[27] These were coded terms that ensured that access to higher education would remain limited to wealthy white, Protestant men.

The 1920s was the definitive decade during which the modern college admissions system as we know it took shape. It was 1926 that saw the arrival of the Scholastic Aptitude Test (SAT). The SAT began as a World War I–era IQ test created by two "intelligence scientists," one of whom, Carl Brigham, taught at Princeton. In general, nonwhite immigration, including that of Jews from eastern Europe, spurred the appearance of this new field of pseudoscience. In 1923, Brigham published *A Study of American Intelligence*, in which he asserted that "the Nordic race group" was intellectually superior to all others. Further, he argued, "the decline of American intelligence will be more rapid than the decline of the intelligence of European national groups, owing to the presence here of the negro."[28] It's true that Brigham would withdraw his more explicitly eugenicist claims by the time he developed the SAT, but he hardly abandoned his belief in white superiority. If anything, we might think of Brigham as a conduit by which eugenicist ideas, once shorn of more distasteful claims to biological inferiority, could go mainstream. To put it quite bluntly, the history of the SAT is steeped in histories of xenophobia, racism, and antisemitism, much like the US higher education system more widely.

The SAT represented one post–World War I gatekeeping tool, but selective universities, such as Columbia, would grow bolder still. Located in New York, the home of the second-largest Jewish population in the country, Columbia was among the first universities to witness the rise in its Jewish student population. Administrators sought a so-called solution to the "Jewish problem" and in 1910 established its first Office of Admission expressly to limit the matriculation of Jewish students and even impose quotas on Jewish applicants.

To address the rising number of Jewish applicants, Columbia admissions officers creatively discouraged Jewish applicants from applying to Columbia. Instead they nudged Jewish would-be students toward the Seth Low Junior College, an extension of Columbia located in Brooklyn. This was the experience of Isaac Asimov, who, in 1935, was denied admission to Columbia but was encouraged to consider Seth Low. As Asimov later recalled, "The interviewer didn't say something that I eventually found to be the case, which was that the Seth Low student body was heavily Jewish, with a strong Italian minority." He added, "It was clear that the purpose of the school was to give bright youngsters of unacceptable social characteristics a Columbia education without too badly contaminating the elite young men of the College itself by their formal presence."[29]

Though Columbia led the way in pioneering an exclusivist admissions process, Harvard, Princeton, and Yale soon followed suit. By 1926, Harvard had adopted an admissions system that required not only demographic information but also a personal essay and a list of extracurricular activities demonstrating character and leadership. Women's colleges were no exception. In the 1930s, Sarah Lawrence implemented a strict quota system to limit the number of Jewish women admitted.[30] Eventually, colleges and universities adopted the practice of interviewing prospective students in order to gauge how well they conformed to appropriate standards of dress, speech, attire, and etiquette becoming of Ivy League gentlemen. This widespread practice served as yet another means of identifying and eliminating Jewish applicants from the rosters.[31] To circumvent their chronic exclusion from higher education, Jews would eventually establish a few of their own institutions, including Brandeis in 1948.

As with the proslavery movement, faculty and college leadership played a large role in imparting antisemitic values to their students. A. Lawrence Lowell, a professor of government at Harvard and a Harvard alumnus himself, supported immigration restrictions during this period, especially from southern and eastern Europe. Lowell even served as the vice president of the Immigrant Restriction League in Boston. As Harvard University president in the 1920s, Lowell tried to expel Black students from campus. Today he is remembered by his alma mater as a distinguished sexist, racist, and antisemite.[32]

Similarly, Princeton president Woodrow Wilson was, even by the standards of his time, a renowned racist. Born in the Deep South and raised in a devoutly religious Christian family, Wilson was a strong proponent of segregation and the disenfranchisement of Black Americans, whom he once referred to as "an ignorant and inferior race."[33] Indeed, Princeton, like Harvard, would not accept Black students until well into the twentieth century.

As before, HWCUs also continued to graduate some of the period's most pernicious racists, including Madison Grant, a Yale alumnus who has been remembered as "the high priest of scientific racism," and Henry Fairfield Osborn, a Princeton alumnus who played a prominent role in the eugenics movement.[34] In 1920, the Harvard graduate Theodore Lothrop Stoddard published *The Rising Tide of Color against the White World-Supremacy*, a work that remains significant for its early articulation of unapologetically white-supremacist ideology. Like Osborn, Stoddard was a prominent eugenicist who took a hard stance against miscegenation, or race mixing.[35] Here, then, we might say that the previous centuries' violent denigration and dehumanization of Native and Black Americans was reconfigured and applied to new "ethnically undesirable" populations.

The ugly cycle of opening the doors to college access ever so slightly to a marginal few, followed by backlash and exclusion, repeated throughout the rest of the twentieth century. And no one would feel that white backlash more acutely than students of color, especially Native and Black students, whose ancestors had made these colleges possible in the first place.

Whitelash

Colonial efforts at Christianizing Natives Americans petered out in the late 1700s. From the early 1800s to the 1950s, the US government took on a more prominent role in Indian education, an era known as the federal period. Rather than use its power to support Native communities, however, the US government instead hollowed out Native education. As before, the goal of primary and secondary education remained to assimilate Natives into the United States and to prepare them to serve as laborers in the racially stratified economy. As a result, the government created nearly insurmountable barriers to Native students' ability to obtain a college education.

Between 1778 and 1871, the United States concluded ninety-seven treaties concerning Native education with tribal communities throughout the country. Treaties forced land sales and also created a trustee responsibility between the federal government and Native communities where education was concerned. The first treaty between the US government and a Native community was signed with the Choctaw Nation in September 1830. It provided for scholarship funds, which, a decade later, Choctaw students made use of when they first attended white institutions.[36]

While treaties earmarked some monies for Indian education, Native communities had no say in what the education of their young would look like. In 1819, the Indian Civilization Act directed federal monies from land sales to mission schools and government-operated schools. Essentially the government contracted with religious organizations, incentivizing them to live among and "educate" tribal communities. Once more, it sought to force Natives to abandon traditional customs and assimilate into the US socioeconomic order as agricultural and industrial laborers. Federally controlled education thus sought explicitly to assimilate Natives into white Christian American culture in the hopes that they might return to their communities and serve as agents of assimilation in their own right.[37]

Some tribal leaders saw federally controlled education as an opportunity to learn the ways of the oppressor and fight back. This was the case for the Choctaw tribe, whose leader, Pushmataha, encouraged participation in mission schools for precisely this reason.[38] But the plan didn't always work as intended. In 1911, US-educated middle-class Natives founded the Society of American Indians. Its purpose was to promote education of Natives in the US education system. Rather than being subversive in orientation, the society and its members instead endorsed the assimilatory aims of US education. As a result, those who obtained an American education found themselves isolated from the home communities they'd left, their experiences echoing that of their ancestors who had attended colonial colleges.

Other tribes tried to obtain a degree of control from the federal government but were rarely successful. This was the case for the Cherokee Nation. In 1851, Cherokees established a Male and Female Seminary in Talequah, Oklahoma. The college for men eventually became Bacone College, still in existence today. Bacone received US government funding as well as white philanthropic support—from the Rockefellers, no less—but only on the condition that it offered Natives a Christian education. Indeed, Bacone's mission statement declares that "its primary objective is to prepare native teachers and preachers for a more effective Christian work among the Indian tribes."[39] Thus, even Indian-run higher education during the federal period was compelled to include white assimilatory aims because it received federal funding.[40]

By the mid-1850s, the Bureau of Indian Affairs began to occupy itself with Native education. The bureau created the notorious boarding school system that ripped Native children from their homes, families, and communities to reeducate them in the ways of white Anglo-Saxon American culture and tradition. By the early 1900s, the government even sanctioned the kidnapping of Indian children to raise in white families and boarding schools. Like early colonial colleges, these boarding schools served as sites of assimilation where youngsters were forced to surrender Native languages, customs, religions, and ways of life. And they were renowned for their cruelty, abuse, and depravity.

White industrialists bankrolled these schools for Native children, seeking to equip the children with practical tools for entering the racially stratified job market. Boarding schools were pivotal in help-ing white capitalists create the racialized workforce they so desired.[41] During the federal era, then, the predominant focus in postsecondary education for Natives was vocational education.[42] This atmosphere was anything but conducive to preparing Natives for US higher education. Then again, that was precisely the point.

At the beginning of the twentieth century, only two schools approx-imating colleges had been founded for Natives. These were Sheldon Jackson College, founded in 1878 to educate Alaskan Natives, and Cro-aton Normal School, founded in 1887 in North Carolina.[43] I say they "approximated" colleges because the education they offered was often high school level, since Native students had been systemically denied an adequate education by the US government. Sheldon Jackson Col-lege would not offer postsecondary classes until 1944, and it became a four-year institution, properly speaking, only in 1981. Similarly, Cro-aton Normal School, now known as Pembroke, was dedicated expressly to Native education, but, like Sheldon Jackson, the so-called university offered a curriculum barely comparable to an eighth-grade education.[44]

It wasn't until the 1921 Snyder Act, which gave Native Americans full citizenship, that the Bureau of Indian Affairs finally began to improve education for Native students. Several years later, a 1928 report by the Indian Office of the Brookings Institution accelerated these efforts. The authors of the Merriam Report found subpar education standards in government-run schools. Among the chief reasons why Natives did not pursue higher education, the report stated, was the inadequacy of secondary-education conditions, including the frequency of harsh dis-ciplinary practices, the poor quality of facilities, and the prevalence of malnutrition and disease.[45]

Moreover, the report determined that a decidedly vocational cur-riculum stunted Native students' learning and growth. According to the Merriam Report, "The secondary work offered at these schools would hardly be accepted by the most reputable universities through-out the United States." The authors of the report called out the lack of teacher preparation among white teachers at Indian schools. Across the board, none had attended four-year colleges, a basic expectation for secondary-education teachers. The report concluded, "So far as can be ascertained no government Indian school meets this minimum requirement."[46] Thanks in part to the Merriam Report, then, the 1930s and 1940s saw calls for more appropriate, less vocational education for Native children.[47]

By 1934, the Indian Reorganization Act paved the way to an "Indian New Deal," in which the US government "granted" Native peoples more rights. In some ways, the fact that Indian interests had a seat at the table within the federal government allowed for marginal improvements in the realm of education. But the ongoing tragedy of boarding schools makes clear how incomplete Native control remained.

Overall, the era of government-controlled Indian education is remembered as an unqualified failure. By systematically denying Native communities a sufficient education that would have allowed them admission to colleges and universities as well as the autonomy to create their own systems of education, the United States perpetuated their ongoing privation, impoverishment, and disenfranchisement. On rare occasions the US government did allocate funds to Native higher education, but only if it furthered the civilizing mission. It would take years before Natives would be able to even begin to overcome the many barriers to an education that the government had erected over the centuries.

For African American communities in the United States, the process of disenfranchisement from higher education proceeded differently. Education in general has a particular historical resonance in African American communities. Under slavery, white slaveholders prohibited African and African-descended persons from learning how to read and write. In 1740, South Carolina was the first colony to forbid teaching the enslaved how to read and write; other Southern states soon followed.[48] Not only did white slaveholders consider an education of no use to the enslaved, but they also worried that an education might actually aid runaways in their quest for freedom. Even under these dangerous conditions, however, some of the enslaved taught themselves how to read and write in secret. They did so at considerable risk of harm and violence under a brutal slave system.

Restrictions on Black schooling intensified between the 1800s and 1830s in the wake of the Haitian Revolution and the string of so-called slave revolts led by Gabriel Prosser, Denmark Vasey, and Nat Turner. In the early nineteenth century, the specter of Black liberation haunted the white imagination, and many white Americans believed that depriving the enslaved of an education would serve as one surefire method of controlling them more effectively. There were, of course, a handful of exceptions. In the 1820s, three African American men received degrees from Middlebury College, Amherst College, and Bowdoin, respectively. It would take more than four decades for an African American woman to do the same. But they were very much the exception, not the rule.[49]

Though free Black Americans had long sought to establish schools for their community in the free states of antebellum New England, they were repeatedly met by whitelash. Consequently, these colleges rose and fell all too rapidly. No Black college, seminary, or academy would ever last in free antebellum New England.[50] The case was similar in the South, where nearly 90 percent of Black Americans resided.

In 1863, just twenty-eight African Americans out of the newly emancipated four million freedmen had received a bachelor's degree.[51] In order to circumvent a racist system that had long excluded them, after emancipation, Black Americans began to found their own institutions of higher education. These are the origins of modern-day historically black colleges and universities (HBCUs).[52] Within just a two-year period from 1865 to 1867, Black leaders established seventeen Black colleges, a testament to the hunger for knowledge among a people who had been systematically denied it. In the 1870s and 1880s, one scholar speculates, about two hundred Black colleges and universities were established. Yet many of these, too, were shuttered for various reasons, above all the Reconstruction consensus that Northern elites struck with the South in order to appease a recently defeated and humiliated people.[53]

Black Americans were not discouraged. To aid their efforts, Black leaders obtained financial assistance from white Protestant missionary organizations in the North and, after the Civil War, from the Freedman's Bureau. It must be said that these bodies were not always driven by benevolent motives. White missionaries and government emissaries hoped to eradicate so-called slave religions and properly Christianize the formerly enslaved. Moreover, they were driven to philanthropy by what they imagined as the menace of uneducated Black Americans unleashed on the United States in the wake of emancipation.

White industrialists also contributed to Black higher-education efforts, but, as was the case for Native students, they directed funds toward education that would prepare Black Americans for lower-class jobs in trades.[54] In other words, as the nineteenth century gave way to the twentieth, wealthy white industrialists used education to groom both Native and Black Americans alike to participate in a racially stratified economy. Unlike white men, colleges did not seek to prepare Native and Black men to take the reins of power in US society, and that's assuming colleges admitted them at all.[55] Insofar as Native and Black students gained exposure to the humanistic disciplines, they learned white European history in which nonwhite peoples featured only as inferiors to be conquered, enslaved, and disenfranchised.[56]

Because of the strong degree of white influence exerted on them, HBCUs could typically offer only primary and secondary education masquerading as higher education. After all, many Southern conservatives still saw Black education as a threat to white supremacy.[57] HBCUs also remained systematically underfunded as compared to HWCUs. They had no schools of law or medicine, nor could they offer PhD programs. Because of the influence of white missionaries and industrialists, few could furnish science or engineering curricula, as they remained financially obligated to provide vocationalist education.[58]

Moreover, the Morrill Act, which established land-grant universities through the seizure of Indigenous land, did not include Black colleges in the Southern states or those colleges in the South that had fought against the Union during the Civil War. By the Progressive Era, this would change. But even then, benefits were ceded to Black colleges only to maintain a structure of racial segregation in higher education, to reinforce the "separate but equal" ethos that guided a post-*Plessy* United States. As the Morrill Act initially dispossessed Natives from their lands, it also disenfranchised Black Americans, and it represents a prime example of how inequality has been layered on inequality in the US.[59]

Hampton Institute and Tuskegee in Alabama were among the most celebrated early HBCUs. In fact, Hampton Institute was initially opened to educate Native communities, and its first students came from displaced southwestern tribes. But like white-funded universities and colleges for Black and Native Americans, their curricula emphasized agricultural and industrial programs, not a liberal arts education.[60] By contrast, post–Civil War HBCUs such as Howard University in Washington, DC, and Fisk Institute in Nashville deliberately set themselves apart from the "industrial-vocational model" of Black colleges. Doing so, however, caused Northern foundations to withdraw financial support.[61]

Though HBCUs offered Black men educational opportunity, Black women were severely underrepresented. In 1920, just two of ten graduates from HBCUs were Black women. Even at HBCUs, Black women contended with pervasive sexism.[62] To circumvent both racism and sexism, Black women founded their own HBCUs, including Bennet College in Greensboro, North Carolina (founded in 1873, coed until 1926); Hartshorn Memorial College for Women in Richmond, Virginia (1883); and the Atlanta Baptist Female Seminary, later Spelman College, in Georgia (1881). By the 1940s, Black women began to outpace their male peers in terms of enrollment and graduation from HBCUs. Unsurprisingly, it would take far longer to see this trend emerge at HWCUs.[63]

At the turn of the century, racial exclusions remained the norm in both Northern and Southern HWCUs. Despite the myth of a tolerant North, racism was less a regional problem than a national one prior to the civil rights movement (and, some might argue, well after).[64] After the Civil War, some Black Americans initially tried their luck at HWCUs up north. Overall, Northern states offered more educational opportunities to African Americans than Southern states, though Black students never accounted for more than 3 percent of total college enrollment.[65] As had become the pattern, in seeking greater opportunity, they were met with a wave of whitelash. White students organized to prevent Black admission to Northern schools. By 1910, less than seven hundred African Americans had graduated from HWCUs. Oberlin, the University of Michigan, and the University of Kansas led the way in graduating African Americans.[66]

In the 1920s, anti-Black racism thrived on college campuses. During this decade, Harvard saw a flurry of Ku Klux Klan activity on its campus. The existence of the KKK was an open secret among students, faculty, and leaders. In 2021, the Harvard undergraduate Simon Levien researched the resurgence of the Klan on Harvard's campus. Among other things, his research surfaced images of Harvard students in Klan garb from a 1924 yearbook. One photo's caption read, "Harvard Klass Kow & Klans—students having fun." In a 1923 *Crimson* article, an unnamed Harvard Klan member of the period is on record as saying, "The Harvard Klan is inactive. But it is very far from being disorganized, nor can I say that even now its influence is unfelt." There is some indication that the KKK's presence hasn't entirely disappeared from campus. Throughout the rest of the twentieth century, as late as 1996, Harvard students would see KKK leaflets, threatening letters, and KKK graffiti on campus.[67]

The resurgence of the Klan took place at the same time as the establishment of major fraternities on US college campuses. Many fraternities of the period included so-called white clauses that effectively prevented Black and Jewish students from joining. Consequently, many Black students created their own fraternities, known today as historically Black Greek Letter Organizations (BGLOs). In addition to social acceptance, Black fraternities offered Black students a measure of

FIGURE 7. Harvard branch of the Ku Klux Klan, 1924. Members of the Harvard branch of the Ku Klux Klan pose for a graduation photo on Class Day 1924 at the foot of the John Harvard statue in Harvard Yard.
Source: Courtesy of the Boston Public Library, Leslie Jones Collection.

safety, a space where they could escape, if only momentarily, from the oppressive white supremacy that pervaded HWCUs.

Where Black students did matriculate, segregation was the ruling principle on both Northern and Southern campuses. From the 1930s to the 1960s, a handful of African Americans sought to challenge the status quo. They strategically applied to segregated universities in the South, expecting the inevitable refusal. These rejections served as a basis for the NAACP to launch antidiscrimination lawsuits against HWCUs that refused to provide education that was "separate but equal." For example, the NAACP mounted considerable legal challenges against UNC Chapel Hill in 1933 and the University of Virginia in 1935 and was successful in its endeavors. Between 1936 and 1950, the organization was similarly successful in lawsuits filed against the University of Maryland, the University of Missouri, the University of Texas, and the University of Oklahoma.

Winning could be cold comfort, though. As had been the tradition for their ancestors brought as property to seventeenth-, eighteenth-, and nineteenth-century college campuses, Black Americans once again endured harassment and violence. In 1914, white students physically accosted a Black dental student from the University of Pennsylvania, throwing stones at him. Even at HBCUs, Black students carried weapons in the event that they had to fend off white attacks. In 1919, Iowa State refused to house Black students in dorms, not even in segregated living arrangements. Local residents took them in as boarders as they completed their studies, turning a profit along the way. Unsurprisingly, as a result of racist campus cultures, HWCUs had exceptionally low retention rates when it came to their small number of Black students. At Cornell, not one of the six Black students who attended in 1904 returned the next year.[68]

The principle of racist exclusion extended to off-campus extracurricular activities as well. Even at Northern schools that admitted Black athletes, coaches refused to allow those athletes to play against Southern teams if the latter didn't permit racial integration.[69] Not only were Black students sidelined on the field, but they were expected to stay in separate hotels and patronize different businesses in the Jim Crow South, which refused to welcome interracial teams well into the 1960s.[70] North or South, white supremacy always won the day.

After World War I and the Great Migration, Black higher education made real gains, but they were concentrated among HBCUs. According to Ibram X. Kendi, "More black students graduated from college between 1926 and 1936 than in the nation's previous 300 years combined."[71] Over time, however, white colleges and universities used HBCUs as a way to maintain racial segregation under the separate-but-equal doctrine, denying admission to Black students with the expectation that HBCUs would simply absorb them.

The Era of Desegregation

The Second World War put an end to business as usual in US higher education. In the United States, the immediate postwar years were characterized by tremendous prosperity. Against the background of the Cold War, US politicians began to see higher education as critical to national defense interests. This was especially the case with science, as the US and USSR engaged in an intense competitive arms race throughout the 1950s and 1960s. As a result, the postwar period witnessed a huge expansion in the number of college-going Americans, who were expected to catapult the United States to world supremacy.[72]

In 1939–40, student enrollment came in at under 1.5 million, but by 1949–50, it was closer to 2.7 million—an 80 percent increase in just one decade. The GI Bill, which helped veterans pay for college, was mostly responsible for this surge.[73] By the 1960s, the postwar baby boom played its part too. Indeed, between 1947 and 1948, the Veteran Affairs Administration paid for nearly half of all American (male) college students to attend university. Meanwhile, the National Defense Education Act extended loans to students in defense-related fields. By 1950, 16 percent of all eligible veterans had opted to pursue a college education.[74] It's no exaggeration to say that higher education became a part of the American way of life in the fifties—for white America, that is.

As before the war, the flexible and highly subjective criteria of character and leadership defined the admissions process. Once more, private colleges enforced racist admissions criteria to maintain a white student body. Though slowly opening the door to American education for a larger number of students, admissions officers and university administrators at selective universities overwhelmingly favored legacy sons. Why? They needed their full tuition. HWCUs also needed to maintain positive relations with alumni to ensure a steady flow of donations. Thus, although the college-going population expanded, the student body remained racially homogenous.

By contrast, public schools, generally more affordable, tended to absorb the wave of first-generation and working-class students who had become eligible for a college education after the war. Here we see the beginning of a stratification in higher education wherein private colleges and universities are reserved for white wealthy men, while public universities increasingly serve a far more diverse college-going population. Though more Americans achieved a college education after the war, the chasm between private and public institutions widened during these decades.[75]

The GI Bill affected college campuses significantly. From one angle, the bill served as a great equalizer, permitting men of all social classes the opportunity to attain a college education. But it was all men. The significant presence of former soldiers reinforced the gendering of fields of study. Men were tracked into business and engineering, women into more ladylike fields. Though female veterans were technically eligible for the GI Bill, it most clearly affected the lives of white men. White women wouldn't regain their footing in higher education or return to their pre–World War II numbers until 1970.

Moreover, male veterans tilted campuses in conservative directions and "masculinized" the postwar campus.[76] Some scholars have described GIs in this period as relatively "unruly," particularly in fraternity settings. And, as before the war, fraternities were organizations that distinguished themselves as particularly discriminatory toward nonwhite students.[77] One Black student who would eventually become a faculty administrator in an early minority affairs office recalled that fraternities at Wake Forest waved Confederate flags and burned black effigies on their lawns to intimidate Black students.[78] It worked.

Technically, the GI Bill included Black and Native veterans. But because of the long historical association between education and disenfranchisement, even abuse, fewer Natives took advantage of it as compared to whites. About twenty-five thousand Natives fought in the Second World War,[79] but by 1957, only about two thousand had enrolled in college.[80] At Dartmouth, a university that boasted one of the oldest Indian colleges in the country, no more than two hundred Natives attended the college from its founding until 1965; fewer than thirty actually graduated.[81]

Black Americans faced additional obstacles. Many HWCUs imposed quotas to limit the number of Black students who could enroll, much as they had for eastern European Jewish students at the turn of the century. This was reflected in the faculty composition as well: in 1948, just sixty Black professors taught at HWCUs throughout the entire nation.[82] At best, the GI Bill sponsored what John Thelin refers to as "inclusion without integration," a story that would repeat itself throughout the twentieth century as well.[83]

The 1954 *Brown v. Board of Education* Supreme Court decision that officially struck down school segregation did little to improve the situation. Many of us may recall learning of *Brown v. Board of Education* in high school and seeing images of "the Little Rock Nine," nine black students encircled by an angry white mob as federal troops escorted them into their new high school. Most colleges and universities didn't experience the kind of violence that accompanied the integration of primary and secondary schools, but some did.

At the University of Mississippi, white students rioted when they learned that James Meredith, an African American student, won his NAACP-backed lawsuit and gained admission to the university. In 1962, white mobs attacked the US marshals who were there to protect Meredith. The violence didn't end until the arrival of federal troops the next day. Two people died and hundreds more were wounded and arrested.

At the University of Alabama and the University of Georgia, the path to racial integration throughout the fifties and sixties was similarly marked by violence and hostility. White student protesters joined forces with local gubernatorial opposition to bar Black students from enrolling at Georgia.[84] Anti-Black opposition among white students was so bad in some places that colleges tried to sneak Black students onto predominantly white campuses during summer sessions, the logic being that if they were quietly enrolled, they wouldn't stir the pot and provoke a whitelash.[85]

After *Brown*, most HWCUs desegregated to give the appearance of compliance with federal mandates. Others remained segregated until the law intervened. In fact, Georgia Tech was the first Southern school to open itself up to Black students without a court order, and that wasn't until 1961. The 1964 Civil Rights Act allowed government agencies to withhold federal money from institutions that continued to enact discriminatory and segregationist practice in spite of the *Brown* decision. But it would appear that this wasn't always enticement enough for HWCUs. As late as April 1965, over ten years after *Brown*, 300 colleges and universities refused to comply with the federal mandate, out of a total of 2,100 colleges that received government assistance.[86] Holdouts were located in the most unyielding states of the Deep South. There, significant opposition to the *Brown* decision thrived, and in some cases, politicians and judicial authorities backed the opposition, conspiring to block Black applicants from Southern HWCUs. The South submitted only gradually and begrudgingly to the changing political tides throughout the late sixties and early seventies.[87]

Arguably, Black students on forcibly desegregated campuses faced a greater degree of violence than those at schools that complied with federal desegregation orders more willingly, if not enthusiastically. In 1961, a mob of white students surrounded Black students' dorms at the University of Georgia, hurling insults at them for beating Georgia Tech at a basketball game. KKK members attended as well, holding signs that read "N----- go home." The mob set fire to their dorm rooms before moving to general rioting. If they sought to register their white displeasure with desegregation, they succeeded.[88] And it wasn't just white *students* whom Black students feared. White Citizens' Councils, organizations of white upper- and middle-class Americans who disputed the *Brown* ruling, collaborated with state legislators to force professors from colleges and universities to get behind the racist imperatives of the day.[89]

Over time, the combination of federal pressure, loosening racial restrictions, and more financial assistance prompted HWCUs to engage in greater outreach and recruitment efforts. As a result, the number of Black students at HWCUs gradually increased. By fall 1965, two hundred thousand Black students were enrolled at HWCUs, representing about 4 percent of total enrolled undergraduates. By 1967, they were closer to 5.15 percent.[90]

As access to a college education progressively expanded during the nineteenth and twentieth centuries, it provoked significant backlash. While white women and Jewish students of eastern European origin constituted early twentieth-century targets, white resistance to Black education stretched back centuries. The violence of integration, the begrudging acceptance of Black students, and the painfully slow progress toward full desegregation reflected the steadfast belief in white dominance that so characterized US state and culture.

Ultimately, democratic expansions in college attendance marched in lockstep with new exclusions, clearly demarcating who was worthy of higher education in this country and who was not. As a college education became more desirable, admissions offices became more selective, their officials serving increasingly as gatekeepers. Rather than seek "diversity" as many of today's colleges and universities do, they instead sought to maintain the homogeneity of the white male student body.[91] But they were not, and could never be, entirely successful in their endeavors to exclude women and people of color. As more and more historically marginalized students arrived at HWCUs, they began to question the ongoing white supremacist legacies that structured their college experience. With strength in numbers, they readied themselves to mount a challenge to the status quo that no one could ignore.

CHAPTER 3

Turning Points

The civil rights movement galvanized a generation. Through protest, civil disobedience, and outright revolt, those who had long endured second-class citizenship in this country rose up to denounce a white-supremacist regime. Rallying civilians throughout the United States, civil rights leaders contributed to a global movement against oppression in all its various forms. From anticolonial struggles to the antiwar movement, college students were often at the center of the fight for freedom both on and off campus. In the US, they fought in particular against racial injustice and helped spur the passage of far-reaching racial justice legislation, including the Civil Rights Act of 1964, which prohibited discrimination, and the Voting Rights Act of 1965, which secured the right to vote for minorities. As youth of color moved to dismantle structural racism in every part of American society, they set their sights on the next frontier—historically white colleges and universities.

Black students, especially, were at the forefront not only of the national struggle for liberation but also of the movement for racial equality at HWCUs. Forging strong multiracial alliances among fellow students, staff, and some faculty, they compelled white senior leaders to confront and dismantle institutional racism. As protests roiled campuses across the nation, students secured some long-lasting wins, including the establishment of interdisciplinary academic departments such as ethnic studies, African American studies, and women's studies.

Significantly, students also fought for the founding of various minority affairs offices and Black student unions, the forerunners of today's diversity, equity, and inclusion (DEI) offices and multicultural student centers.[1] While their activities often overlapped, racial affinity centers were more likely to be involved in the provision of social support services to students of color. Consequently, it was common for these centers to be located in divisions of student affairs, which, as we will see, often limited what they could accomplish. By contrast, offices of minority affairs, typically headed by faculty members, tended to have a greater ability to effect wider institutional change. Both administrative branches were united in common cause to improve the experiences of students of color at HWCUs, but the distinction between where they "lived" within the university's organizational structure would have important consequences in the decades ahead.

Animated by the ambient spirit of moral rebellion, staff, faculty, and student leaders couched their struggles in the vernacular of antiracism and antioppression. They used a social justice framework that explicitly acknowledged how power operated in our society. But that liberatory political moment was short lived, stalled not only by an unforgiving global economic recession but also by whitelash that struck in the 1980s and 1990s. During these decades, the political Right was reconfigured around conservative values that united a broad swath of right-wing actors who hadn't taken kindly to the uprisings of the 1960s and 1970s. Colleges slowly chipped away at the hard-won victories of the previous decades. The backlash against progressive platforms—most of which had only just begun to usher in much-needed change at HWCUs—stalled the fight for racial progress on college campuses.

As US culture lurched further rightward, minority affairs officers and racial affinity center leaders found themselves in a bind. How could they assert the original antiracist goals of their offices without inciting further backlash? In order to survive the eighties and nineties, they changed tack. Instead of missions dedicated to eradicating racism, they searched for a new vocabulary that would allow them to pursue what equity work they could without ruffling feathers. In so doing, they adopted both power-blind and color-blind languages and approaches that de-emphasized histories of racism and oppression and declared that, because everyone was the same, antiracist and antioppression practices were no longer necessary. The eighties and nineties thus witnessed a shift toward what Sarah Ahmed calls "diversity talk," or a sort of bland appreciation of "difference" in all its various forms.[2]

This chapter recounts that rocky journey, as directors of offices of minority affairs and multicultural student centers struggled to survive changing political winds, find new ways to keep the interests of marginalized students on the institutional agenda, and, overall, stay relevant throughout the last two decades of the twentieth century.

Revolt

Advances in education for Native communities proceeded on a parallel and mostly alternate path from that of other racially marginalized groups. While many Native American students at HWCUs participated in campus-wide student movements in the 1960s and 1970s, the community as a whole commanded their own anticolonial liberation struggle focused on beating back federal control over all facets of Native life. Above all, they wanted both the return of stolen lands and resources and a guarantee for the proper education of Native history, tradition, and custom for their people. Though they had much in common with other people of color in the United States, the historical situation of Native communities—a dispossessed, colonized, and bereaved people— was in many ways unique.

The shift from federal rule toward self-determination began to take shape in 1961, when the American Indian Chicago Conference gathered Natives from throughout the country. Together they composed a Declaration of Indian Purpose that equated Natives with other colonized peoples throughout the world. Significantly, the authors of the declaration placed self-determination squarely at the center of Native activism and their policy agenda, later submitted to President John F. Kennedy. These were also the central platforms of the wider American Indian Movement, which began in Minneapolis in 1968. In line with the spirit of the times, activists opted for mass action, militant tactics, and civil disobedience as opposed to pointless treaties and negotiations with the US government as their ancestors had long tried. This was particularly the case for Native youth of the newly formed Red Power Movement, a far more radical group that fought for Native self-determination and liberation.

The manifold failures of HWCUs to meet the needs of Native students drove the battle for Native-controlled education. In spite of overwhelming odds, about 2,000 Native students attended HWCUs in the

FIGURE 8. President John F. Kennedy with delegates from the American Indian Chicago Confer-
ence, August 15, 1961. From left to right in the foreground: Eleanor Red Fawn Smooth, of the
Mohawk and Cherokee Nations; President Kennedy; Chief Calvin W. McGhee, of the Creek Nation
East of the Mississippi; Kathitha Addison, of the Narragansett Nation.
Source: Abbie Rowe. White House Photographs. John F. Kennedy Presidential Library and Museum, Boston.

late 1950s, increasing to about 3,500 a decade later.[3] Only 18 percent
of Native American students, however, went on to pursue a college
degree, and nearly 97 percent of those who did dropped out along the
way. Nine out of ten Native students dropped out of college in 1960,
and just sixty-six Native students graduated from college throughout
the entire United States in the following year.[4] When asked why they
dropped out, they stated the obvious: poor academic preparation as
a direct result of federal negligence, mismanagement, and attendant
trauma in primary and secondary educational institutions, not to mention financial insecurity, institutional racism, and an overall cultural
mismatch with HWCUs.[5]

Even the US government couldn't ignore how profoundly it had
failed Native communities. Forty years after the Merriam Report, the
Kennedy Report on Indian Education noted how little progress had
been made. The title of the report really says it all: *Indian Education:*

A National Tragedy—a National Challenge. In the 1960s, a congressional committee presented its findings on Native education by federally run schools in the following terms: "We conclude that our national policies for educating American Indians are a failure of major proportions."[6]

Following the publication of the Kennedy Report, the government made marginal improvements, such as increasing scholarships allocated to Native American students. The Bureau of Indian Affairs (BIA) also partially funded three community colleges for Natives, including the Haskell Institute, founded in 1884 as an Indian boarding school. The Haskell Institute was the first BIA-funded degree-granting school. Other two-year colleges soon followed.[7]

Significantly, the Kennedy Report catalyzed the passage of key pieces of federal legislation related to Native American self-determination. These included the Indian Education Act of 1972 and the Indian Self-Determination and Assistance Act of 1975, both of which allowed for more Native control over their own education.[8] In many ways, the laws themselves were an acknowledgment of how enormously deficient federal efforts to provide Native education had been. Above all, however, the Kennedy Report provided justification for what Native communities had demanded for over a century: Native-controlled education.

During this period, Native communities began to exercise increasing influence over the management of their own education. By the 1960s, many off-reservation boarding schools introduced postsecondary-level courses for the first time.[9] More significantly, they established their own colleges in order to address the scandalously high Native dropout rate at HWCUs.[10]

In 1968, the Navajo Nation founded the very first tribal college in the United States in Tsaile, Arizona. Navajo Community College offered students a curriculum that diverged starkly from the vocational training funded by white industrialists throughout the late nineteenth and early twentieth centuries. Instead, Native curricula sought to teach students about Native history, language, and culture.[11] In other words, higher education in tribally controlled colleges was what today we might call culturally relevant, meaning that it helped Native students bridge the cultural divide between the white American world and their own cultures and communities. Tribal colleges offered other benefits too. Students did not have to move away from home for their education, as these newly founded colleges were closer to tribal lands. As a result, they enjoyed community support as opposed to the isolation that HWCUs had to offer.[12] Today, over thirty-five tribal colleges exist in the United States.

For Native Americans, the civil rights movement offered an opportunity to get out from under the shadow of federally controlled education that drastically limited their life possibilities. As a result, they sought self-determination, autonomy, and sovereignty above all else. By contrast, the small handful of those who attended HWCUs joined with students of color, and Black students especially, to demand equity and an end to institutional racism. While in the 1940s and 1950s students of color sought simply to keep their heads down on all-white campuses, as more students from historically marginalized backgrounds enrolled, they found strength in numbers. In keeping with the times, many dared to move in more radical directions ushered in by the civil rights era. Black, Native, Latinx, Asian American, and other nonwhite students in HWCUs sought nothing less than to overhaul higher education in the United States. And in many ways, they succeeded.

Like white women and Jews before them, African American students gained critical mass in the sixties, provoking significant whitelash. After the *Brown v. Board of Education* decision, which officially desegregated education, more Black students started to attend HWCUs. Additionally, the 1964 Civil Rights Act and the 1965 Higher Education Act that provided financial assistance to college students allowed government agencies to withhold federal money from institutions that continued to engage in discriminatory and segregationist practice. Recall that as late as April 1965—over ten years after the *Brown* decision was issued—a good 300 colleges and universities still refused to comply with the law, out of a total of 2,100 HWCUs that received government assistance.

Due to federal pressure, loosening restrictions, and the growth of the civil rights movement, the number of Black students at HWCUs eventually increased, notwithstanding the reluctance and outright resistance of some HWCUs. By fall 1965, two hundred thousand Black students had enrolled at HWCUs, representing about 4 percent of total enrolled undergraduates. By 1967, they represented 5.15 percent of college students, even though the total Black population in the United States was at that time closer to 12 percent.[13] These weren't huge strides, but they were something.

HBCUs were at the forefront of Black campus movements. HBCU graduates orchestrated the well-known Woolworth lunch counter protest after Black students were denied service at a whites-only diner in Greensboro, North Carolina. Black students brought tactics they had learned in the civil rights movement to the next battle to be waged—the one on college campuses. They organized protests, demonstrations, and sit-ins at HBCUs such as Jackson State, Alcorn State, Norfolk State, and Howard, where faculty remained overwhelmingly white. As HBCU leaders gradually transitioned away from white to Black leadership, administrators grew more responsive to student dissent. These pioneers inspired Black students throughout the country to follow their lead.

From 1965 to 1972, HWCUs experienced the roiling. As more Black students attended HWCUs, they found campuses that were wholly unprepared for them. Black-led campus activism blossomed on at least 150 campuses from 1967 to 1968.[14] By 1969, another 269 campus protests swept across the country.[15] At the height of student activism in the 1960s, one in five student protests demanded an end to racial discrimination on campus.[16] By some estimates, at least a quarter of all Black college students were directly involved in campus activism. Another quarter sympathized with Black activists.[17] Together, they outlined agenda-setting goals for their various institutions.

While Black students certainly were at the center of justice movements, they forged meaningful relationships with other nonwhites, including Natives, Latinx, and a growing number of Asian and Asian American students who entered the United States in increasing numbers once the US finally lifted the ban on Asian migration in 1965. In 1969 at the City College of New York, for instance, Puerto Rican and Black students as well as poor white students joined forces, organizing a protest and submitting five demands to the university. Specifically, they requested a separate school for Black and Puerto Rican studies; a separate orientation program for Black and Puerto Rican first-year students; a decision-making role in faculty selection, promotion, and firing; new admissions practices that would mandate that the student body reflect the diversity within Harlem; and that Black and Puerto Rican history and Spanish language be required for all education majors.[18]

Although student activists found support among some faculty, in general such alliances were not easy to come by. As time progressed, faculty drifted into two camps: one conservative, one radical. Most opposed student protests; others supported them. Some objected to the swift institutional change; others advocated for more of it. These latter wanted their universities and professional organizations to declare solidarity with marginalized students and to endorse some of the other leftist positions of the era, such as the antiwar movement.[19] Across the board, having radical faculty willing to join the student movement, as they did at Buffalo and San Francisco State University (SFSU), was a boon to student activists. Faculty made for powerful allies.[20]

To accomplish their goals, student activists turned their attention toward building community among themselves. They did so by establishing student unions that brought students together by racial or ethnic identity—what today we would call racial affinity groups. The vast majority of today's Black student unions on college campuses can trace their origins to the ferment of the 1960s and 1970s. As is still the case, groups functioned both as a source of community support and as a political base from which to demand administrative and academic change in HWCUs.[21]

In an era well before social media, they also connected with one another at conferences, built national student networks, and organized across the country. And they engaged in larger community-wide education efforts to help highlight Black culture and restore Black dignity in a world bent on destroying it. Students brought Black speakers to campus during Black Cultural Weeks they organized. These organized events featured speeches, films, panel discussions, and social and artistic events. We might even say that they created one of the few places on campus where all students, especially white students, could learn about African American history and culture.[22]

As the movement progressed, students' aims evolved and they broadened their range of demands. In their fight against structural oppression, students, in addition to some sympathetic staff and faculty, proposed a very specific list of recommendations. Foremost among them was a demand for administrators to expand the recruitment and admission of Black students. They also called for the recruitment and hiring of Black faculty and the dismissal of openly racist white faculty.[23] Students wanted to see more Black administrators and to fill university boards with trustees who looked like them and who thus understood the plight of students of color at HWCUs. They demanded Black affinity housing and reforms for Black athletes. In response, some more progressive institutions like UCLA, Occidental, Rutgers, and Wesleyan did indeed increase their outreach and recruitment efforts. Several even established summer support programs for Black students that sought to help them "acculturate" to predominantly white colleges and universities.

In their efforts to transform the university, students did not neglect the members of the wider university community, whose fates were tied to that of HWCUs. They fought for better working conditions for Black workers on campus, who in turn joined them in their struggle.[24] As Black student unions continued to build power on college campuses throughout the country, their leaders also voiced objections to the construction and expansion of HWCUs in urban settings, which typically came at the expense of communities of color, especially Black urban neighborhoods.[25] The University of Pennsylvania, for example, expanded its presence by encroaching into Black neighborhoods and communities in Philadelphia. The same can be said of the University of Chicago, which has a tense relationship with the surrounding community to this day.[26] Black students were thus at the forefront of mending community relations between HWCUs and the wider Black communities that they had steadily displaced. In other words, student activists joined in broad solidarity with the wider local community, an undertaking that reflected their steadfast dedication to social justice beyond the narrow confines of higher education.

The upheaval at San Francisco State University provides the most vivid example of student activism during the civil rights era. SFSU was nothing less than a raging hotbed of campus dissent. In 1968, its Black student union initiated the longest strike in US history, a strike that lasted five months. In solidarity with a diverse mix of fellow students, it established the Third World Liberation Front and advocated for a Third World Revolution. In a multiracial coalition, the Black student union led students, staff, and faculty in a war against the administration and called for more inclusive admissions practices as well as more support for faculty of color. They also demanded a more diverse curriculum. In the end, they managed to spur the establishment of the first ethnic studies department and the first Black studies program in the United States in 1969.[27]

When news spread that SFSU students had managed to effect such large-scale change at their university (a feat achieved solely through student protest), Black student unions throughout the country amplified their demands for Black studies departments, programs, and courses.[28] Following in SFSU's footsteps, many institutions began to establish ethnic studies programs. From 1968 to 1969 alone, HWCUs instituted nearly seven hundred interdisciplinary programs, centers, and departments.[29] By 1971, HWCUs had founded more than five hundred African American studies programs, departments, and institutes.[30] Women's colleges, which had long sidelined Black women and excluded them from their campuses, similarly bowed to student pressure. In 1969, thirty-four Black female students occupied Vassar College's Main

FIGURE 9. Student protesters on strike at San Francisco State University, 1968.
Source: University Archives, SF State Strike Collection, SFSU Photo Binder 20: 1989.4.01.

Building and demanded courses that dealt with the Black experience. By fall, Vassar unveiled its first Black studies program.[31]

The push for African American studies inspired demands for similar interdisciplinary studies movements on behalf of marginalized members long excluded from the existing canon and curriculum of traditional higher education. The Chicano studies movement, for instance, was founded in April 1969 after a meeting of organizers in Santa Barbara, California.[32] The women's liberation movement also took a page out of the student activism playbook, fighting for women's studies departments through the late 1960s and early 1970s. Between 1969 and 1982, 330 women's studies departments were founded.[33] It's thanks to the student movements of the civil rights era that these interdisciplinary fields exist today.

Advance

In addition to the establishment of ethnic studies, African American studies, women's studies, and other interdisciplinary programs

FIGURE 10. Asian American Political Alliance members who joined the Third World Liberation Front in 1968–69. The Third World Liberation Front united students of color in a common struggle against oppression.
Source: Christina Lee, Danielle Lo, and Eliana Mugar, "Third World Liberation Strikes [National History Day 2018]," YouTube video, 9:59, March 5, 2018, https://www.youtube.com/watch?v=8eqGjdF69n4.

and departments, arguably the most enduring achievement of the student movements was the creation of campus centers for different racial groups and minority affairs offices.[34] With few exceptions, many current-day DEI offices and multicultural centers trace their origins to racial affinity centers established in 1968 and 1969. At more conservative Ivy League institutions, these campus spaces may have been called Third World Centers. This was the case at Princeton and Brown, both of which opened centers in the 1970s that were later renamed the Carl A. Fields Center and the Brown Center for Students of Color, respectively.[35] Yale also built culturally distinct centers around the same time, which included the Afro-American Cultural Center, which opened in 1969, and Casa Boricua, which opened in 1974.[36] Similarly, following student protests, USC established El Centro Chicano in 1973 and, four years later, the Black Cultural Center.[37]

Early directors of racial affinity centers provided safe harbor for marginalized students where they could experience community rather than alienation. These directors helped African American students in particular to navigate the hardship, racist violence, and hostility they endured on campus for the crime of simply existing.[38] They taught students of color, who had grown so accustomed to withstanding a constant barrage of aggression, to demand more of white institutions. Most center representatives I spoke with highlighted their efforts in trying to help Black students "survive" a white institution. When pressed, they were quick to remind me that Black students' lives were often on the line.

To meet the needs of minority students, racial affinity centers primarily undertook cocurricular programming. At Oregon State University, the Lonnie B. Harris Black Cultural Center aimed to "complement" academic programs at the university.[39] As a result, these early offices could serve as sites of politicization where students learned about social causes of the day, as was the case at SFSU.[40] Eventually they transformed into resource centers. For some, like those at Swarthmore and the University of Illinois, part of the mission was also to educate the wider (and whiter) campus community about the history, culture, and contributions of Black Americans.[41] Centers offered one of the few places where students would have the opportunity to learn about non-European cultures, histories, traditions, and values. In that sense, they countered centuries of academic scholarship steeped in histories of white supremacy and race science that had long dominated in the academy. In short, early racial affinity centers offered both a social support system and a more dignity-affirming curriculum that provided students of color with a sanctuary from the wider white-supremacist campus culture that they raged against.

Though uncommon, these centers managed to offer both cocurricular and curricular support services to contribute to not just recruitment but retention of students of color, something that remains a challenge for many of today's HWCUs. For example, the forty Black students enrolled at Colorado State in 1968 demanded more academic support to assist Black and Latino/a students. This led to the establishment of Project GO (Generating Opportunities), which later evolved into what is now the Black/African American Cultural Center and El Centro.[42] Institutions such as Boise State and Texas A&M introduced both academic and social support efforts at once, offering tutoring services and other programs to incorporate predominantly Black and Chicano students.[43] On the whole, however, most of these offices could offer only limited academic support because they were located not in academic affairs but in student affairs. As a result, they were left encouraging student success from the margins.

In other cases, newly established African American studies departments and their faculty undertook some of the student academic and social support services offered by these centers.[44] At the University of Tennessee, Knoxville, the Black Cultural Center began as an academic unit under the cultural studies program in the College of Liberal Arts and derived its funding from the Liberal Arts budget.[45] This was also the case at the University of Wisconsin–Madison once the university closed its short-lived Center for Afro-American and Race Relations. By 1971, the new Afro-American Studies Department had taken over many of the academic functions of the erstwhile center.[46] Similarly, the Intergroup Center at California State University, Long Beach, was partially dissolved in the wake of the establishment of ethnic and women's studies programs.[47] The message at these HWCUs was clear: students could either have a support center or an ethnic studies program, but not both.

Institutional commitment, then as now, varied, determining the overall success and longevity of these offices. At the University of Washington, the Office of Special Education was granted a budget of $60,000 as well as ten staff members.[48] Other offices were not as fortunate. Harvard-Radcliffe's Afro-American Cultural Center, established in 1969, received no funding from the university and eventually closed in 1974.[49] At the University of Wisconsin–Madison, the Center for Afro-American and Race Relations opened in 1968 but was quickly shuttered by the administration in 1973, reopening only with renewed student protests in 2017.[50]

As racial affinity centers spread like wildfire throughout the country, colleges and universities turned their attention to recruiting folks to take on these administrative roles and functions. Naturally, they turned to people of color in student affairs positions who already worked at the university. These professionals offered many benefits, primarily because they were already at the center of student life. As HWCUs sought personnel to staff these new offices, they hired principals and vice principals of predominantly Black high schools. They also hired from their limited Black alumni networks.

In most of my interviews, early directors of student centers explained that part of what motivated them to take on these positions was their experience as students in these same institutions. They understood intimately the institutional racism that other students of color were likely to face, and thus the institutional gaps in the university's student support. As one recalled, alumni also had "the benefit of historical record and institutional memory."[51] The combination of insider knowledge and preexisting relationships with the movers and shakers at their institutions set them up well for leadership positions in these newly established centers.

During the civil rights era, many Black women distinguished themselves as fierce supporters of student activism and helped shepherd students through a tumultuous time.[52] Take Augustine Pounds, an undergraduate and graduate alumna of Oakland University in Rochester, Michigan. Pounds began her career in 1971 in commuter services. In 1973, she took on the role of assistant director of Oakland's Student Center and adviser to Oakland's Black Student Association. As the student movement gained momentum, she found herself playing the role of counselor and adviser to student leaders, since she was one of only a handful of Black administrators on the college campus. In so doing, she, like so many others, drew directly on her own experiences with racism at Oakland University—both as a student and as a staff member.[53]

Veronica Cade had similar experiences. A native of Newark, New Jersey, Cade attended a large public research institution in the Mountain West region from 1965 to 1969, during the heyday of the Black campus movement. Not only was Cade involved in student protests at her university, but she also helped organize a sit-in on the president's lawn. She did so because, in her words, coming to the university was "like a slap in the face." She was used to moving through majority-Black communities, but there were almost no Black people at the university, let alone in the surrounding area. "There were some places you just knew not to go," she told me, remembering a local town where the vestiges of the Jim Crow era lingered still. In fact, in another nearby town, there were still laws on the books forcing Black Americans to leave by sunset. It was just one of hundreds of "sundown towns" throughout the nation responsible for today's ongoing racial segregation.[54]

In interview after interview, early center directors like Veronica Cade recounted what it was like growing up in a white-supremacist society. Though Cade experienced this most sharply after leaving home, many other Black administrators described what it was like to live in 1950s- and 1960s-era segregated towns and cities, to attend segregated schools as children.[55] They spoke of being bussed out of their communities. They spoke of parents and grandparents who were community organizers and civil rights activists, of nuclear and extended families who were migrant farmworkers and manual laborers. They grew up in an era when Cesar Chavez and Dolores Huerta, Malcom X and the Black Panthers inspired their communities to demand more. Like Veronica Cade, many themselves would go on to participate in the Black campus movement. They were, in other words, formed in the cauldron of freedom struggles. Undoubtedly, their upbringings shaped their values and moral outlooks, thus influencing the vision and goals of the early offices they would come to direct.

In those days, there was no playbook and no best practices that spoke to how one should pursue equity work within HWCUs. There was no research or scholarship on student support. Educators had yet to speak in the accents of multicultural education, student equity, or student success outcomes. There were only a handful of professional organizations, and even those were small affairs bringing together tiny groups of professionals who, at best, might swap promising ideas. In other words, early administrators had to learn on the fly. Of course, the student movements had pointedly outlined the most immediate items on the agenda—student and faculty recruitment and retention, curricular diversity, and support services for historically marginalized students. But administrators from the 1970s readily confess that they were making it up as they went.

Veronica Cade does, though, offer one success story. In 1968, she and fellow student protesters pushed senior administrators to grant them funds to establish a program focused on outreach, recruitment, and retention of both students and faculty of color. Shockingly, the center was entirely student run, indicative of a university that was looking to appease students of color but not entirely invest in their success. After graduating, Cade would return to the program, transform it from top to bottom, and help separate the program into two distinct but complementary wings—one for Black students and another for Latinx students.

As the first director of the Black Student Services Center, Cade managed to accomplish what few in her position could: real curricular change. Students had of course demanded a more diverse curriculum during the protest movement, but Cade actually succeeded in pulling it off, offering courses for credit under the auspices of the student center. This was despite the fact that her office, like so many similar offices throughout the country, was located under Student Affairs. When asked how she achieved such a feat, Cade responded candidly, "We didn't want to work with just Student Affairs. We had to ask, where's the power on this campus? We need Academic Affairs."[56]

In order to provide academic offerings through her office, Cade applied for a federal grant that supported academic success programs. Such things were still relatively rare. Administrators signed off on the grant proposal, perhaps not really understanding what it was. Sure, STEM research brought in money, but what could the Black Student Services Center possibly have to offer? It's also possible that they underestimated Cade. When she received the grant, they were shocked, but they certainly weren't about to turn down free money.[57]

While Cade's work at her university constitutes one powerful example of what early racial affinity centers could accomplish, hers is in many ways a singular case. On the whole, those centers located in student affairs were limited in their reach, at least in an institutional sense. Certainly, they provided critical cocurricular support services for students of color and occasionally a supplemental curriculum that accurately reflected their own communities, but they could rarely effect larger organizational change because of where they were located in the university hierarchy. By contrast, the faculty directors who often led offices of minority affairs could leverage their considerable power by virtue of their position in the university's pecking order.

Unlike racial affinity centers, minority affairs offices tended to hire faculty rather than staff directors. From the institution's perspective, tapping faculty of color for minority affairs offices was the most effective option. It is true that, as part of a very small handful of minority faculty, they were more likely to have already formed strong attachments with students of color who sought them out for mentorship and counsel at hostile HWCUs. But faculty appointed to director positions also came cheap, as most contributed their time and energy for little to no compensation. An example is Professor Mary Elizabeth Townsend, one of a small number of Black students at the University of Kansas in the 1960s, who rose to the rank of faculty in the Psychology Department by 1965. By 1974, she had accepted the offer to serve both as faculty and as director of the Office of Minority Affairs at KU, which had originally been called the Office of Urban Affairs in the early 1970s.

Like all early directors, Townsend's own experiences with racism as a student and faculty member motivated her to adopt this role. As a student, a white professor had ordered her to sit in the back of the classroom. When she refused, the faculty member threatened to kick her out of the class. Drawing on her experiences with institutional discrimination at KU, Townsend oversaw the transformation of the Black students' meeting place into an academic and social enrichment center. She is remembered for her staunch advocacy on behalf of marginalized students.[58]

Professor Reginald Thomas provides another interesting case. As an undergraduate in the late 1960s, Thomas had participated in the student uprisings at his own school, a public state university in the mid-Atlantic. He later pursued a PhD at a private university in the South, becoming the campus's first Black PhD and, following graduation, the university's first Black faculty member. He knew from personal experience that, as the saying goes, Black Americans had to work twice as hard to get half as much. As he rose to prominence within the institution, he leveraged his relationships with white administrators, pitching the idea of establishing an Office of Minority Affairs. He succeeded, and the office opened its doors in 1978. It would be the first such office at any southern HWCU.

The office's first director, a history professor, instituted academic support services, promoted leadership skills, worked with the admissions office on recruitment, and, with faculty support, grew the number of multicultural courses offered by the university.[59] But when that director left two years later, Thomas worried that administrators might no longer see a need for a fully functional office for marginalized students. As a result, he took on the role while remaining an active faculty member. Though he served as interim director from 1980 to 1984, he still remembers the pushback he received from white faculty and administrators. When they pointed out that there was no corresponding "Office of Majority Affairs," he reminded them tersely that every office at an HWCU was de facto an Office of Majority Affairs. What was the reaction? "You could have heard a pin drop," he recalls with a grin.[60]

Many student affairs professionals who ran racial affinity centers would likely marvel at Thomas's cheek, seeing in this exchange the kind of power flex that faculty alone could exercise. As one former director of a Black student services center mused, "This was really a student programming office."[61] This was a critical observation: as a result of being situated in student affairs, racial affinity center directors often found themselves hemmed in, their reach within the institution narrow.

By virtue of their enviable positions within the university hierarchy, faculty directors could, by contrast, push offices and centers in more academic directions. In so doing, they managed to situate their offices at the critical intersection of student affairs, academic affairs, and faculty affairs. While some racial affinity centers created programming that approximated seminars, they were rarely a formal part of the curriculum and certainly never credit bearing. Academic change that racial affinity center staff advocated for existed largely at the margins.

Conversely, faculty directors had the privilege of being able to leverage their power in multiple domains to initiate broader transformation in both curriculum and policy. From the start, then, equity work located in academic affairs had the greatest potential to effect institutional change, if only because of academic affairs units' location in the institutional hierarchy.

While it's true that faculty were afforded greater power than most student affairs professionals in their dealings with the university, as people of color in predominantly white institutions, both groups confronted similar difficulties. Among the biggest hurdles they faced were their conflicting loyalties. On the one hand, they had been appointed during a period of great tumult to serve as racial crisis managers on behalf of their institutions. On the other, they wanted to serve as student advocates who fought against structural racism and institutional whiteness.[62] As Pounds phrased it, "Could I represent the university and support the students without any conflict?"[63] This profound tension between serving the interests of the institution and serving the interests of students of color meant a constant struggle for early directors. As we will see in chapter 4, it remains so.

To resolve this tension, many undertook what we might call covert operations in order to help students drive equity work on campuses. Others called it "infiltration."[64] Indeed, social justice proponents within education settings, both then and now, speak in a frankly military vernacular, in the language of tactics, strategies, and precision targets, suggesting in part their embattled positions within HWCUs.

As they reflect back on their roles in those heady days of student protest, early directors recall that they wanted above all to teach their students how to protest more effectively to help create institutional change. Consequently, and perhaps unbeknownst to white senior administrators, many taught their Black students how to organize, how to protest, and how to make sure they would be heard. They taught their students how to win over white student voters in order to rise to campus leadership positions and thus advocate for minority students from a position of power. They therefore imparted a political education to Black students modeled on their own activist years.

Of course, faculty and student affairs professionals alike knew that their students could succeed only if they had enough support from white administrators and faculty. To win hearts and minds, they taught students to adopt different tactics at different moments. There were times to speak out and times to bite your tongue. Like them, Black students needed to be able to walk into a room, size everyone up, identify allies and opponents, and develop a strategy to maneuver accordingly. They had to learn to court white opinion and mobilize white allies, sometimes in the interest of their very survival. Thomas, for instance, often advised his Black students who planned to protest and march to take their white friends just to make sure that police officers wouldn't open fire on them. You see, unlike assaulting Black individuals, manhandling white students was a total nonstarter for police officers. Just think of the fuss their parents would kick up.[65]

Whether staff or faculty, directors had to accept when their influence inevitably diminished, when their voices no longer packed the same punch as they once did. Again, this was more often the situation for racial affinity center staff than for faculty directors of minority affairs offices. Ernest Thomas Cooper remarked that, when he was director of the Black Student Center at a research university in Texas, white faculty and administrators got "tired of hearing just another Black man screaming about all the injustices." In response, he hired a white woman to deliver the message for him. She led trainings with white faculty and administrators and, as he recalls, was quite successful. Cooper believes that white faculty and administrators were willing to actually listen to her, whereas he would have been roundly ignored. His experience resonates with current debates in the DEI world about the racial politics and ethical considerations of who does this work for which audiences and why.

On the whole, early directors of both minority affairs offices and racial affinity centers do not recall faculty as very supportive figures in the 1970s and 1980s. While white faculty were rarely on board, many faculty of color were afraid to speak up lest they risk permanent damage to their careers. Indeed, they could face significant repercussions, including being denied tenure.[66] In other words, white faculty and faculty of color didn't always ally with these programs, but for manifestly different reasons.

Today, early directors regret the lack of faculty participation since, as Cooper says, "they can really make a difference—especially white [faculty]." There were, of course, always one or two history, sociology, or psychology professors who pitched in, especially if they had tenure. But unless minority affairs faculty and staff had personal relationships with white faculty, they were not likely to be institutional partners.[67]

Directors encountered other formidable, if wholly unsurprising, institutional obstacles. Just as students fought against the insidiousness of institutional racism, staff and faculty directors of offices and centers had to put up with their fair share of prejudice. This was particularly the case for student affairs professionals because their arrival signaled massive institutional change. To put it bluntly, many white administrators found them threatening. After a particularly challenging conversation with her white supervisor, Pounds learned years later that he was terrified she might physically attack him. He drew, of course, on the pervasive stereotype of the "angry Black woman" so often promoted in media and culture. Similarly, Black administrators from the 1970s to the present disclose having to be very selective in their expression of anger in order to avoid inciting fears about so-called Black rage that haunted the imaginations of white colleagues and supervisors. Basically, leaders of these offices have always worked hard to counter the racist stereotypes flung at them while also dismantling institutional racism on behalf of students of color.[68]

Under the auspices of student affairs, administrators' power to effect change was undeniably limited. While they could introduce cocurricular supports, such as workshops on how to take notes, how to participate in a class discussion, or how to refine writing skills, they could rarely implement curricular change the way that some faculty directors could, as a result of where they sat in the university structure. That said, both faculty and administrative directors recall that their early visions and office missions were straightforwardly rooted and couched in the terms of fighting institutional racism and systemic oppression in higher-education institutions, as in US society, writ large. The minority rights revolution thus introduced significant changes in the structure, organization, and culture of higher education. Unfortunately, not all were fated to last.

Retreat

Even as offices of minority affairs and racial affinity centers proliferated throughout the late 1960s and 1970s, trouble was already brewing. Whitelash, of course, burst forth fast and furious as ever. From the start of the Black campus movement, conservative student organizations banded together to thwart progressive changes on university campuses.[69] But backlash was also helped along by a series of global calamities. When oil-exporting Arab countries placed an embargo on Western states that supported Israel, the world experienced its first oil shock. The United States was particularly affected by the oil crisis, which lasted from 1973 to 1975. During that period, US unemploy-ment skyrocketed from 5.7 percent to 7.5 percent. Meanwhile, inflation doubled to 12.4 percent.[70] Americans suffered under the weight of gen-eral wage stagnation. And by the late 1970s, the United States found itself knee deep in an economic recession the likes of which hadn't been seen since the Great Depression.

The financial crisis didn't spare colleges and universities. As the economy went into a tailspin, college and university presidents scram-bled to keep institutions afloat. In general, there was a shift toward privatization in higher education and the government that intensified throughout the eighties. In response, colleges and universities shifted the financial burden to students and their families. During the seven-ties, tuition costs had increased sharply; indeed, we can trace today's skyrocketing student loan crisis to this period. Meanwhile, the govern-ment decreased Pell Grant funding, which had promised aid to lower-income students. These developments signaled the end of the "golden era" of higher education that had promised greater college access to all Americans.[71]

Perhaps no event marked the beginning of the end of the progressive era of higher education more than the 1978 *Bakke v. Regents of California* decision, which mandated limits on affirmative action. In 1965, Lyn-don B. Johnson had signed Executive Order 11246, which demanded that contractors "take affirmative action to ensure that applicants are employed, and that employees are treated during employment, without regard to their race, color, religion, sex, or national origin." Richard Nixon extended affirmative action to include government employees. In the late 1960s and early 1970s, many selective colleges adopted affir-mative action policies as a way to diversify their student bodies, just as student activists had demanded.[72]

Enter Allan Bakke. Bakke was not the first white student to chal-lenge affirmative action in college admissions in a court of law, but he was the most significant. Bakke sued UC Davis Medical School because he was twice denied admission. His case made it all the way to the US Supreme Court, which eventually struck down racial quotas in college admissions decisions. The justices claimed that the imposition of racial quotas violated the Fourteenth Amendment's equal protec-tion clause. In particular, they believed it was unfair to punish white students who were entirely innocent of the sins of their forefathers. It was tantamount to reverse discrimination, they and many others would later suggest.

The *Bakke* ruling rolled back one of the most significant wins that civil rights and student activists had secured over the previous decade. It also ushered in a sea change in higher education. The court conceded that universities could take "diversity" into account in college admissions but maintained that race could serve as only one of several factors considered. In so doing, the decision declared that *any form* of so-called difference counted as diversity. According to Richard Thompson Ford, Justice Lewis Powell equated race and ethnicity, reducing both to varieties of "cultural" experience and ensuring that "'diversity' would tend to focus only on cultural difference and would ignore or play down the history of racism and the relevance of status hierarchy."[73] As such, affirmative action went from a practice to address histories of discrimination to a more general expression of support for all kinds of student diversity, one that relied on what Angela Castagno has called "power-blindness."[74] The ruling foreshadowed a shift away from acknowledging how power operated in this country to marginalize some in favor of others and toward a flat understanding of diversity as any form of difference. In short, it created the conditions for the diversity regime to come.

The *Bakke* decision was a legal battle, but it reflected broader cultural and political transitions. It signaled not only an adoption of power-blindness but also the increasingly pervasive ideology of color-blindness. As the sociologist Eduardo Bonilla-Silva has argued, color-blindness, or color-blind racism, was a powerful new sociopolitical force that took hold in the United States after the civil rights era. According to Bonilla-Silva, color-blindness—the idea that "we don't see color" and thus that racial difference is insignificant—suffused the American imagination from Right to Left. As he describes it, this "New Racism" was "subtle, institutional, and apparently non-racial." Eventually color-blindness became its own unique form of racism because it upheld the status quo and white supremacy in Reagan's America and long after.

Because color-blind racism explained away contemporary racial inequality through nonracial, power-blind dynamics, it dovetailed neatly with the broader global swing toward neoliberalism. Neoliberal ideology places primacy on the individual above all else. At the policy level, neoliberals favor a laissez-faire approach to the economy because, as they see it, the free market alone can liberate individuals. Those neoliberal arguments about the free market fed color-blind racism because they rearticulated elements of traditional liberalism in the grammar of "work ethic, rewards by merit, equal opportunity, individualism, etc.," as Bonilla-Silva puts it.[75] From there, it's only a short step to Bakke—a white student who claimed that he "deserved" admission and that students of color were merely "special admits." Indeed, the decision itself coincided with another neoliberal shift in higher education: a shift from a general consensus about higher ed's institutional responsibility to educate all US students, toward a new consensus that underscored the notion of students' "right" to college admission. And, as we've seen in previous chapters, it was only white Christian men who ever enjoyed that kind of privilege in the United States.

The *Bakke* decision opened the floodgates to wave after wave of lawsuits challenging affirmative action throughout the 1980s and 1990s. From the University of Georgia and the University of Texas to the University of Michigan and the entire University of California system, HWCUs reversed course throughout these decades, erasing some of the advances of the 1960s and 1970s when students and, to some extent, the wider public held them responsible for dealing with the historical injustices they had had a hand in creating.[76] To provide but one example: throughout the 1980s, there was no increase in the percentage of Black students enrolled in college.[77]

In many ways, these rollbacks reflected the changing political winds. The sixties and seventies reconfigured the Left around progressive political ideals. The Cold War played a part here too. Soviets could easily point to the United States' violent repression of people of color in order to make the moral case—to formerly colonized regions of the world, especially—that their Communist model was far superior. In response, US leaders found themselves in the unenviable position of having to adopt antidiscriminatory legislation in order to maintain some semblance of moral legitimacy on the global stage.[78] I raise this point for one reason alone: US commitment to the struggle for social justice receded at the same moment that Soviet Russia was on the decline. I can't help but wonder whether at least part of the story of the conservative retrenchment of the eighties and nineties is not attributable to the declining external pressure on the United States to address systemic racism.

Fed in part by the economic crisis and, perhaps, by the waning of the Cold War, the eighties and nineties witnessed the reconstitution of the Right. The National Rifle Association, the Moral Majority, and evangelical Christian groups forged a powerful New Right that breathed life into the Republican Party and catapulted Reagan to the presidency from 1981 to 1989. During the Reagan era, the rise of the neoliberal state, the emergence of the new economy, and the dismantling of federal antidiscrimination programs, including affirmative action programs, paved the way back to an inequitable admissions process that continues to favor wealthy white students. In line with a fervent faith in doctrinaire free-market beliefs, and in response to the specter of a nation run by radical leftists who believed in racial equality, the Reagan administration rescinded federal support of higher education.[79] As one student affairs administrator remembers, "It was every man for himself."[80]

During the 1980s and 1990s, Republicans successfully destroyed the fragile wins of the previous decades that had only just begun to show signs of success, especially those that sought to lift Black Americans out of centuries of generational poverty. Then as now, obtaining a college degree powered socioeconomic mobility. But under Reagan-era rollbacks, Black unemployment soared once again, reaching 15.5 percent, a figure not seen since the Great Depression. As the state chipped away at social services and other supports, there was also an expansion in mass incarceration, the beginning of the so-called war on poverty, and a precipitous growth in poverty among marginalized communities.[81] How could this phenomenon not affect HWCUs? Black student enrollment plummeted in the early 1980s compared to the mid-1970s.[82] Similarly, the mid-1990s saw a new low point in federal funding for Native American higher education. Tribally controlled colleges received less than half the funds promised.[83]

As the culture wars raged throughout the 1980s and 1990s, offices of minority affairs and racial affinity centers found themselves caught in the crossfire. As an administrator at a large public research university in the eighties put it bluntly, "A wave of antipathy landed at my doorstep."[84] Indeed, every faculty member and administrator I interviewed who served in these offices during the eighties and nineties shared his sentiments. Senior administrative leaders, they believed, began to send the message, "We'll give you enough to keep you quiet, but we're not going to change who we really are as a higher education institution—[for instance] the elitist values upon which we're founded." Simply put, they no longer saw these offices as "a good return on investment."[85]

Senior leaders of HWCUs pulled the rug out from under directors and coordinators of these newly founded offices. As a former director of Black student services at a large public flagship in the West put it, "When the financial crisis hit, funding for minority student programs were the first to go."[86] She speculated, "When the civil rights movement died down . . . [administrators] didn't see the need to have so many separate offices." Though the recession certainly played its part, defunding minority affairs offices and racial affinity centers was also the outcome of decades of complaints from white students and parents who, as early as the sixties, declared that special services for minority students constituted both "special treatment" and "reverse discrimination."[87] These were the inevitable consequences of the *Bakke* decision.

In the tumultuous 1960s and 1970s, many senior leaders at HWCUs begrudgingly accepted that, in order to protect and preserve their institutions, they simply had to bring them into line with society's growing expectation of equality for all. To refuse to do so was to condemn the university to chaos, to risk its reputation in a marketplace where their primary clientele—students—refused to endure second-class citizenship any longer.[88] It's no exaggeration to say that, to assure their very future, leaders of HWCUs adjusted to changing times by adopting the logic of Allan Bakke's argument that white students were entitled to admission to college, while minority students were qualified only because of their status as underrepresented.

The events of the 1980s and 1990s removed the imperative to evolve. Many senior leaders at HWCUs turned their backs on their obligation to dismantle injustice. They started to rethink the mission and purpose of these centers, seeing them now as not only unfair but divisive of the campus community. Recall that Harvard established a center for minority students in 1969, only to shutter it five years later in 1974. Students renewed their demands two decades later, in 1995. Dean of students Archie C. Epps III fiercely opposed them, stating, "It would be inconsistent with [Harvard's] purpose to set aside space for racial, ethnic and cultural groups." According to Epps, "Third-World or multicultural centers promote racial separation."[89]

As was the case at Harvard, the Black Cultural Center at the University of Tennessee, Knoxville, closed and then reopened following renewed student protest in 1980, at which point it was renamed the Office of Minority Affairs and oversaw the operations of the Black Cultural Center. Importantly, though, the office's mission further distanced itself from its early promotion of "understanding and appreciation of the black experience" and increasingly moved toward "serving all students regardless of race, religion, or background."[90] Such attitudes led to the liquidation of specific ethnic organizations in favor of lumping them all under a central multicultural office limited to cultural programming. Again, this was a response to growing discomfort in white America about addressing historical injustices and signaled a preference for a flat understanding of cultural differences, also known as multiculturalism.

HWCUs welcomed the ideology and language of multiculturalism, prompting in the late eighties and nineties the transformation of many offices of minority affairs and racial affinity centers into varieties of multicultural centers that celebrated all manner of "difference" among the student body. The move away from addressing structural inequities head-on was apparent in the centers' new mission statements. Throughout the late eighties and nineties, institutions as varied as Wake Forest, Texas State, and Mount Holyoke transformed faculty-led minority affairs offices into multicultural centers.[91] The reorganization reflected a larger shift toward feel-good "diversity" programming for the whole campus community.[92] Later in 1999, the University of Kansas Office of Minority Affairs morphed into the Multicultural Resource Center, "designed to enhance cultural awareness and appreciation of cultures among all ethnic groups on campus" and "celebrate the diverse composition of the Lawrence Campus population."[93]

Multiculturalism was not all bad. It was clearly influenced by the movements of the 1960s and 1970s and was a response to the steady diversification of the US population that had taken place during those years. In 1965, white Americans counted for 84 percent of the US population; by 1995, they accounted for 72 percent.[94] The term "multiculturalism," then, accounted for the presence of an ever-growing array of people of color in the United States. In that sense it could be seen as a more "inclusive" term. The issue that concerns us, however, is what was lost in translation, as struggles for equity and justice morphed into a bland celebration of cultural difference. This is where we see the reappearance of the language of "tolerance." "Tolerance" discourse was rooted in the 1940s, specifically in efforts toward intercultural and interfaith harmony, but the 1980s refurbished those notions and added a neoliberal twist: tolerance was now about how individuals relate to one another, not about state law and policy that countered structural racism. Roughly translated, 1980s-era tolerance meant, "You do not have to like people who are different from you, but you do have to put up with them." The reduction of the social justice struggle to an apolitical interpersonal conflict management philosophy is rooted in this period and continues to this day.

It's possible that minority affairs offices may have survived the political maelstrom. After all, we saw a resurgence of student activism in the 1980s and 1990s centered, for example, on the antiapartheid struggle.

But it wasn't enough, and faculty were otherwise engaged. Throughout the short existence of minority affairs offices, though lead staff didn't find all faculty receptive to their cause, they could always rely on at least some faculty in interdisciplinary departments and programs, which were uncoincidentally among the most racially diverse academic units at HWCUs. But in the 1990s and early 2000s, faculty attentions turned elsewhere. Specifically, scholars found themselves in the throes of what have been remembered as "the canon wars."

The canon wars occurred when faculty in interdisciplinary departments mounted a challenge to the traditional canon in fields like literature and history. They asked: which authors should constitute "the canon," and was it not time to revise it? Traditionalists argued that all students needed exposure to the great Western classics authored by Shakespeare, Faulkner, and Fitzgerald, and the canon reflected this, consisting almost entirely of works written by elite white men. By contrast, multiculturalists believed that the moment demanded a rethinking of who and what had been left out. Specifically, they called for the inclusion of works by those long ignored, including women and people of color, on humanities syllabi: for example, Virginia Woolf, Toni Morrison, and James Baldwin.[95] It wasn't the first time academics had questioned the content of the traditional college curriculum. It wasn't even the first time that century.[96] But the canon wars took place at an undeniably contentious political moment.

Traditionalists weren't shy about calling out multiculturalists for their overtly "political" agenda. When Allan Bloom, a philosopher and professor at the University of Chicago, published *The Closing of the American Mind* in 1987, he argued that the canon wars were yet another detrimental outcome of the 1960s and 1970s when, he claimed, universities had confused their mission to educate students about "superior" moral truths with a new mission to educate them about structural racism and social justice. He was just the first of many to make such an argument.[97] In the end, traditionalists perhaps exaggerated the extent to which women, people of color, or both colonized syllabi. In fact, courses featuring diverse authors remained ancillary, often addenda to "great books" courses, relegated to electives on the fringes of the curriculum.[98] But that was hardly the point. It was yet another backlash against the progressive ideals ushered in by the civil rights era.

While the canon wars are not a direct concern of this book, they do play a tangential role in our story. Although faculty allies steadily worked toward the diversification of the curriculum, their efforts took place separately from the evolution of DEI offices, mired as they were in the multicultural morass.[99] "In the canon wars, how would you put DEI into practice?" one senior practitioner asked.[100] It is here we start to see a separation between how DEI issues were addressed in curricular versus cocurricular spaces.

The same practitioner recalled that over time, "faculty retreated to their academic corners" and became "less involved" than the first generation of scholar activists. She took pains to point out, however, that what she saw was less "a schism" than the evolving culture of the academy, which included greater demands on faculty—specifically the dawn of the publish-or-perish mindset.[101] In other words, it's not necessarily that faculty consciously rescinded support. Rather, they responded naturally to the kinds of structural pressures under which they increasingly found themselves. As administrators lost the participation of what few powerful allies they had, DEI measures were further emptied of their social justice meanings. This is a state of affairs that, as chapter 5 will show, requires immediate redress.

Without the fire of the civil rights era, support for ethnic studies, African and African American studies, and other departments similarly subsided. From the start, these programs had often incited hostility from white students as well as many white administrators and faculty, perceived, according to David Yamane, as "academically immature and misguided stepchildren borne of the wildly radical sixties."[102] But the political climate of the 1980s and 1990s allowed opponents to express those opinions more loudly. Combined with the financial squeeze of the 1980s, interdisciplinary programs and departments struggled to stay afloat. Administrators refused to approve hires or budget increases.[103] For educational institutions, it was an opportunity to reconsider the very existence of these academic programs in the modern university.

While universities sapped resources from interdisciplinary fields and departments, philanthropic foundations also played a role. The Ford Foundation, for instance, refused to fund Black studies programs it deemed too radical. Instead, funders offered support to departments that were less political, less activist, and more interested in "integrating" into the university.[104] Just as racial affinity centers and offices of minority affairs found themselves increasingly under attack, foundations assisted universities in neutralizing the galvanizing power of one of the only academic spaces on college campuses invested in the structural critique of the university system and of society at large. Interdisciplinary departments and programs that refused to fall in line suffered.

As political and financial support from universities and funders dried up, many interdisciplinary programs were dissolved. They were reestablished in the twenty-first century only thanks to renewed student activism.[105]

Diversity Dawns

By the end of the twentieth century, affirmative action was under attack throughout the country, and the fight for social justice along with it. The story of Proposition 209 provides one illustrative case. In 1996, Prop. 209 passed in California, effectively eliminating the use of affirmative-action policies throughout the state, including in higher-education admissions processes. The trend was particularly accentuated at the University of California's two most selective universities. At both UCLA and UC Berkeley, the percentage of Black and Hispanic students fell by more than half between 1995 and 1998.[106] I spoke about the fallout of Prop. 209 with one longtime social justice advocate in California who spent most of her career fighting for educational equity. As she remembered, "The number of Black and Latino students plummeted, and we've spent the last twenty-five years trying to get back to where we were."[107] In other words, Prop. 209's impact on communities of color was devastating.

This practitioner also recalled that, after the passage of Prop. 209, "all the language had to change." Whether in local college access programs or institutions of higher learning, the terms "race" and "ethnicity" were now prohibited. Instead, missions were reframed as seeking "to prepare students from backgrounds and communities that are underrepresented in higher education." As she noted, "It was the only way to get around legal barriers [about] what we had always been open and honest about in the past."[108] Her experience reflects what scholars have documented too. According to Anthony Platt, "Future historians might very well note 1954, the year of *Brown v. Board of Education*, and 1996 [the year of Prop. 209] as the markers of the rise and fall of the post-World War II Civil Rights Movement."[109]

As US culture lurched rightward throughout the 1980s and 1990s, college faculty and administrators grew tired of equity language. Institutional representatives of predominantly white institutions no longer wished to debate equal opportunity and affirmative action. "We could read the tea leaves," said one chief diversity officer who served at a large midwestern public research university from 1990 to 2020.[110]

As the days of justice, equality, and equity waned, terms like "oppression" that implied critique and elicited sharper, more defensive reactions from white students, faculty, and administrators also disappeared.[111] Instead, practitioners adapted by grasping for more "neutral," acceptable, feel-good terms in order to disarm powerful white senior administrators and faculty who had reversed course.[112] These adaptations created a slow slippage toward power-blind "diversity" language as a way of managing so-called difference.[113] By the early 2000s, "diversity" replaced terms like "institutional racism."[114] To survive the political storm that engulfed universities, directors of these offices resigned themselves to the language of diversity as the only way to get things done.

CHAPTER 4

Diversity Practitioners and Institutional Whiteness

The "diversity regime," as James M. Thomas calls it, dawned in a number of industries, not just higher education.[1] The notion of "managing diversity" rose to popularity in corporate environments in the 1990s. By the midnineties, 70 percent of fifty Fortune 500 companies had diversity management programs. But there were ulterior motives in play. According to Will Kymlicka, corporations managed to "reduce multiculturalism to a marketing ploy, as if the goal of multiculturalism is not to challenge inherited racial and ethnic hierarchies, but rather to repackage cultural differences as an economic asset in a global economy and/or as a commodity or lifestyle good that can be marketed and consumed."[2]

To their great dismay, lead practitioners watched as institutional leaders in higher education similarly engaged in the commodification of diversity, especially student diversity. Senior leaders at HWCUs learned that there was a profit to be made in drawing public attention to Black and brown bodies, providing what Sara Ahmed calls "a multicultural aesthetic" to university websites and brochures with the goal of demonstrating how very progressive institutions were.[3] But practitioners almost unanimously agree that this obsession with collecting and displaying bodies of different colors in HWCU university materials and on websites was simply a means of *deflecting* attention away from the abandonment of the fight for social justice. At the start of the 2000s, then, a bizarre situation arose: more and more students of color arrived on college campuses, shoring up institutions' image as bastions of diversity, yet campuses themselves had not dismantled the infrastructure of institutional whiteness that posed significant obstacles to the academic success and well-being of "nontraditional" students. Since then, the main function of diversity practitioners has been to bridge that gap.

Diversity practitioners support students in critical ways, but they also increasingly make up for institutional shortfalls. Drawing on their own personal backgrounds and experiences with systems of inequality, diversity practitioners bring a structural lens to their work that allows them to see students holistically, as connected to communities that contend with broader systems of oppression. And it's because they employ a social justice framework that diversity practitioners are so successful in their one-on-one work with students. But as soon as they start working within institutional parameters, everything changes. Under the power-blind diversity regime, structural inequality and institutional whiteness cannot be named, and as a result, diversity practitioners at every level wind up instead playing the part of "minority managers"— that is, staff who are regularly called on to manage identity-based crises on behalf of all-white, or majority-white, faculty, administrators, and senior leaders in ways that pacify students of color while papering over institutional failings.[4] And while the last several years, especially, have witnessed an explosion of chief diversity officers who, theoretically anyway, have more power, more authority, and more institutional pull than ever before, institutional whiteness prevents them, too, from doing their jobs effectively. As we'll soon see, the power-blind diversity regime feeds institutional whiteness, constrains diversity practitioners at all levels, and ultimately prevents HWCUs from responding to the imperative to change.

The Practitioners

Diversity practitioners forge strong relationships with the students they serve, in part because they share similar backgrounds, experiences, and upbringings. Black, Latina, and other woman-identifying people of color predominate in the field of DEI today. Though there are some South and East Asian Americans and white practitioners in the field, we tend to be few and far between. Many practitioners, though not all, also identify as first generation and working class. Some are immigrant-descended, others perhaps undocumented, DACA-mented, or DREAM-ers. Like early practitioners, we come to the work informed by our own early and intimate experiences with sexism, racism, classism, and other forms of oppression. And like our predecessors, we found our political causes during our college careers, even in the notoriously apathetic 1990s and 2000s. Those who came of age in the late 1980s and 1990s participated in antiapartheid and divestment rallies.[5] Similarly, those of us who came of age in the 2000s may have protested the invasion of Afghanistan. In more recent decades, practitioners have supported and participated in the Black Lives Matter movements. Times change, but we are all marked by our era.

Most of us also experienced institutional bias while attending HWCUs and predominantly white institutions and so readily relate to students who experience something similar at today's colleges and universities. When asked about the defining moment that made them want to become DEI administrators, nearly every interviewee I spoke with instantly relayed a story of being on the receiving end of bias, prejudice, and discrimination from peers, staff, and faculty members while in college. I recall the story of one practitioner in particular—a first-generation working-class Latina at an HWCU in the 1990s. She recounted a time when a white faculty member told her that if she didn't feel comfortable on campus, then maybe that campus wasn't for her.[6] A Black transfer student who would later go on to become an affirmative action officer remembered that, when he met with a dean at UCLA, he was told he would never make it into the university. As it turned out, not only did he get into UCLA, but he was voted one of the fifty most outstanding students in his graduating class. On graduation day, he approached that dean and asked, "Do you remember me?" The dean claimed not to. "Yeah you do," he said, and walked out.[7]

Over time, we are radicalized by these experiences. They make us want to change the ways universities operate, if not for ourselves, then for the students who come after us. And so we enter administrative roles with a desire to improve the college climate, create community, and enact structural change—whatever we can do given our role and our position in the university hierarchy.

So what does the day-to-day look like? Let's start with student-facing administrators who work most closely with historically marginalized undergraduates. We're familiar, perhaps, with the bland bullet points that dot position descriptions, dully laying out "expectations" and "responsibilities": "Advise students." "Manage programs." "Work closely with colleagues across campus units." The list is long and doesn't make for the most inspiring reading. But these jobs require much more than meets the eye.

In addition to all the normal administrative work you would expect with any university staff position, we must at all times be attentive to how national political turmoil plays out concretely in the lives of our students. That means that we often support students who are in crisis not only as a result of the academic and social stress they experience on campus, but because of what is taking place off campus—from death, illness, and general strife in their families to the impact of police violence, ICE raids, or deportations on their communities. Because diversity staff approach students holistically, we are better able to connect the dots when, say, their academic performance takes a sudden nosedive during periods of personal turmoil. From our perspective, then, we come to understand that expanding access to students from so-called nontraditional backgrounds means that we're also opening the doors to marginalized communities in the United States who face the kind of challenges that more "traditional" student populations do not. Diversity practitioners thus find themselves in an odd position: their success with students depends on their awareness of structural oppression at large, and yet, as we'll see, their professional success depends on operating within a power-blind diversity regime at work.

Diversity practitioners' awareness of and experience with structural and social inequality in the wider world helps us make other connections that our colleagues might not. For example, some of our students have never had steady access to health care, let alone free, high-quality health care. A trip to the doctor could have meant breaking the bank. Consequently, they may make decisions that, on the surface, are hard to comprehend for those of us, including myself, who take health insurance for granted. I once had a student whose grades went south and whose academic advisers couldn't figure out why. When I spoke with her, she explained that she was having trouble with her eyesight, that she couldn't see her professor's PowerPoint slides, and that she was too embarrassed to tell anyone. She'd written off the possibility of addressing the problem because, in the past, that kind of medical support was inaccessible and unaffordable. Interestingly, I heard the exact same story from a diversity program administrator from the 1980s.[8] Our role in this instance is to orient students to resource-rich environments that offer them benefits that were unheard of in their lives before college.

Mental health offers another example of how and why diversity practitioners bring a more all-encompassing lens to bear in their work. In 2023, the National Education Association revealed that the majority of college students suffer from one or more mental-health problems, including anxiety, depression, and suicidal ideation. While students from all backgrounds experience these symptoms, students of color and students from rural backgrounds are less likely to seek treatment than their peers. Indeed, white students are twice as likely to seek treatment as Black and Asian students.[9] For many students that diversity practitioners work with, however, discussions about mental health are a nonstarter. Some students have received messages their whole lives that one's struggles are simply not to be discussed. I, too, was raised thinking that in the face of crisis, you're supposed to just muscle through and keep a stiff upper lip. It comes as a revelation to them that, as college students, not only do they have access to free university health care, but, in fact, mental health services are strongly encouraged for all students. Once again, diversity practitioners draw on their personal experience as well as their knowledge of wider structural inequality to support student well-being and, by extension, academic success. In so doing, they are making up for institutions that see diverse students as colorful additions to a predominantly white student body as opposed to members of historically marginalized communities who arrive at college with different cultural norms, beliefs, and experiences that impact their college success.

In individual interactions with students, diversity practitioners have the autonomy to integrate a much-needed equity lens even under the auspices of the diversity regime. But there are limits to what they can accomplish when their work involves others on campus who operate within a power-blind framework. Although it's not part of the formal job description, diversity practitioners, especially those who work closely with students, serve as microaggression managers on behalf of our institutions. Certainly other students contribute to that state of affairs, since many confront large numbers of peers from different racial backgrounds for the first time when they go off to college, making microaggressions distressingly common. But other students aren't the only—or even the primary—source of microaggressions.

One situation that comes to mind reveals multiple institutional failings that hamper the work of diversity practitioners. I remember a young Asian American student from a first-generation, low-income background who came to me shaking because a white STEM faculty member had told them that they were not capable of taking any advanced math course. I looped in an academic adviser to advise and intervene, though not without first finding myself in the uncomfortable situation of managing the professor who called me unexpectedly to insist he had done nothing wrong.

What's wrong with this picture? In the first place, institutions simply do not equip PhDs to work with historically marginalized students. Like many of us, this faculty member needed pedagogical guidance and, without that support, reacted as many would—defensively and belligerently, from a place of fear rather than curiosity. Being a microaggression manager between students and faculty, then, maintains the status quo wherein faculty do not have—*and do not need to have*—the proper preparation for working with student populations who increasingly make up the undergraduate student body.

Second, the incident also demonstrates how, when supporting students, those with little power (student-facing diversity staff) can find themselves going toe to toe with those with considerably more institutional power (in this case, faculty). That puts diversity practitioners in the uncomfortable—and unnecessary—role of "diversity cop." That kind of antagonistic setup does little to foster trusting relationships with faculty, who, as we've seen, can be their most powerful allies.

Third, while student-facing diversity practitioners can indeed provide solace and emotional support to students who have experienced microaggressions, they have little to no institutional power to do anything more about it. Why? For one, they're limited by their placement in the university hierarchy and their resulting lack of institutional authority. But the issue of positionality is compounded by the fact that they wouldn't be able to name racialized power dynamics under the dominant diversity regime even if they wanted to. This is a pattern that repeats itself in many interactions with other members of the university community.

As microaggression managers at HWCUs, diversity practitioners also find themselves in challenging situations vis-à-vis colleagues in a variety of offices and departments on campus. I once counseled an African American student who was advised by career services staff to write about what it was like growing up in "an urban high school" for their law school application—an experience that the student did not in fact have growing up. Similarly, another staffer in that office praised an Asian American student that I was advising for not being "a quiet Asian girl," letting them know that this would be an advantage in the

competitive hunt for summer internships. After these incidents, I suggested to career services leaders that they might want to implement
antiracist training for their staff. I have no idea if they actually did.
Here, again, we see the same institutional gaps: a lack of racial literacy
skills among university staff, the inability of a diversity practitioner to
effect any meaningful institutional change, and the necessity of the
diversity practitioner to manage the fallout from microaggressions on
behalf of the institution by offering individual support to students. It's
in this manner that diversity practitioners fill institutional gaps in ways
that leave institutional whiteness in place and let HWCUs off the hook.

Although we are hired to support students, our efforts are hampered
not just by our lack of power to effect change but also by the institutional cultures of HWCUs, where microaggressions among colleagues
are still regrettably common. Indeed, the same "-isms" that thwarted
us as students are waiting right where they ever were when we become
staff members. Though women of color, especially Black and Latina
women, overwhelmingly make up the field of DEI practitioners in
higher education, the institutions we work in are of course predominantly white. There are now ample studies demonstrating what all of us
already know: that the social identities of higher-education professionals at HWCUs affect their experiences as staff members. This is especially true when it comes to our racial identity/ies.[10] As is the case for
students, day-to-day microaggressions exact a significant psychosocial
toll on equity practitioners.[11] As one former senior leader confided, "As
a Black woman, I felt on some days, how many more insults will I have
to endure, how many more slights?"[12] As we'll see, it's even worse for
senior leaders. Unsurprisingly, then, as W. Carson Byrd and his coauthors observe, "Faculty and staff of color have a higher likelihood of
experiencing isolation, marginalization, tokenization, and alienation
within campus communities." They often lack mentorship and they
suffer worse working conditions.[13] In short, diversity practitioners
are managing microaggressions on behalf of students while navigating microaggressions themselves. These working conditions are hardly
conducive to doing one's job effectively.

Things aren't always so bleak, of course. Since about 2010, and
especially after summer 2020, many of our colleagues have shown a
greater willingness to consider how power, oppression, and privilege
work and to partner with us. This is particularly the case with white
colleagues, who, as we saw in the previous chapter, have always been
key allies in the struggle against institutional oppression in HWCUs. In

a post-BLM, post–George Floyd world, more white administrators can readily acknowledge that they face fewer challenges in the workplace environment where it concerns racism and, if they are men, sexism. One interviewee who identified as a cisgender white man suspected that his privileged social identities accorded him more status with senior leaders who share those identities. He noticed that at times he seemed more capable of moving his agenda forward through the administrative morass than others did, and with significantly less blowback. In the case of this particular practitioner, he readily recognized the leeway afforded him and tried to use it on behalf of his marginalized colleagues. As he reflected, "I'm just less likely to be punished for what I say."[14] In so doing, he engages in what social justice circles call everyday acts of allyship—that is, a racial-identity consciousness that allows more privileged individuals to occasionally mobilize their power in order to say and do what more marginalized members of society often cannot.

Such acts of professional allyship require a knowledge and recognition of how structural racism shapes the workplace and how each of us can—and cannot—move through it. That awareness can go far in creating a productive, collaborative environment with diversity practitioners, most of whom are women of color. According to one white woman, "I'm a feminine-presenting white lady with an extroverted personality, [so] I have to be aware of that when I work in this space."[15] Another practitioner said that he also makes it a point to acknowledge identity-based power dynamics in the workplace. He might preface his comments with phrases like, "Of course, I'm the white man saying this, but . . ."[16] This is not to undermine his expertise and authority, but rather to acknowledge that due to his worldview and experiences, he may have a different perspective on the issue at hand than other people in the room.

Though a basic awareness of identity-based power dynamics makes for strong allies, as we've seen time and again, it's not something diversity practitioners can always count on. Although we rarely discuss it openly, diversity practitioners often encounter problems in their working relationships with white women specifically. Indeed, nearly every woman of color interviewee who served as a diversity practitioner from the 1960s onward implored me to take a moment in this book to discuss their fraught professional relationships with white women. On the one hand, white women certainly make for strong allies, but they must be able to understand and attend to racial power dynamics in the workplace. One senior DEI practitioner active since the 2000s recalled,

"White women were quite frankly perhaps as notorious for using their privilege to dismiss the concerns of women of color [as white men]." She remembered in particular that they talked over her in meetings. When she raised the issue, she was told, "We're just doing what the guys do."[17] In other words, in some white women's quest to fight sexism in the academy, they adopted precisely those patriarchal habits that had once oppressed them, and then wielded their newfound power over women of color. Based on my conversations with today's diversity practitioners, these challenges persist.

While race poses problems at an interpersonal level between white women administrators, on the one hand, and the women of color who lead DEI offices, on the other, there's more to it than just that. Because of their gender and race positionality, white women can have difficulty forming strong relationships with students of color. In some cases, the experiential disconnect between white women and students of color can lead to unpleasant, even dangerous, situations. One former DEI administrator, Elena Gonzalez, told me about a fraught encounter between a Latinx student and a white female administrator who threatened to call the Department of Public Safety on him. When Gonzalez learned of the incident, she had to pull her colleague aside and explain that, for an inner-city kid of color, police did not represent community safety but state-sanctioned violence and brutality. She explained that white women have certain kinds of privilege in their interactions with police that people of color may not, and that such interactions don't always end well for them. In this case, it was a successful teachable moment: the white female administrator apologized to the student for her ignorance and went about thinking through more culturally responsive actions she could have taken.[18] This is a story with a happy ending, but it's more the exception than the rule. As today's diversity practitioners attest, a conversation like the one Gonzalez had with her colleague would more likely raise hackles and elicit defensiveness than lead to a mutually agreeable resolution.

At the end of the day, diversity practitioners who work closely with students are critical to the institution's daily functioning. They are successful in their jobs because they develop strong relationships with students; they know they have to approach them holistically, not just as individuals severed from their communities and the wider world. By taking into account how wider systems of violence can impact students, they are bringing an equity and justice lens to their work. But they can do so only so long as they avoid words like "oppression," "inequality," and especially "racism." Moreover, as they navigate their own daily slights and humiliations, as they cope with the realities of having low status in the university hierarchy, student-facing diversity practitioners often find themselves in a precarious position vis-à-vis other university community members. Since they can't actually make broader institutional changes, their main job function is to manage campus microaggressions and, by extension, manage minority students in ways that shield institutions. Unfortunately, that's also the lot of the chief diversity officer.

The Rise of the CDO

Until around the late 1990s, DEI practitioners were still a relatively rare presence in the world of university governance. If they were on the executive leadership team, they may have had a legal background and handled compliance issues around, for example, affirmative action, Title IX, and the Americans with Disabilities Act. One former affirmative action officer I spoke with reported to Human Resources, while others sat in the president's cabinet. To some extent, that hasn't entirely changed. These sorts of positions still exist and take on similar legal, regulatory, and institutional equity work. Increasingly, however, they are also responsible for helping adjudicate bias and discrimination cases on campus. They may oversee workplace discrimination cases and handle other issues traditionally housed in Human Resources. They remain critical to the day-to-day operations of a university.[19]

After BLM and especially after summer 2020, we saw a massive expansion of these senior-level roles. And they have very different portfolios than their predecessors did. They go by many names: dean, vice chancellor, chief diversity officer (CDO), vice president for diversity, equity, inclusion. As lead diversity officers for their institutions, they have the power to elevate student issues to institutional priorities and to centralize and synchronize often wildly disparate DEI visions, programs, and strategies that have emerged across campus.[20] Those who sit in the president's cabinet have broader organizational purview and access to power.[21].

Because senior-level diversity practitioners have a bird's-eye view of the university, typically their first responsibility is to develop, coordinate, and/or implement DEI strategic plans. Now, strategic plans have a pretty bad rap among students, faculty, and some alumni. To some, strategic plans are really nothing more than hollow political gestures.[22]

While more than a little skepticism surrounds the idea of DEI strategic plans, most practitioners nevertheless agree that it's better to have something than nothing. "They're a pain in the ass," said one, "but I understand why people do them."[23] If nothing else, it is productive to write down on paper where the institution needs to focus and develop its DEI efforts. In fact, the hiring of lead diversity officers is often item number one on these strategic plans.

The content of strategic plans depends entirely on institutional context. At minimum, lead diversity officers manage the deans and directors of various campus affinity centers—the women's center, the LGBTQ center, and the racial affinity centers. Most function as chief student affairs officers with exclusively DEI portfolios. This has been something of a game changer. As one CDO put it, in the past, DEI coordinators of affinity centers could think only programmatically, which limited their institutional reach.[24] In order to even have a chance of creating broader organizational change, they had to rely on their influence, not power, and, as one former CDO reminded me, influence is hard to come by when your job is to shift culture in ways that make people feel uncomfortable.[25] Now senior-level administrators can think more institutionally about student-facing work. They can devote their attention to matters of policy, decision-making, and strategy.[26]

In addition to overseeing student affairs centers, lead diversity officers are also responsible for establishing metrics for success, implementing surveys, and producing incontrovertible proof that these programs and others are effective.[27] There is, then, an institutional research component to CDO jobs. Luckily, they have help from social science researchers, who provide scholarship on the ways that HWCUs fail to create inclusive and equitable environments for students of color, especially when they are low income, first generation, and/or genderqueer. Such scholars have furnished practitioners with much-needed evidence that practitioners then mobilize when bargaining with senior leaders. Moreover, in concert with institutional research offices, diversity practitioners are better able to track and evaluate student success outcomes, including GPAs, retention, years to graduation, and metrics demonstrating student belonging. Though rarely required of other campus centers and programs, this mountain of information has immense benefits. It's a veritable arsenal of evidence for practitioners who must constantly assert and defend why DEI work is so urgent and important.

Senior-level diversity practitioners' portfolios are also increasingly attentive to the recruitment, retention, and advancement of historically marginalized faculty. Despite attempts by the academy to diversify faculty, white men and women still outnumber faculty of color by a very large margin at all ranks.[28] In the wake of 2020, we saw the appearance of the hashtag #BlackInTheIvory, where Black faculty, especially Black female faculty, disclosed on social media the onslaught of microaggressions they contend with day to day.[29] Not too long after, in May 2021, the *Chronicle of Higher Education* published a digital tool that allowed readers to look up how many Black female faculty work at their institutions.[30] As you might imagine, the numbers were dismal. In some ways, these developments are in line with a disturbing and growing subgenre in the field of education where faculty of color, especially female faculty of color, describe their challenges navigating the racist and sexist culture of the academy.[31] In fact, the post-2020 "Great Resignation" that swept through the academy hewed closely to racial and gender lines, as it is women and people of color who tend to take on child-care responsibilities and unpaid labor at work, not least of all on DEI committees.[32] All this has dragged into the light how much more work HWCUs need to do to not only recruit but retain their faculty of color.

On the face of it, then, it would appear that HWCUs have given CDOs an extensive mandate to introduce sweeping change. Certainly, like any senior administrator, they have to learn the art of politicking, deciding when and how to expend political capital, identifying so-called red flags, and avoiding the proverbial land mines. And like other senior leaders, because they are situated so high in the university hierarchy, their professional difficulties are often amplified: they are highly visible and under constant scrutiny, and they suffer worse consequences if they run afoul of the institution. But for a professional to be asked to deliver wide-ranging institutional change that chips away at the structures on which the institution was founded—that's a uniquely tall order.

Some of the obstacles CDOs face are all too familiar. Senior leadership in HWCUs is overwhelmingly white. In 2013, a study found that people of color accounted for only 14 percent of senior leaders on campus at four-year institutions in the United States. At doctoral-degree-granting institutions, senior leaders are even less diverse and skew older.[33] Consequently, CDOs, who are mostly women of color, frequently attest to experiencing daily slights and humiliations.[34] That is, while pushing back against oppression on behalf of their students, they themselves must navigate microaggressions from their colleagues. And unlike student-facing diversity staff at the university, the fact that they occupy the topmost rungs of the white university hierarchy creates a special kind of loneliness and alienation that they must keep private, if for no other reason than to protect their own professional future.

Other challenges that CDOs face are uniquely burdensome. As Sara Ahmed has written, many HWCUs showcase their DEI hires and the existence of DEI positions as evidence that they're "doing something" about racism and other systems of oppression. Just as the diverse bodies of students are used to shore up the institution's image, the diverse bodies of DEI practitioners are put in service of the institution, providing evidence of their newfound moral rectitude. In other words, DEI positions, and the very bodies of those who occupy them, offer institutions a way to publicly break with their racist pasts. But as Ahmed puts it succinctly, "Diversity changes perceptions of whiteness rather than changing the whiteness of organizations."[35]

From one angle, we might appreciate the elevation of women of color and other marginalized people to the upper echelons of university leadership as a step forward. It is, after all, a move toward greater representational diversity. But while there is a lot of good to be said about representational diversity, I would be remiss if I didn't acknowledge that it, too, has a dark side. Because high-profile DEI positions and the people of color who occupy them can become more about changing the *image* of a thing (in this case, HWCUs), rather than changing the *thing* itself, HWCUs and their leaders may, unintentionally or otherwise, engage in tokenization—that is, symbolic gestures of showcasing those with marginalized identities as a way of deflecting criticism that an organization is behind the times.

As several CDOs attested with substantial frustration, they're trotted out to speak with students every time a calamity befalls the institution, whether it's a protest outside the president's office or an all-night vigil in the main campus center. In a system characterized by institutional whiteness, it can be challenging for people of color to avoid getting co-opted in the process. After all, they might see the benefits of striking a certain kind of bargain: you use my image so long as I get to enact the agenda I want. To some extent, then, CDOs must agree, tacitly or otherwise, to their own tokenization—that is, they must accept that they have been hired at least in part to give the appearance of equality within an institution without necessarily changing the institution itself. Consequently, CDOs find themselves compromised, lending their credibility and legitimacy with students in service of an institution that is ill equipped to handle situations that require a fundamental reckoning with how legacies of white supremacy persist in today's modern universities.

Under these working conditions, CDOs have developed coping tools. Above all, they self-police and self-silence so as not to incite white defensiveness among majority-white colleagues. As Ahmed discovered in the course of her own conversations with diversity professionals in the UK and Australia, "There is an implicit injunction not to speak about racism to protect whiteness from being hurt."[36] In my interviews with practitioners, I heard this theme loud and clear. "We have to be very careful and say things in a particular way," Mary Elizabeth Brown, a dean of diversity and inclusion in student affairs, reflected. "I'm always cautious, calculated, and mindful of language." Fearful of whitelash, many of today's practitioners tread lightly. This is problematic because, as more than one DEI practitioner explained, they need to be able to name white supremacy, institutional whiteness, and all associated challenges if they are to do their jobs effectively. As Brown says, "You can't always be walking on eggshells because it leads nowhere."[37] Like student-facing diversity professionals, then, CDOs find themselves in a tricky position even though they theoretically enjoy status, authority, and an institutional mandate to make reforms.

Self-silencing poses other conundrums as well. As many confided, they constantly confront the ethical challenge of mediating between student needs and institutional needs. Some senior-level DEI practitioners use the vernacular of "code switching" when describing how it is they manage these tensions in their day-to-day work. They change vocabulary, tack, and strategy depending on whether they are communicating with students or colleagues, especially fellow senior leaders. They do so in order to better advocate for the needs of students and reframe student demands through the prism of what is in the institution's best interest. Doing so allows them to demonstrate interest convergence—what is good for "diverse" students is also good for the institution. "Is it good or bad?" Brown asked herself aloud, deciding, "It's a necessity to be that way to get stuff done." The real issue, she said, is "how do you be authentic without stepping on toes."[38] I would go a step further: how can you be effective when you can't name the problem—how power and oppression function within HWCUs? How can you be effective when you have to constantly self-police so as not to cause your majority-white colleagues the slightest bit of emotional discomfort?

In order to mitigate their silencing by HWCUs, some CDOs have increasingly turned to consultants. Indeed, as Pamela Newkirk has written, DEI consultants have become another major feature of the DEI landscape across industries.[39] Speaking strictly from my own experience, I can say that external DEI consultants offer many benefits. First, they allow uncompensated people of color in the university who are often approached for DEI work to say no to institutional leaders seeking their help. Instead these individuals can find a practitioner who will do that work and suggest, at least implicitly, that it is a job that requires remuneration. Second, external consultants can be of use to lead practitioners. As we've seen, CDOs must soften their tone in professional settings in order to navigate predominantly white institutions. Again, this is the natural consequence of a diversity-and-inclusion regime that demands that practitioners speak in the vernacular of bland difference without reference to hierarchies of power. By contrast, external consultants can more easily sidestep internal organizational politics. They are in a better position to provide honest assessments to senior leaders. In the process, they often echo what diversity practitioners have advocated for with little success. Above all, external consultants have the opportunity to name power, oppression, and historical marginalization. That doesn't mean that they will, of course—only that they have more choices available to them as outsiders.

In the final analysis, a complicated picture emerges: CDOs enjoy more status and visibility than ever before. Their expansive portfolios give them the power to provide direction and purpose to otherwise scattered, insufficiently supported DEI programs and centers. But in addition to the standard difficulties any senior administrator faces, they confront unique challenges that limit their ability to execute the very institutional change that HWCUs supposedly hire them to make. If institutional leaders really want to transform their colleges and universities, to renovate their institutions from top to bottom as position descriptions suggest, they must move beyond the power-blind diversity-and-inclusion regime and toward a power-conscious equity-and-justice framework that allows diversity professionals to name and counter institutional whiteness.

Between a Rock and a Hard Place

In my conversations with those individuals who participated in the Black campus movement, who were at the forefront of establishing minority affairs offices, racial affinity centers, and scholars' programs for historically marginalized students, I noticed a recurring theme.

Many perceived a shift in the way that some diversity practitioners operate today. Ernest Thomas Cooper, who worked with students of color in the 1970s and 1980s, worried that today's practitioners are more "timid" than they used to be. For him, they are further from their "roots." When I asked him to elaborate, he explained, "They went to fancy schools and colleges, they weren't that impacted by racism and sexism. But others like me really lived it, so [DEI work] has a different meaning."[40]

Cooper wasn't the only former practitioner I spoke with who felt this way. You may recall Reginald Thomas, the faculty director of a southern university's first Office of Minority Affairs, whom we first encountered in chapter 3. Thomas agreed with Cooper's assessment, similarly claiming that diversity professionals are too "timid," while adding, "They don't want to rock the boat." In particular, Thomas blamed careerism in a field that has significantly expanded and professionalized since the 2010s or so. Cooper echoed this point, saying that a new generation of practitioners seems more interested in "being part of the old boys' club." Consequently, in his consulting work today, Cooper takes a hard line: "I tell [today's practitioners] to do their job. They need to be more courageous. When they're scared and they don't speak out, who suffers? The students."[41]

Thomas and Cooper aren't wrong, per se. But their appraisals overlook a larger structural and cultural problem and the ways that diversity practitioners have had to adapt in order to navigate through the morass. The present moment is a tricky one. According to one CDO, "It used to be that you could just deal with racism—now there's a lot of massaging of language and approach, and worrying about who will I offend."[42] Thomas was even more blunt: "White capacity for understanding truths has gone down. DEI work today now requires a lot of coddling bullshit with white people. [Diversity practitioners] can't call it like it is anymore. That's what's wrong. White people can't stand that they have privilege." He added, "You don't have to be mean or rude, but people need to know that they're born into systems of privilege. We need to tell them what they need to hear, not what they want to hear."[43]

Their observations are in line with this chapter's principal argument: ultimately, cultures of institutional whiteness will always limit what diversity professionals can do. In the worst-case scenario, diversity practitioners are reduced to low-level microaggression managers because they operate within an ecosystem where structural racism can't be named. Those constraints are part of the reason why we see such incredibly high DEI staff turnover.[44] As onlookers have begun to realize, diversity practitioners cycle in and out of roles at an alarming rate. They do so because they bump up against the same institutional barriers at every turn. Manufacturing an endless series of senior leadership roles is ultimately inadequate if institutions cannot address structural inequalities that run deep in HWCUs. It is a stark reminder that if institutions remain in thrall to power-blind notions of diversity and inclusion, no amount of (over)work or politicking on the part of practitioners will ever be enough to usher in much-needed change.

CHAPTER 5

The Classroom and the Culture Wars

As we've seen throughout, the majority of diversity practitioners are cordoned off into offices of student affairs, and as a result their work with students falls outside the classroom. But so-called DEI is more than a student life issue, and these days it's the college classroom that's at the center of the ideological maelstrom gripping our country. Importantly, it's not just what faculty teach in college classrooms or even how they teach it. Academic freedom, safe spaces, trigger warnings, the rigor wars—this is how DEI issues present in the classroom for faculty, and they've become proxy conflicts in the wider culture wars. That puts faculty front and center in the battle for the soul of the nation.

I want to provide a snapshot of the ideological battles gripping higher ed because those debates still unfold in ways that overlook histories of structural oppression, legacies of racist exclusion, and the unjust distribution of resources in the United States. Because we lack a structural lens, we haven't found structural solutions to structural problems. Instead we've arrived at piecemeal semisolutions, the likes of which inclusive teaching most clearly represents. Inclusive teaching has gained purchase since the 2010s as a means of acknowledging, addressing, and managing classroom "diversity." But ultimately I fear that inclusive teaching alone is simply not up to the task. As with all power-blind frameworks, ultimately inclusive teaching permits changes only at the margins. What we really need in our deeply divided multi-racial democracy is nothing less than the total transformation of the academy as we know it.

In keeping with the spirit of this enterprise, this chapter employs an equity-and-justice approach to help us move beyond petty grumbling over "emotionally fragile" and "academically unprepared" students and toward a keener understanding of how academia reproduces structural barriers that hinder student (and faculty) success and well-being. As we consider earlier traditions of liberatory pedagogy in the United States from which inclusive teaching descends, we'll see what we've lost over the years. In the end, I believe that inclusive teaching is an easy and useful way to implement equitable pedagogical practices. But as educators have argued for over a century, an education system forged in the cauldron of white supremacy will ultimately require more transformative pedagogies.

Academic Freedom

Today's academic culture wars are inseparable from the political schisms currently dividing the United States. In the 1980s and 1990s, the culture wars presented in the academy through the canon wars—who and what was on the syllabus. Today, the nation is up in arms about critical race theory, with many on the far right accusing lefty educators of seeking to indoctrinate students with "woke" politics and divisive ideologies.[1] By February 2022, lawmakers in at least thirty-six states had attempted to restrict teaching about race, racism, and other "divisive concepts" in K–12 schools, especially in social studies and humanities curricula.[2] The thrust of such meddling is to ensure that US schoolchildren receive a sanitized version of the nation's history that de-emphasizes its more unsavory features.[3] Similarly, in higher ed, some disciplines, above all history and literature, find themselves more regularly caught up in the churn than others. But the truth is that the culture wars have always been about much more than content and curriculum.

As ever, culture wars are about values and worldviews, and they represent a clash between fundamentally different versions of our shared national past and our common future. In higher education, academic freedom is at the heart of these conversations. As a concept, it's been around for at least one hundred years. In the United States, it actually started with a conflict between a professor and his university. As Emily Levine has written, Edward A. Ross, the professor in question, was

expressing opinions that were contrary to Stanford University's economic interests. That controversy eventually led to the establishment of
the American Association of University Professors (AAUP) in 1915. In
the organization's Declaration of Principles of Academic Freedom and
Academic Tenure, it defined academic freedom narrowly, as protection
from removal. But as Levine points out, "The declaration left the scope
and purpose of academic freedom undefined. By focusing on protection from removal, the AAUP created what the philosopher Isaiah Berlin called a negative rather than positive liberty—a freedom from rather
than a freedom for." The problem, then, is that "it never spelled out
exactly what scholars were gaining freedom to do."[4]

It's been more than a century, and unfortunately things haven't
changed much. As of 2023, the AAUP defines academic freedom as "the
freedom of a teacher or researcher in higher education to investigate
and discuss the issues in his or her academic field, and to teach or
publish findings without interference from political figures, boards of
trustees, donors, or other entities. Academic freedom also protects the
right of a faculty member to speak freely when participating in institutional governance, as well as to speak freely as a citizen."[5] But when the
thrust of academic freedom is so closely centered on faculty's relationship to their institution, we overlook the bigger issue—namely, social
responsibility. As Levine argues, we need a new definition of academic
freedom with what she calls "an academic social contract at its heart."[6]

What would it mean to develop a new academic social contract?
In the first place, it would demand that we account for the changing
times. As we've seen, the concept of academic freedom dates to the late
nineteenth century, a period when the faculty body and the student
body were largely one and the same—that is, elite white men. Because
of legacies of white supremacy, that state of affairs remained largely
the same until about the 1970s. As Kevin Gannon has explained, that
demographic overlap made for a very different kind of faculty-student
dynamic. Gannon writes, "[White male] faculty with endowed professorships could offer biologically deterministic arguments about a
hierarchy of racial types, or make claims allegedly grounded in analytic psychology that women's capacity for scientific reasoning was
inherently inferior to that of men." But times have changed, and so
has the student body. As Gannon concludes, "Groups that have traditionally held sway over the discourse, and indeed, much of the very
agenda, of higher education, are seeing that hegemony challenged, even
rejected, by large numbers of students and faculty who do not accept

an environment that considers them as less-than."[7] To be sure, the academic freedom wars aren't simply a race issue, but it would be folly to pretend that there isn't at least some racial component in play.

In the absence of a framework for academic freedom that acknowledges the persistence of structural injustice, it is students—and especially historically marginalized students—who become the target of the higher-education culture wars. In their popular book *The Coddling of the American Mind*, Greg Lukianoff and Jonathan Haidt provide a glorious example of that mess. Haidt is a social psychologist at the Stern School of Business at New York University. Lukianoff is the CEO of the litigious Foundation for Individual Rights and Expression (FIRE), an organization bankrolled by donors who support conservative causes. In their 2018 book, they were among the first to articulate the concerns of a number of conservatives—and liberals—that paint today's college students as an existential threat to academic freedom and higher ed as we know it.

Lukianoff and Haidt offer a very specific perspective on the fraught racial climate on many college campuses. They argue that a "culture of safetyism" has taken root in colleges and universities, curtailing freedom of speech and producing fragile, overly emotional students who rely on feelings-driven arguments to get their way. For them, microaggressions are really just a failure to expect the best from people or give them the benefit of the doubt; demands for safe spaces are about fears of facing life's toughest questions; claims of "victimhood" are based in catastrophizing patterns of thought and oversensitivity; student involvement in social justice movements blinds them to the meanings of true justice; and so on. Basically, they claim that Gen Z suffers from "cognitive distortions" and that it is woke students and their radical ideas who are to blame.[8]

To Sara Ahmed, these characterizations rely on three manufactured archetypes: the consuming student, the censoring student, and the oversensitive student. According to this line of thinking, the consuming student views the relationship between them and the university as that between client and service provider. It is a transactional relationship—I give you money, you give me a degree. According to this vein of thought, students are seen as singularly responsible for the corporatization of modern-day universities. The censoring student, on the other hand, is a member of the so-called woke generation who zealously polices the line between right and wrong, moral and immoral. Finally, the oversensitive student fails to understand complexity and seeks to preserve their psychological safety even if it negatively impacts their education and that of their peers.[9] In other words, they are the products of the culture of safetyism against which Lukianoff and Haidt rage.

It's against this background that high-profile controversies over safe spaces and trigger warnings unfold. Since the end of World War II, students who were once formerly excluded from institutions of higher education have entered college in greater numbers. But as we've seen time and time again, people from historically marginalized communities have different relationships with systems of power and oppression. Consequently, they've experienced society in concretely different ways than their whiter, wealthier, continuing-generation peers *and* faculty. As Gannon has put it, "As our student body continues to diversify—in areas like gender identity, ethnicity, immigration, and veteran status, for example—the traumas embedded in some of our students' experiences are part of the package."[10] In short, we must reframe the question of trigger warnings from one that centers the emotional failings of students to one that centers how structural injustice (e.g., overpolicing, sexual assault, lack of medical care, and the early, sometimes violent, death of loved ones) has done real harm to historically marginalized communities. For Ahmed, that means that trigger warnings and safe spaces are actually just "partial and necessarily inadequate measure[s] to enable some people to stay in the room so that 'difficult issues' can be discussed." She argues that "safe spaces are another technique for dealing with the consequences of histories that are not over."[11] In the end, we must recenter histories of oppression when we seek to understand student requests for things like safe spaces or trigger warnings.[12] We must also historicize the concept of academic freedom by applying a power-conscious lens to what has been falsely construed as a "universal" value. If we don't, we'll continue to find ourselves mired in a semantic war playing out on the bland terms and intellectually impoverished foundations of the power-blind diversity-and-inclusion regime.

This is a culture war, to be sure, but I'd be remiss if I didn't point out that there are material consequences, and, simply put, the "Right" and "Left" don't experience the fallout in the same ways. Though they are still in the minority, there has been a precipitous rise in women and people of color in the graduate and faculty bodies as compared to five decades ago.[13] Like historically marginalized undergraduates, they, too, bring new perspectives on how power, oppression, and inequality operate in societies. Many on the right and especially on the far right experience this scholarship as an affront and the values it espouses as limiting what they can and can't say, what they can and can't do. They experience, that is, real emotional discomfort and blame an ambiguously defined culture of wokeness. But lives are at stake when colleges and universities platform speakers who openly endorse white supremacy and other oppressive ideologies. With the arrival of Trump's America, in general, faculty face terrifying attacks from the Far Right, and it's predominantly women, people of color, and Black women especially who bear the brunt of threats of physical violence.[14] There is massive asymmetry, then, in how "both sides" experience the fallout of the culture war.

We need to acknowledge history and engage in structural analyses of the culture wars. Doing so reveals the ongoing legacies of white supremacy in the academy. It reveals, too, that the academic culture wars are their own particular form of whitelash to the expansion of access in higher education over the last several decades. To my mind, debates over academic freedom really boil down to questions of power—who had it and whether they can hold on to it in the face of changing social mores. It is, in short, the last gasp of a dying era.

Academic Rigor

The hidden legacies of white supremacy inform not just the ideological contours of academia but also educators' practices in the college classroom. Every day, we're discovering how faculty often unconsciously use biased criteria to talk about and assess students. The recent debates over the meaning of rigor in higher education provide a good example of how those biases functionally obscure the role of structural oppression, individualize blame, and conceal all the different ways institutions fail students.

From nearly the start, HWCUs saw maintaining the elite stature of the university and providing increased access to nontraditional students as conflicting imperatives. For instance, from the mid-1800s onward, senior administrators at the University of Michigan believed exclusion was, according to Matthew Johnson, "a necessary price to pay" for creating and maintaining a top-notch university.[15] College officials used the language of quality and merit expressly to keep lower-income and non-white students out. In that sense, Michigan was representative of other HWCUs that prevented the enrollment of Jews and Black Americans in the early and mid-twentieth century.

Today, many continue to employ the language of rigor to call out the so-called failings of historically marginalized college students.

According to this logic, the current student body across the country—which, it bears repeating, is more socioeconomically and racially diverse than ever before—has caused institutions to water down curricula and lower academic standards.[16] From this perspective, historically marginalized students are viewed solely through the prism of their deficits rather than their assets, what they take away from the university as opposed to what they bring to it. In that sense, rigor is of a piece with the concurrent intensification of fears that unprepared students of color "dumb down" higher education, the implicit suggestion being that admitting white students shores up a university's prestige, whereas admitting historically marginalized students diminishes its selectivity. In this manner, recourse to the language of rigor becomes a way for some college leaders and faculty to draw a distinction between the students they "want" (qualified) and the students they "get" (diverse).

The debate over rigor is not just undergirded by racist and classist assumptions. It's also shot through with ableist assumptions that shape pedagogical practices. As we saw in previous chapters, higher education helped manufacture and disseminate eugenicist thought that asserted the inferiority of nonwhite peoples. Eugenicist ideology also pathologized a number of other groups, including those with mental and physical disabilities. As Cate Denial observes, "We have not shaken off the dirt that clings to these roots." Denial names a number of ways those legacies persist, from how easily people with disabilities can move through physical academic spaces to how readily they can conform to disciplinary expectations that privilege certain kinds of learners over others.[17] Because faculty don't always have a good grasp on this history, they sometimes approach student requests for accommodations with a fair amount of skepticism. As Katie Pryal has written in the *Chronicle of Higher Education*, "Mistrust of disabled students sounds like this: 'Not *another* student with a disability note. Honestly, how does every kid have a diagnosis these days? I'm teaching to the lowest common denominator. They're faking ADHD to get extra time on tests.'"[18] Rigor, when employed in this manner, then, creates a culture of suspicion between faculty and students that gets in the way of both effective teaching and learning.

How do we move past a model of teaching that relies on an ideology of rigor steeped in the biases and prejudices of another era? Cate Denial once again offers us a way forward. She advocates moving away from a "combative way of approaching teaching," because it undermines relationships with students. Instead we must employ "a pedagogy of kindness."[19] For Denial, a pedagogy of kindness is not about being nice, but about leading with compassion. It boils down to three things: "attending to justice, believing people, and believing *in* people." It is, in short, "a discipline." What does that mean in a practical sense? Denial suggests that faculty move away from stringent attendance policies and hard and fast deadlines, which in addition to putting pressure on students can also put them in the uncomfortable position of having to share intimate details of their lives with professors just to explain why they can't submit that midterm paper by, say, Thursday at noon.[20] It's clear how easily this pedagogical orientation met students' needs during an ongoing global pandemic when, as the director of the CDC put it in April 2022, adolescents experienced the worst mental health crisis we had seen in decades.[21]

Gannon also suggests new ways of thinking about rigor that help us get to the heart of the matter—namely, how to hold students to high academic standards in a way that also centers equity. Specifically, he recommends that faculty separate what he calls intellectual rigor from logistical rigor. In an interview for the *Chronicle of Higher Education*, he explains that intellectual rigor "challenges students' assumptions, spurs their motivation, requires their effort, increases their skills." At the end of the day, intellectual rigor "push[es] students to learn." By contrast, logistical rigor expects obedience to stringent classroom policies about, for instance, when to turn in work and what penalties accrue for late work. Such policies are undergirded by the assumption that adherence to policy matters more than producing higher-quality work. It shifts emphasis away from a demonstration of intellectual growth and learning in favor of evidence of obedience to authority.[22]

In the face of a culture of institutional whiteness that a priori presumes their inability to make the cut, what resources do so-called nontraditional students have at their disposal? Increasingly, they've been encouraged to develop greater grit and resilience. In 2016, "grit guru" Angela Duckworth published *Grit: The Power of Passion and Perseverance*, which, as the subtitle indicates, defined grit as perseverance and passion for long-term goals.[23] But as the education professor Bettina Love argues, the concept of grit that has gained traction among educators in the last few decades is, in fact, a racially coded concept to denote "character education" of the variety that we saw in the early twentieth century when HWCU leaders implemented new admissions policies to keep ethnically undesirable Jews out of higher education.[24] What's worse, those historically marginalized students who make it far are praised for their grit, then encouraged to draw on more of it when they face academic and social challenges in college. In many ways, then, they are used as proof both that the system is working and that some students just aren't trying hard enough.

Certainly, most reasonable people would agree that some degree of grit, resilience, and perseverance are essential life skills. But Love's point is that an uncritical use of grit and its corollary, resilience, erases the unjust distribution of power and resources in the United States. Instead these concepts place blame on society's most marginalized individuals. As she observes so poignantly, "Measuring African-American students' grit while removing no institutional barriers, then watching to see who beats the odds makes for great Hollywood movies (i.e., 'Dangerous Minds,' 'The Blind Side,' 'Freedom Writers') and leaves us all feeling good because the gritty black kid made it out of the 'hood.'" But in doing so, she reminds us, "we fail to acknowledge the hundreds of kids who are left behind because we are rooting for what we are told is an anomaly."[25] Grit, then, is the natural outcome of a belief system that endorses the idea that we can all bootstrap our way out of structural oppression and that those who fail have only themselves to blame.

The global pandemic offers a very recent concrete example of the dangers of wielding rigor as a weapon. When the pandemic started, many faculty engaged in robust discussions over rigor—that is, how to balance the imperative to educate with the recognition that COVID-19 was understandably affecting the academic performance of their students, especially their low-income and underrepresented minority students. At the height of the pandemic, low-income students who moved back home like everyone else had less reliable access to Wi-Fi, laptops, and other devices, preventing them from participating in what was a global shift to online learning. At home, they may have also lacked the physical space and privacy necessary for their schooling. Further, many found themselves called on to take care of younger siblings or to help their families earn income during an acute recession brought on by COVID-19. We also know that the pandemic hit low-income communities of color hardest because so many were classified as "essential workers," and since essential workers were concentrated in the service sector, most couldn't afford to take time off from work. Consequently, they were exposed to COVID-19 at far higher rates than those who were able to work from home.[26] Adding insult to injury, should they become very ill, low-income individuals would scarcely be able to pay off hefty hospital fees as a result of our broken health care system. Using rigor as a framework to assess student performance and achievement during the pandemic renders these phenomena invisible, unfairly blaming and punishing students for things that lie well beyond their control, and ours.

By individualizing blame, the language of rigor deflects attention away from institutions that have consciously wooed students from historically marginalized backgrounds onto their campuses. As Jordynn Jack and Viji Sathy have written, placing blame on students from historically marginalized backgrounds for their failure to succeed overlooks how institutions of higher education recreate the conditions in which students "fail." As they point out, "It's the system we should be questioning when it erects barriers for students to surmount or makes them feel that they don't belong."[27] To be clear, faculty should absolutely expect academic excellence from all students, but we need to also ask what assumptions we are making about students. Are we imagining the "traditional" student for whom the university was constructed? If so, what access to K–12 educational resources and prior exposure to college-going culture are we expecting them to have had? With that in mind, are we setting all our students up for success? If not, we're no longer talking about students' poor performance. At that point, we're talking about institutional failures.

The Road to Inclusive Teaching

When we fail to acknowledge structural realities and institutional whiteness, we land on solutions that allow only for tinkering at the margins, and unfortunately I think inclusive teaching falls into this category. In the last several decades, the concept of inclusive teaching has taken the higher-education world by storm. It's no exaggeration to say that it's become the preeminent way to address so-called DEI issues in the classroom. Though inclusive teaching does indeed offer benefits, at the end of the day, it's a power-blind way of addressing inequities in the classroom and, in that sense, yet another inadequate by-product of the diversity-and-inclusion regime. By contrast, there are numerous pedagogical traditions that preceded our present inclusive teaching moment and that reveal with piercing clarity what inclusive teaching is, what it offers, and most significantly how it falls short.

Experiments to change the nature and practice of education can be traced back to the progressive education movement that took place in the United States from roughly the 1880s to 1916 and again from 1916 to 1957. Those early movements sought to shift away from a traditional education model whereby different social classes received different training based on what seemed suitable to their life station. Black educators played an important role in those movements, infusing them with more explicitly emancipatory aims along the way. Take Carter G. Woodson, a Harvard-trained African American historian and central figure in the Black education movement. As Michael Hines and Thomas Fallace have written, "Like other pedagogical progressives, Woodson saw the educational system that surrounded him as fundamentally flawed, characterized by 'rigidity, a hopelessly old-fashioned curriculum,' and a 'neglect of student interests' (Snyder, 2015, p. 278)." They add that "Woodson, however, recognized that for Black students these problems were rooted in and exacerbated by 'the spirit, point of view, and content of the curriculum,' which sought to impose White worldviews, histories, values, and cultural norms onto non-White students."[28] Essentially, then, Black K–12 educators have long experimented with what today we might call antiracist or social justice pedagogy.

While the radical Black education movement represented a world of innovative liberatory pedagogy, current iterations of social justice pedagogy in US higher education are more often credited to the theoretical work of the Brazilian educator Paulo Freire. Based on direct observations educating manual laborers in Brazil, Freire offered readers a unified system of thought that aimed to liberate "the oppressed" in the so-called Third World through a radical form of education. His work *Pedagogy of the Oppressed* first appeared on the global scene in 1968 and in English translation in 1970. In theorizing his educational philosophy, Freire draws on Marxist thinking. Above all, he insists that the existing system of education encourages a rigid social, political, and intellectual order that keeps historically marginalized individuals ("the oppressed") subservient to the dominant class ("the oppressors"). Freire calls attention to and rejects the "banking system of education," which centers on an all-knowing teacher who unilaterally transmits knowledge to students, who are presumed to be empty vessels. For him, this type of pedagogy fosters a static understanding of knowledge and prevents students from seeing themselves as anything but Objects *to whom* knowledge is imparted, as opposed to Subjects *with whom* knowledge is created through dialogue. As Freire saw it, an educational system that failed to develop students' critical awareness by encouraging them to engage with the world around them was at the root of social injustice in the modern world. He introduced the notion of educating for what he called critical consciousness, and because his work arrived at a very specific historical moment, when people around the world were engaging in passionate conversations about systems of power and oppression, *Pedagogy of the Oppressed* attracted a large audience, especially among formerly colonized peoples and racial minorities in the United States.[29]

As we saw in chapter 3, multicultural education was one particular strain of progressive education that came out of this Freirean moment. While multicultural education was certainly inspired by civil-rights-era ideals and driven by good intentions, I suggested that it ultimately proved too limiting. As a reminder, multicultural education was all about educating for pluralism. Proponents of multicultural education recognized that US society was growing steadily more racially diverse and that the traditional Euro American way of educating left some youth behind. Subsequently, many educators shifted toward what the prominent education theorist James A. Banks calls "the heroes and holidays approach to curriculum reform."[30] According to this logic, teachers could occasionally add women and other marginalized peoples to the curriculum. In its worst forms, then, the multicultural approach was additive, not integrated, and it did little to advance real equity in the classroom. It wasn't all bad, of course. As Banks highlights, because adding content related to women, people of color, and LGBT figures was a relatively light lift, educators could respond quickly to calls for more diverse content raised in racially and ethnically diverse communities.[31] But once again, that's the problem with diversity as representation—it loses a lot along the way.

Education scholars such as Lisa Delpit, Gloria Ladson-Billings, and Geneva Gay sought in part to address these limitations of multicultural education. While offering different critiques and recommendations for how to improve the K–12 education system, all three believed that, beyond curriculum, educators needed to change their very practice. Along Freire-esque lines, they reconceived of schools as transformational sites that required paradigmatic shifts not just in the curriculum but also in teacher attitudes, policies, assessment practices, and so on. For Ladson-Billings, that looked like "culturally relevant teaching."[32] For Geneva Gay, it was "culturally responsive teaching."[33] Both Ladson-Billings and Gay argued that low-income students of color brought important cultural strengths to the table. These scholars were thus emblematic of the movement away from deficit thinking and toward assets-based thinking that is so central to inclusive teaching today.

As critical as these pedagogical conversations were, they mostly took place among K–12 educators. It's bell hooks who raised these questions for higher education and translated these debates to that field. In her 1994 book *Teaching to Transgress*, hooks offers a set of essays that examines teaching through a Freireian lens. She writes of teaching as awakening, as consciousness raising, refocuses faculty attention on the higher-education system writ large, and asks what norms, politics, and pedagogy have been built into it. As such, hooks resituates higher education in a wider sociopolitical framework shaped by histories of power and oppression in the United States.

Teaching to Transgress is filled with fascinating insights and observations that help recenter the question of power in the classroom. For example, hooks describes how she experienced the shift from all-Black to all-white schools during the era of desegregation as profoundly alienating. For hooks, all joy, human contact, and relationships were stripped from the learning process. She and her Black peers went from being subjects to being objects.[34] White K–12 schools and then HWCUs seemed less interested in "the practice of freedom" than in "obedience to authority."[35] As hooks remembers, the college classroom was a space "to enact rituals of control that were about domination and the unjust exercise of power." There, Black students were expected to become "clones" of their white peers.[36]

Drawing on her own experiences with the US schooling system, hooks advocates for the dismantling of rigid power hierarchies in the college classroom. She enjoins fellow faculty to "mak[e] the classroom a democratic setting where everyone feels a responsibility to contribute." As she puts it concisely, "More radical subject matter does not create a liberatory pedagogy." Rather, liberatory practice decenters the authority of the professor and allows students to generate knowledge together.[37] Through what she calls transformative pedagogy, hooks makes a forceful argument in favor of returning to Freirean pedagogies. Even more importantly, her ideas gained traction among higher-education faculty.

Thanks in part to public intellectuals like hooks, the 1990s saw the appearance of a variety of disruptive pedagogies—critical pedagogy, feminist pedagogy, antiracist pedagogy—all of which challenged the dominance of traditional educational models. To be fair, faculty interest in and enthusiasm for new ways of teaching took firmer hold in some disciplines than in others. Recall once again the canon wars that unfolded in the humanities in the 1990s and 2000s. It was a battle over curriculum and content, to be sure, but for many humanities faculty it was also an invitation to rethink pedagogy. "We were reading bell hooks and Paulo Freire," recalls Judith DeGroat, emeritus professor of history at St. Lawrence University. "We wanted to use the classroom to model a way of being in society, living together collaboratively, asking hard questions." But DeGroat also wonders whether this tendency was more pronounced at teaching-centric small liberal arts colleges that offered faculty the requisite time and funding they needed to engage in such conversations.[38]

Twenty-first-century inclusive teaching is the distant descendant of these varied pedagogical traditions. I won't describe here all the best practices associated with inclusive teaching. That has been done well and concisely by many others.[39] But here are some basics: the focus is on clarity of expectations and communication, more transparent and robust course structure, and laying bare at all times the hidden curriculum. Philosophically, faculty who implement inclusive teaching practices tend to agree that intelligence is not fixed but can be nurtured and grown (this is growth mindset). They convey high expectations and their belief in students' ability to reach those expectations (this is wise feedback). Above all, they believe in the centrality of relationship building to student success. In short, these educators would argue that teaching isn't "good" unless it's inclusive, that learning can take place only if faculty create safe learning environments.

Just as the concept of safe spaces is tied to the broader ideological culture war, so, too, are they at the heart of present-day conversations about creating inclusive classrooms. This raises the question: what does it actually mean to create a safe learning environment? Safe space discourse has circulated in education circles since the 1990s but became enmeshed with the culture wars only in the 2010s or so. Like Lukianoff and Haidt, detractors see the concept of safe space as a means of coddling pampered millennials and, now, Gen Z-ers. But this simply isn't true. Faculty who want to create safe spaces do not seek the avoidance of all stress. In fact, the safe classroom is supposed to be a space for uncomfortable critical reflection, because being safe isn't the same thing as being comfortable. Safe space, then, is about creating an environment of psychological and emotional safety *in order to* have difficult and uncomfortable conversations. Or, as Sara Ahmed has put it, "We have safe spaces *so* we can talk about racism, not so we can avoid talking about racism!"[40]

How do faculty create a safe learning environment? Rather than teachers asking students to keep their opinions to themselves, all students should be invited to explore the biases and beliefs that undergird their opinions. Contrary to popular wisdom, this does not have to be an antagonistic project. Challenging students to dig deeper should invite them to base their thoughts and opinions on facts and thus make informed contributions in the classroom and, eventually, society. As Robert Boostrom summarizes it:

> It's one thing to say that students should not be laughed at for posing a question or for offering a wrong answer. It's another to say that students must never be conscious of their ignorance. It's one thing to say that students should not be belittled for a personal preference or harassed because of an unpopular opinion. It's another to say that students must never be asked why their preferences and opinions are different from those of others. *It's one thing to say that students should be capable of self-revelation. It's another to say that they must always like what they see revealed.* (emphasis mine)[41]

One form of pushback against the safe space movement claims that the classroom should not be a place to discuss controversial issues. Proponents of this viewpoint might consider the classroom a neutral site where students should play the part of detached scholars. But that's simply unrealistic. Much of what we discuss in the humanistic disciplines are what I'd call "live" issues—that is, they should, and usually do, elicit strong emotions because they address complex issues that plague our current world. That's not something for educators to avoid; that's a moment of opportunity that every professor dreams of.

Safe classrooms are not spaces where scary topics are avoided; rather, they are learning environments where students develop habits of mind necessary for an informed citizenry, including how to engage in a fact-based conversation that steers clear of useless ad hominem attacks. Faculty are in a privileged position to model for their students those habits of mind. A fair amount of resources now offer step-by-step instructions about how to create learning environments that push students out of their comfort zones in humane ways. I, for one, favor the approach put forward by Diana Hess and Paula McAvoy. In *The Political Classroom*, Hess and McAvoy argue that there is a difference between partisan education and political education. While the former imparts dogma to students, the latter should equip students with the necessary skills and mindsets to be democratic citizens. For Hess and McAvoy, schools are and ought to be political sites, and the political classroom creates the conditions in which students learn to deliberate all sorts of questions, including political ones.[42]

There is, of course, an ethical challenge when attempting to balance political and partisan education or, as Hess and McAvoy put it, "determining where political education ends and partisan proselytizing begins." The skills important in a political education include "teaching students to weigh evidence, consider competing views, form an opinion, articulate that opinion, and respond to those who disagree." Moreover, proponents of political education "seek to teach young people to see each other as political equals and to inculcate them into the practice of reason-giving and considering how their views and behaviors affect others."[43] Hess and McAvoy encourage educators not to shy away from political controversy but instead to help students develop the intellectual skills and dispositions necessary to deliberate. Here again, they agree that faculty are in an ideal position to model the kind of civic behavior for which we, as a society, currently lack suitable models. Rethinking the purpose of the safe space debate through the prism of good citizenship (e.g., knowing how to make fact-based arguments and engage in civil discourse) is a step in the right direction toward getting us back to critical consciousness development in the college classroom.

Without a doubt, inclusive teaching is having a moment. But after summer 2020, pedagogies of the Freirean variety have also made a big comeback in higher education.[44] Since the George Floyd protests, we've seen increasing faculty interest in what Kyoko Kishimoto calls antiracist pedagogy. Some of it is familiar. According to Kishimoto, antiracist pedagogy requires the inclusion of course content on race and inequality, including in STEM classes; it requires innovative pedagogy that emphasizes critical skill development rather than rote memorization; and it requires faculty to decenter their authority and instead empower students to take control over their own learning. But for Kishimoto, antiracist pedagogy is impossible unless faculty cultivate an awareness of and engage in constant self-reflection about their multiple social identities that afford them more or less power in classroom settings and, of course, in the world.[45] In that sense, antiracist pedagogy sets its sights as much on educator development as on student learning.

Kishimoto's work echoes that of the K–12 educator Zaretta Hammond, who similarly argues that educators must develop a consciousness of self, which includes an understanding of structural racism in our society and an awareness of their own cultural lenses (not just those of students). Drawing on a substantial literature on the neuroscience of learning, Hammond further suggests that faculty must learn how to identify their own socioemotional response to student diversity in order to truly be effective.[46] Personally, I believe this question is among the most overlooked when it comes to pedagogical training for faculty. Indeed, if we know we need to approach students holistically, why wouldn't we do the same for faculty? Just as historically marginalized students confront new environments, so, too, are the majority of faculty coming into contact with a student body whose lives they may not completely understand. Part of the bridging between them will necessarily require a socioemotional awareness of self among faculty—for instance, recognizing how parts of *us* are "triggered" in the college classroom when students point out what we ourselves may not have considered.

Finally, there is another pedagogical trend currently sweeping higher education—"decolonizing the curriculum." Advocates start from the same basic premise as earlier educational theorists: that the conventional Euro American classroom is a space of inequality and domination, that it is imbued with values, culture, and practices that seek to mold students in the image of the white, wealthy, male ruling classes. Where the philosophy departs from others is in its emphasis on the classroom as a cultural artifact shaped by histories of imperialism and colonialism. As such, decolonizing the curriculum calls into question the privileging of Western knowledge itself and the way it has marginalized, if not erased entirely, other cultural traditions, primarily those belonging to the colonized and other historically oppressed peoples. For Kishimoto, that would mean posing questions like the following: "How was the discipline developed and what was the political, social, economic, and racial context in the U.S. and the world in which certain theories, research methods, and paradigms became legitimized? What was the role of the discipline within the dominant ideologies of U.S. society? Who was involved in the creation and perpetuation of the discipline, who had access to the disciplines and its knowledge, and who benefited from it?"[47]

Growing interest in decolonizing the curriculum raises tough questions, though—not least of all the erasure and co-optation of Indigenous ways of thinking. In an article entitled "Decolonization Is Not a Metaphor," the prominent Native scholars Eve Tuck and K. Wayne Yang remind readers that decolonial education is very specifically rooted in efforts to recuperate Indigenous systems of knowledge and ways of knowing. According to Tuck and Yang, understanding decolonial education requires analyses of how settler colonialism operates

in two contexts: schooling and education research. In terms of schooling, settler colonialism refers to "how the invisibilized dynamics of
settler colonialism mark the organization, governance, curricula, and
assessment of compulsory learning." In terms of education research,
settler colonialism is "concerned with how settler perspectives and
worldviews get to count as knowledge and research and how these
perspectives—repackaged as data and findings—are activated in order
to rationalize and maintain unfair social structures."[48] Critically, Tuck
and Yang state in no uncertain terms that they view the use of the term
"decolonial education" by social justice educators as its own form of
colonial appropriation. As they point out, the term seems stripped of
any context. To them, those who use the phrase often fail to recognize its specific meanings for Indigenous peoples. As a result, they also
fail to acknowledge the intellectual labor of Indigenous scholars who
first formulated the colonial critique of the US schooling system. As
such, Tuck and Yang reclaim the specificity of the term for Indigenous
peoples for whom decolonization means unequivocally the return of
land to Natives.[49]

Should we dispense with the term altogether? Maybe. All I can say is
that it's undeniable that many scholars and educators find the decolonial education framework useful. For them, it offers a theoretical tool
to interrogate how the oppression of other historically oppressed peoples and the suppression of non-Western histories and ways of knowing
have come to pass. For all its flaws, decolonial education as it is pres-
ently understood invites us to see how bodies of knowledge in the Euro
American academy privilege Western perspectives and ways of knowing.
I think that's valuable because, whether we realize it or not, those of us
educated in the Euro American classroom are predisposed to see Western knowledge as "Truth" and Western ways of knowing as the only way
to arrive at said Truth. From this angle, decolonizing the curriculum
has provided scholars with an opportunity not just to recenter educator
practices in the college classroom but to reconsider the construction
of knowledge itself—what historical views and biases knowledge con-
tains and who has been sidelined in the process of academic knowledge creation. That mandate goes well beyond imbuing classrooms with
diversity and inclusion. It's about history and justice, and as such it represents a return to and an extension of the original civil rights impetus
for meaningful educational reform à la Freire and others.

What might decolonial education look like in practice? Let's start
with decolonizing the curriculum, a fuzzy concept but one with which

many faculty are probably familiar. Like multiculturalists, antiracist pedagogues, and inclusive-teaching enthusiasts, most proponents of decolonizing the curriculum would agree that incorporating "diverse" scholars on the syllabus is important. But while those pedagogies largely encourage such a choice as a way to get at more diverse representation, decolonizing education would take it a step further. For advocates of decolonial education, diversifying the syllabus is about acknowledging not just that whole groups have been historically underrepresented in the academy but also that colonial practices shape the existing canon and thus require the construction of an alternative canon. In that sense, decolonizing the curriculum is a more academic project with greater ambitions than inclusive teaching.

In *Teaching to Transgress*, bell hooks provides what I consider other useful examples that embody the spirit of decolonial pedagogy, though that's not the term she uses. If we acknowledge that classrooms are sites of power and hierarchy, what does that mean in terms of what counts as "class participation"? In hooks's experience, white male students tend to dominate classroom discussion. This observation led her to pose the questions, "Who speaks? Who listens? And why?"[50] Is the monologuing she witnessed a sign of active engagement, or does faculty's expectation of filling silence with talking just reproduce racist, sexist, classist, heterosexist, ableist, and other ways of thinking that privilege whiteness, maleness, middle-classness, straightness, able-bodiedness, and so forth? In short, how do power dynamics related to social identity and structural inequality show up in the college classroom, and what should educators do to address that?[51]

If we imagine education reform possibilities ranged along a spectrum, multicultural education would be at one end, decolonial education would be at the other, and inclusive teaching would probably fall somewhere in the middle. Critical pedagogy, feminist pedagogy, antiracist pedagogy, decolonial pedagogy—they all get us closer to a truly transformative education model *and* they are frustratingly elusive. Such pedagogies require imagination, design, experimentation, inevitable failure, and reexperimentation. Inclusive teaching has none of those drawbacks. It doesn't really call for the overhaul of curriculum and pedagogy, and it certainly doesn't require that faculty learn how their academic disciplines have been historically constructed to the exclusion of non-Western peoples and perspectives. Rather, inclusive teaching proffers a series of light lifts and easy-to-implement solutions that are more like what Viji Sathy and Kelly A. Hogan call "an overlay" to teaching practices.[52] It's perfect for beginners who crave tips on how to improve accessibility quickly in their college classrooms.

I'm glad that individuals, departments, and institutions have begun to see the merit of inclusive teaching practices. But for those of us who want to see historically marginalized students succeed academically, inclusive teaching can sometimes feel more like improvements at the margins that prevent us from imagining major structural and cultural changes, varieties of which antiracist pedagogy and decolonizing the curriculum would more closely approximate. Inclusive teaching has the potential to do precisely what I argue against: remove the classroom from a wider sociohistorical framework. It provides an easy, palatable way to adapt teaching methods without provoking too much backlash. It is perfectly suited, in other words, to our current social and political climate.

This chapter has offered new ways to think about the major ideological debates gripping higher education today. By incorporating a historically informed equity-and-justice framework, it exposes oversights and biases that fundamentally structure academia and shape the college classroom. Are faculty single-handedly responsible for the pedagogical overhaul of higher education? Hardly. Such an argument flies in the face of what this book is about—namely, refocusing on systems and structures as opposed to individuals. Transforming one's teaching doesn't happen overnight. It takes time and energy on the part of faculty who have less and less of both. Thankfully, there are increasing numbers of initiatives to address these issues: improvements in graduate pedagogical training, the development of new faculty onboarding programming, the implementation of faculty coaching and other professional development opportunities, reforms in the reward structure of teaching, shifts in faculty hiring and retention practices, and so on. If we want to actually improve equity in the classroom, faculty require real structural and cultural reform in higher education, and, in fact, that's not nearly as impossible as we've been led to believe.

The pandemic showed us how rapidly academia can adapt to a changed, and constantly changing, world. Take tenure—among the most ossified traditions in the academy and a perennial bottleneck to the advancement of many, but especially women and faculty of color. We've all been so conditioned to seeing tenure processes as incapable of being reformed, but now we know that's simply not the case. COVID-19 fundamentally altered the tenure process by accounting for the care responsibilities that suddenly fell to faculty, especially female faculty.[53] This happened rapidly, in response to a frightening global crisis that, at the time of this writing, lives with us still. Imagine if we could thoughtfully and intentionally plan a smooth transition to altered tenure expectations. It's yet another way that COVID-19 offers a blueprint for how quickly things can change if institutions just have the imagination to think big and the courage to try.

CHAPTER 6

Programs and Pedagogical Innovation

While previous chapters focused on diversity practitioners and faculty, ultimately this book is about what it would take to improve the student experience. First-generation, low-income students, who are disproportionately students of color, constitute the undergraduate student body of colleges and universities in ever greater numbers. But there are persistent disparities in so-called achievement between them and their whiter, wealthier, continuing-generation peers. As the education expert Gloria Ladson-Billings notes, approaching this problem through the lens of the achievement gap is a mischaracterization. It makes more sense to consider those disparities as the outcome of "educational debt," which is to say it's the direct result of structural inequality in this country.[1]

Selective HWCUs have sought to rectify this situation, often through piecemeal research-based interventions and student affairs programming. Racial affinity groups have become one especially common way in which institutions attempt to support historically marginalized students and promote their sense of belonging. Certainly, we've seen how HWCUs produce environments that make it necessary for first-generation, low-income students of color to find community in racial-ethnic affinity groups, and as Micere Keels has proven, those "campus counterspaces" do indeed create meaningful spaces for connection among students of color.[2] But isolating DEI issues in student affairs prevents us from approaching students holistically. We need to bring the classroom back into the discussion and, I would argue, place it at the very center of equity initiatives in higher education. Academic affairs units have the institutional pull necessary to drive major curricular change, making it possible to involve faculty in that process. And there's more good news. There are plenty of models for these kinds of collaborations, partnerships, and experimentation, and they've been around for a while.

Enter scholars' programs. In broad terms, scholars' programs take a small cohort of students and provide them with tailored and mutually reinforcing curricular and cocurricular supports. Among the many reasons that these programs are so successful is the centrality of the academic experience, which facilitates collaboration between diversity practitioners and faculty. But scholars' programs are also successful because of the degree of control and involvement that diversity practitioners have in this domain. As we'll see, scholars' programs give diversity practitioners the rare opportunity to influence curriculum, guide faculty, and create an integrated system wherein students receive support both outside and inside the classroom. Scholars' programs are collaborative sites of structural transformation and pedagogical innovation. They offer a model that selective institutions can adopt, refine, and eventually scale up and out to support all students at their institutions. And the research is clear on how to do that.[3]

This chapter surveys the design, structure, and implementation of some of the most effective and innovative scholars' programs. As such, it offers institutions a roadmap for how to build programs of their own that meet the specific needs of low-income, first-generation students and/or students of color. While the exact details will differ according to institution, there are broad principles we can use to inform our process and guide our efforts. Above all, the most impactful scholars' programs tend to be multiyear, have strong curricular components, and offer a finely tuned cocurriculum calibrated to each stage of the undergraduate career. Consider this chapter, then, both a plea and a plan: a plea for diversity practitioners and faculty in both humanities and STEM fields to work together, and a plan for how we might do so.

The Scholars

Scholars' programs for historically marginalized students should be considered a basic requirement at selective HWCUs, if for no other reason than because institutions need to keep up with the evolving racial realities of this country. Since about the 1970s, the demographic makeup of the US population has shifted dramatically. In 1965, whites in the United States accounted for 84 percent of the population; in 2015, they accounted for 62 percent. The largest increase during that period has been in the Hispanic population, which almost quintupled during this period, from 4 percent in 1965 to 18 percent in 2015.[4] While Latinx communities represent the fastest-growing domestic multicultural population in the United States, Asians account for the fastest-growing immigrant population. What does it all add up to? By 2045, the United States will phase into a majority-minority country, a trend that will be particularly accentuated among American youth.[5] In fact, apart from the Midwest and Great Plains states, in many major metropolitan areas in the West, in the South, and on the East Coast, this process is already well underway.[6]

What have these massive demographic shifts meant for higher education? As Stacey Abrams reminds us, "Demography is not destiny; it is opportunity."[7] We saw in earlier chapters that the mere existence of people of color in the United States didn't automatically lead to their greater inclusion in HWCUs, let alone in the political, economic, and social life of the nation. To the contrary, deep, persistent legacies of white supremacy posed what at times seemed like insurmountable obstacles to the right to access a college education. It took the hard work of student activists in the 1960s and 1970s to ensure that the undergraduate student body would reflect the racial and ethnic diversity of the US. While in 1976, students of color accounted for just 13.9 percent of college students, by fall 2017, 33.5 percent of the US undergraduate population comprised Black/African American, Hispanic/Latino, Pacific Islander, and American Indian/Alaska Native students.[8]

Thanks to the efforts of generations of activists who came before us, the undergraduate student population is more racially and ethnically diverse than ever before, but that's less true of selective HWCUs than it is of other two- and four-year institutions. In part, that's because selective HWCUs serve such a small slice of the college-going population. In fact, three-quarters of college students in this country attend community colleges and regional state colleges and universities.[9] That means it's primarily less well-funded institutions that have "absorbed" the majority of racially minoritized students. By contrast, the lion's share (82 percent) of new white enrollment has gone to the 468 most selective and well-funded colleges. There's not necessarily a vast conspiracy behind all this. As I've argued throughout, it's about history. HWCUs enroll a disproportionate amount of white students because, in the admissions process, they privilege legacy students, those who attended private high schools, and students who are able to cover the full costs of attending college without financial aid—all categories in which white students are overrepresented.[10] These are just a few reasons why selective HWCUs remain not just historically white but predominantly white.

These days, HWCUs have begun to focus more attention on recruiting first-generation students and students from lower-income backgrounds—often, though not always, overlapping categories. Though definitions of who "counts" as a first-generation student vary across institutions, the National Association of Student Personnel Administrators (NASPA) in higher education defines first-generation students as students who come from a household where neither parent or guardian obtained a four-year degree.[11] Since the early 2010s, nearly one-third of all college students were the first in their families to attend college. Similarly, it's hard to know for sure how many college students come from low-income households, but Pell Grants are one useful measure. Pell Grants are a 1970s-era government assistance program that offer grant aid for college students from households demonstrating "exceptional family need." And the number of students who receive Pell assistance has grown substantially since the 1980s.[12]

As we've seen time and again, inequality compounds on itself, and trying to get a college education can be especially harrowing for students who come from multiply marginalized communities. Certainly, first-generation students are less likely to receive a degree within six years. They also tend to come from households with lower median incomes. As a result, only 21 percent of low-income, first-generation college students will have a college degree within six years of enrolling in school, compared to 57 percent of their peers who are neither low-income nor first-generation students. And there are grave material consequences for those who take longer to finish their degrees.[13]

First-generation and low-income students who don't finish their degrees within four years often have to take out more loans and thus leave school saddled with more debt than their continuing-generation and better-off peers. In fact, even though an increasing number of students receive Pell Grants, tuition continues to soar. Consequently, federal assistance that was once a godsend to students from lower-income backgrounds simply does not cover as much as it used to. And it should come as little surprise that underrepresented minority students are more likely than white students to be first generation and low income. Black and Latinx students in particular are more likely to have significant loan debt than white students.[14]

To address these disparities, scholars have suggested a variety of low-stakes, piecemeal interventions. We are particularly indebted to social psychologists who have contributed substantially to this literature. Nicole Stephens, for example, has analyzed the values mismatch between universities and the increasingly first-generation, low-income students they admit. In one study, she and a team of coauthors determined that university cultures tend to place a greater emphasis on the middle-class norm of independence, which is to say that institutions of higher education put forward a narrative that it's up to you, and only you, to forge your own path to success. But, they assert, this message is inconsistent with the norms and values of many working-class students. They recommend that universities instead adopt messaging that centers interdependence, or the notion that we're learning in a supportive community, so we're in this together. According to Stephens and her colleagues, small interventions like this can go a long way toward closing the social class "achievement gap" between working-class students and their middle- and upper-class peers.[15]

Interventions like this one complement other university supports for historically marginalized students who attend HWCUs. In the wake of BLM-era student protests, there's been a sharp shift back to the racial affinity group model, a model that recalls the 1960s, when Black, Chicano, Native, and Asian American student groups first materialized. As Keels has shown, these spaces are critical for underrepresented minority students who, again, are also disproportionately first generation and low income. Keels is keen to point out that historically marginalized students need these spaces because of how thoroughly the K–12 educational system has failed them and how many of the institutional structures and cultures of HCWUs continue to fail them as well. Keels notes that, in general, most institutions work off an assimilatory model, trying to integrate students into HWCUs without changing anything about the institution itself, which she contends is responsible for both poor retention and psychological pain, even among high-performing students of color. By contrast, Keels argues that rather than continue with "universal programming" when selecting courses, engaging in cocurricular activities, and adjusting to dorm life, students need HWCUs to provide "identity-conscious supports" that help them establish a sense of belonging and ultimately improve their academic confidence. In sum, they need what Keels calls "campus counterspaces," which she defines as "safe spaces that simultaneously validate and critique one's interconnected self and group identity" to enable "radical growth."[16]

Racial affinity groups or, as Keels calls them, campus counterspaces, offer clear benefits for historically marginalized students. After all, gathering in community was one of the primary strategies that early students of color adopted as they sought reprieve from hostile campus cultures. Still, I'd contend that racial affinity groups don't go far enough. Certainly, the data tell us that these initiatives are effective, but, like small-scale institutional interventions, they are limited in what they can accomplish. Racial affinity groups are just about as extracurricular as you can get. They are, by definition, an additive feature of college going. They do, of course, furnish spaces where students of color can celebrate their culture, forge community, and in the process come to see that the challenges they face in HWCUs are not specific to them as individuals. But ultimately racial affinity groups that hardworking student affairs staff help organize and run give the institution a pass, relieving colleges and universities of the responsibility to engage in structural change that would better support marginalized students by instead sponsoring spaces in which students can process how they're being marginalized. To put an even finer point on it, I'd say that, for all the good that racial affinity groups do, they risk placing the onus on students to simply get used to institutions that were constructed to exclude them. It's yet another stark reminder that we need to approach DEI as more than a student life issue. Instead, we need to embrace curricular structures and pedagogical practices that transcend inclusive teaching and guarantee more equitable outcomes for all students no matter what their background.

From College Access to College Success

Since the early 2000s, we've seen a transition from questions of pure "access" (i.e., who's in and who's out) to questions of college success (i.e., who stays and who graduates). That's meant a shift in emphasis from outreach and recruitment to attainment and retention. In the words of one longtime education equity advocate, "It's not enough just to get students of color from different economic backgrounds into college; it's about getting them out of college within a reasonable timeframe."[17] Indeed, a narrow institutional focus on "diversity" just changes the compositional character of an institution; it doesn't address the structures and cultures of institutional whiteness that hamper student success.

Scholars' programs represent one of the most successful ways that selective HWCUs can support the college success of historically marginalized students, and they're hardly new. TRIO programs rank among the earliest such programs serving first-generation, low-income students. Part of President Lyndon Johnson's War on Poverty, the Economic Opportunity Act of 1964 and the Higher Education Act of 1965 created TRIO. Established in the 1960s and 1970s, TRIO programs represented a significant federal investment in improving college access for all youth. Those programs included Upward Bound (a college readiness program), Talent Search (a community-run talent agency), and Special Services (college success offices on HWCU campuses). While the first two were college access programs geared toward first-generation students from lower-income backgrounds, Special Services sought to improve retention among college students from historically marginalized communities. All TRIO programs, then and now, aimed to provide academic assistance to first-generation, low-income students. They are not expressly race based, but because students of color are overrepresented in those categories, TRIO has gone a long way toward facilitating their college access for the first time.[18]

In addition to federally funded TRIO programs, state-funded Educational Opportunity Programs (EOPs) were founded throughout the late 1960s. Though state funded, they are not offered in every state, nor are they offered at every public university in every state. In fact, they are concentrated in New York, New Jersey, Pennsylvania, and California. Each EOP office has a slightly different history, but most seek out students with significant financial need and a history of educational disadvantage, including a lack of access to rigorous college preparatory schools and programs. EOPs now have a private-school corollary: the Higher Education Opportunity Program (HEOP). Like EOPs, HEOPs are funded by state departments of education, and each institution more or less matches the federal grant. As a result, unlike EOPs, many HEOPs can guarantee their students full financial aid for all four years.

TRIO programs and EOPs have a proven record of success.[19] In addition to passionate and devoted staff, EOPs and HEOPs are successful for several other reasons. First, they are embedded within institutions. Program leaders are familiar with how the college or university operates, so they can offer students academic and social support designed to meet the unique culture and structure of the institution. Second, because most programs receive generous and continuous state and institutional funding, they have enough resources to offer a high-touch program model with a high cost-per-student ratio. Offices may have two or three staffers to serve fifty students, as opposed to one DEI staffer who serves one hundred or more, as is sometimes the case at HWCUs. Consequently, EOPs and HEOPs have high rates of success in terms of student academic performance, retention, and graduation.

Some of these programs have been around for nearly sixty years. That means generations of staff have experimented and refined their approach, design, and implementation over several decades. We might even say they've produced, in industry-speak, a high-quality product with proven results. Why wouldn't we look to these programs for inspiration? In multiple conversations with current program directors, I learned that there are at least five major features at play in each of these highly successful models.

1. Outreach and Recruitment

High-functioning college success programs develop strong relationships with college access and readiness programs. To a large extent, college access and readiness programs teach their scholars how to surmount the steepest admissions hurdles. Nearly all provide in-depth guidance and summer workshops on how to present oneself in personal statements in a way that will most "appeal" to admissions readers. College matching programs like QuestBridge and College Match also help fill the gap. Such programs exist because many talented low-income, first-generation students of color wind up going to colleges and universities for which they are overqualified. They do so because they know little about the college admissions process and lack guidance. Programs like these partner with selective colleges and universities to provide matching services.

While college matching programs are a step in the right direction, ultimately they affect a small number of students who would benefit from them. To chip away at the centuries of inequality that suffuse our public education system, college success program directors encourage their institutions to make significant investments in local K–12 schools. They offer after-school and/or summer courses to K–12 students who otherwise do not have access to academic enrichment opportunities. In the best-case scenario, program offices help develop pipeline programs that prepare local students from underresourced schools and communities to go to college.

2. Admissions and Financial Aid

Impactful scholars' programs include diversity practitioners' participation in the outreach and recruitment stage, involvement in a holistic admissions review process, and close collaboration with financial aid and admissions representatives. Already, most admissions officers have made it a practice to consider specific school contexts during the admissions process. That is, they assess student applications in the context of other factors including the school's graduation rates, absentee rates, and average SAT scores. In so doing, they render visible structural inequities, which allows them to identify promising students who come from underresourced schools and communities.

EOP and HEOP program directors assist admissions officers as they increasingly look beyond formal markers of academic achievement to account for the full range of student circumstances. At the most practical level, diversity practitioners prove a valuable asset to chronically overtaxed admissions officers. But more importantly, they know to look for students who show an inexplicable dip in academic performance. Such downturns often point to a larger crisis in students' lives. Death or illness, homelessness and food insecurity, arrests and gun violence—these are everyday realities that can affect the lives of many historically marginalized students. If students choose to disclose these factors in their personal statements, they may be able to catch the attention of an admissions officer or two. If not, it's unlikely they'll make it to the next round.

3. Summer Bridge Programs

Once students are accepted, EOP and HEOP program directors require them to participate in intensive and immersive summer residential programs with rigorous credit-bearing courses taught by university faculty. In summer bridge programs, students usually take two credit-bearing classes: one writing course and one math or science course. They must also attend supplemental instruction sessions for both courses, led by either graduate students or advanced upper-class program alumni. They participate in workshops, seminars, and learning labs that help them build cocurricular skills and thus prepare them to navigate college. Workshops focus on helping students decode the hidden curriculum of college going, such as how to take class notes, how to use office hours, or how to talk to professors who are at times intimidating. Throughout, students may also gain cultural enrichment in the form of extracurricular activities (for example, excursions to local museums). It would be an understatement to say that summer bridge programs are rigorous immersive experiences that keep students—and the programs' staff—busy around the clock.

4. Multiyear Programming

The most effective programs extend into the academic year, providing ongoing mentoring, tutoring, and advising, particularly during that pesky first year. The transition to college can be more challenging for students who come from different classes, cultures, and racial/ethnic communities than for those for whom historically white colleges and universities were first intended. Extending their reach into the classroom during the academic year has thus long been a key goal of many EOPs and HEOPs. These courses are credit bearing and they also satisfy general-education requirements. Most programs require first-year students to meet with academic advisers, but other programs demand even more. One HEOP director told me that first-year students must meet with their academic counselor every week, every other week during their sophomore year, once a month during their junior year, and as needed in their senior year. This approach creates a strong academic support structure that keeps students on track.

5. Scaffolded, Finely Calibrated Programming

High-performing programs offer robust curricular and cocurricular programming to help students decode the academic, social, and cultural hidden curriculum of college going. They help determine essential academic, social, and cultural skills, competencies, and knowledge that students must master at each stage of their undergraduate careers. EOP and HEOP program support thus shifts emphasis across the four years in tandem with students' shifting needs. While the first and second years primarily focus on easing the academic and social transition to college, the third and fourth years are geared more toward students' postgraduate futures. This includes additional support to help students learn how and why to secure internships, pursue study abroad opportunities, prepare graduate school applications, and compose job application materials, among other things. In the best-case scenarios, programs thoughtfully calibrate both curricular and cocurricular support to the specific needs of undergraduates as they progress through their college careers.

Recognizing the success of federal and state college success programs, many selective HWCUs began to undertake similar efforts. While most scholars' programs have appeared since the early 2000s, a handful of institution-specific scholars' programs have roots in the late 1960s and 1970s. They appeared in the wake of the student protests that so characterized the era. Take, for instance, UCLA, which established the High Potential Program (HPP) in 1968. The HPP would eventually become UCLA's EOP in 1971, but before that it was one of the first special admissions programs in the country. That said, it relied heavily on the labor and enthusiasm of student volunteers, most of whom came from underrepresented minority backgrounds themselves. In other words, institutions did not devote a lot of resources to early programs that served only students of color, especially Black students.

The shifting political winds in this country played a larger role in the evolution of scholars' programs at HWCUs than they did in the development of EOPs and HEOPs. In the 1960s and early 1970s, programs targeted students of color, especially Black and Latinx students. But by the 1980s, that began to change. For example, Greg Collins was a student volunteer at UCLA who helped put the early HPP program together in the 1960s. Twenty years later, Collins found himself at a small private university in the Northeast, where he served as an affirmative action officer. He wanted to establish a program similar to what he had a hand in creating at UCLA as a student, but during the conservative cultural backlash of the 1980s, he had to adjust his vision to the new realities of the political and social climate. Initially, the Admissions Office assumed this would be a program strictly for students of color. But Collins knew that if he pursued that path, he would very likely have to contend with a tidal wave of resentment from prospective white students and parents. To avoid accusations of reverse racism, he pushed to include low-income white students in the program.

To be fair, it wasn't all about strategy and tactics. Collins recognized that the public school system was failing white students in South

Boston too. But the point is that, by including white students, he not only preemptively deflected criticism but also accessed more institutional resources. This was a pattern among HWCUs. Ironically, then, whitelash fueled the development of scholars' programs at HWCUs, ensuring that they became increasingly formalized and better funded so long as they shifted their emphasis from race-based legacies of exclusion to other factors, such as socioeconomic status, that included white students.

The program Collins ultimately founded bears a striking resemblance to the successful EOPs and HEOPs described above, though he had to contend with both political and institutional obstacles at his HWCU. As I've mentioned, he preemptively countered accusations of antiwhite racism even down to the tiniest details. At the most basic level, he called the program, founded in 1988, the Contract Agreement Program (CAP), purposely giving it a kind of no-nonsense apolitical name that bore no mention of the students of color it would primarily serve. In addition, Collins went to great lengths to recruit faculty to support the program. In order to ensure that CAP incorporated strong academic elements, he purposefully sought out five or so faculty members to sit on the program's advisory committee. Collins knew that faculty, especially white tenured faculty, held a tremendous amount of institutional power and that their backing would guarantee the program's success. In short, he strategically engineered the program's governance and leadership structure to ensure maximum institutional pull.

Collins's decision to center the classroom experience reflects a recurring theme that emerged in my conversations with directors of scholars' programs at HWCUs. They were in universal agreement that the programs must be located in the academic affairs division. For all the important work that student affairs personnel do individually with students, student affairs *as a division* lacks the institutional pull that academic affairs enjoys. In the words of Malcom Washington, associate vice provost at a large premier public institution, "Student affairs is always considered an add-on, not essential to the university."[20] Many practitioners agreed. "People talk to us [academic affairs staff] differently," said one director of a program for first-generation, low-income students at a small selective institution in the Northeast. "Colleges look at student affairs as babysitters, as protest prevention," she observed, suggesting that when scholars' programs are located in academic affairs units, they have a greater impact.[21]

Funding is another reason why scholars' programs must be located in academic affairs units. EOPs and their scholars' programs are guaranteed state funding, sometimes more, sometimes less, but that's not necessarily the case at HWCUs. As many scholars' program directors explained to me, student affairs can't always rely on consistent funding. This is all the more likely at large public institutions. When programs sit in academic affairs, they are less likely to see their budgets slashed, which is often the plight of student affairs offices that compete with each other over a limited amount of funding. "When academic departments get funding, we [the scholars' program] get funding too," said Washington, adding, "It's consistent year after year so we never have to worry about our core funding." Indeed, it was only once the scholars' program was moved into the Division of Academic Affairs, Washington remarked, that the program really took off.[22]

Finally, scholars' programs being located in academic affairs facilitates partnerships and collaborations between diversity practitioners and faculty who are so critical to students' college success. It also provides the supportive conditions in which faculty can engage in pedagogical experiments, which has been proven time and again to improve the academic experience of all students. As we're about to see, that's true of both humanities and STEM faculty.

Beyond Inclusive Teaching: Writing

When considering how to go about building a multiyear scholars' program with strong curricular components, writing courses offer a particularly effective yet frequently overlooked opportunity to engage with historically marginalized students. Writing is a logical place to start because it's a skill every college student needs, whether they're majoring in STEM or humanities fields. Writing courses are also a good logistical fit. Many colleges and universities make writing courses a general-education requirement for first-year students. Consequently, writing courses often provide that crucial introduction to the structure and culture of the university that can make or break students. As mandatory classes, writing courses also provide a relatively easy touchpoint to engage a large number of students. Moreover, given that they tend to be much smaller than other general-education courses, they are more conducive to relationship building between faculty and students, and, as we know, low student-to-faculty ratios are correlated with higher student academic performance.

Writing courses are more than just a good strategic and logistical fit for scholars' programs. As Bridget Draxler, associate director of writing, speaking, and academic support at St. Olaf College, told me, writing is at the center of the hidden curriculum in higher education. "When we think of assumed knowledge, there is so much surrounding writing and research," she said. Writing is thus a good pedagogical fit for helping students adjust to the academic culture of higher education. In terms of how to teach writing, instructors might craft writing prompts that invite students to reflect on their identities. "There aren't opportunities in every class to reflect on things like identity and power," Draxler observed. She and her colleagues have even suggested that, when approached in the right way, sentence-level support can be an act of "linguistic social justice."[23] Overall, Draxler explained, "writing classes have a unique ability to give students a sense of belonging at the institution."

First-year writing courses are also a relatively easy way to extend the curricular reach of summer bridge programs into the academic year in ways that avoid common pitfalls that unnecessarily stigmatize historically marginalized students. Typically, universities use GPAs, standardized test scores, and/or writing samples to place students in writing courses. Again, educational inequities in K–12 schools mean that students from historically marginalized backgrounds can wind up clustered in lower-level writing classrooms that may be viewed by the wider university community as "remedial." By contrast, under a scholars' program framework, first-year writing courses become just another program requirement like any other. Those courses should provide supplemental writing instruction sessions that give students the opportunity to learn the basics of academic writing—for example, how to identify an argument, how to structure a research paper, how to read in different disciplines, and so on. Supplemental writing sessions offer other ways to support students during that rocky first year. For instance, peer academic support embedded in writing courses creates opportunities for upper-class program alumni to develop relationships with students who share similar backgrounds and experiences. Writing courses, then, become a way to foster community and strengthen a sense of belonging among historically marginalized students.

Writing courses also offer opportunities to experiment with more equitable grading and assessment practices. Take labor-based contract grading. Around the same time that multicultural education was taking off, educators began to experiment with grading and assessment practices that were more mindful of student "differences," which, again, are products of fundamental inequalities in our education system. Labor-based contract grading separates evaluation from grades so that grades reward labor, not quality alone. Contract grading requires extensive teacher feedback whose primary purpose is less evaluative than substantive, directive, and intensive. Though there are a variety of models, generally labor-based contract grading emphasizes process over product. It decenters getting the grade and recenters learning; it focuses on quality, on labor, or on both. Insofar as writing is a process that consists—rather maddeningly—of brainstorming, outlining, and refining draft after draft, the emphasis on process is yet again a good pedagogical fit.

Labor-based contract grading has much to offer. It incentivizes students to take risks they might not otherwise take if they were focused only on getting the grade. It also encourages more engaged faculty feedback, thereby bringing assessment practices into alignment with inclusive pedagogical values. But more importantly, according to Professor of Rhetoric and Composition Asao Inoue, contract grading ensures that students from underresourced schools are not penalized for what they've never been taught. Contract grading thus promotes a degree of equity in the classroom.[24] While not unproblematic, labor-based contract grading can serve as one approach to mitigating the effects of structural inequities in the education system.[25]

Ungrading provides yet another example of pedagogical innovation that faculty who teach in scholars' programs have more freedom to experiment with. The basic gist is this: involve students in a reflective learning process throughout the course, ultimately asking them to grade themselves. Not only does this lift the tremendous burden on faculty whose time is perennially in short supply, but it also makes students the authors of their own learning. By asking students to constantly engage in self-reflection about the course and its content, faculty ensure that they develop a deeper, more meaningful relationship to knowledge.[26] As Cate Denial has shown, rethinking our assessment practices allows us to focus on what really matters: not the grade, but the learning.[27]

In sum, writing is—and should be—at the center of the college curriculum because writing is a critical skill for all students, no matter what their major. It's a relatively easy way for selective HWCUs to extend scholars' programs into the academic year while creating the conditions necessary for faculty to experiment with more equitable practices.

Beyond Inclusive Teaching: STEM Programs

Because of the stark inequities in student outcomes we see in STEM disciplines, it's important to shine a light on scholars' programs that are specifically for STEM students. Poor retention rates have long been the driving force behind STEM equity-and-inclusion efforts. Indeed, many scholars' programs at colleges and universities began exclusively as STEM summer bridge programs and only later expanded to include humanities components. In spite of how long these programs have been around, though, student of color attrition in STEM fields remains a monumental challenge. In 2016, African Americans constituted 13 percent of the US population and Latinos 18 percent, but they made up only 4 and 5 percent of doctorates in the natural sciences and engineering, respectively.[28] Moreover, since the 2010s, degrees awarded to African American students have stagnated in the biological and life sciences as well as the earth and physical sciences. Meanwhile, the percentages of African American and Latinx students in engineering, mathematics, and statistics have also declined.[29]

The highly successful Meyerhoff Scholars Program at the University of Maryland, Baltimore County (UMBC), is in every way the gold standard of STEM scholars' programs. Established in response to student protests in the 1980s, the program sought to address the dismally low numbers of African American men in college and, in particular, the dearth of Black men with PhDs in STEM fields. When founded in 1989, Meyerhoff served only young African American men. The following year, it expanded to include African American women. Following a lawsuit against affirmative action launched against the University of Maryland College Park, the Meyerhoff Program changed its program requirements. From then on, it recruited students who "demonstrate[d] commitment to diversity and inclusion." That is, it expanded beyond race-specific admissions criteria, securing, perhaps, more institutional funding in the process.

Meyerhoff's mission is to recruit talented students in the sciences who are interested in the advancement of minorities in the sciences and related fields. In the 1990s, that yielded a program that was composed entirely of African American students. Fast forward thirty years later, and the program's 270 students were 57 percent African American, 15 percent white, 15 percent Asian, 12 percent Hispanic, and 1 percent Native American.[30]

UMBC vice provost and later president Freeman A. Hrabowski III played a key role in the design, development, and implementation of the Meyerhoff Program. To be sure, he was influenced by his colleague Uri Treisman's calculus program, which sought to help minority students excel rather than simply "avoid failure." Hrabowski and others considered Treisman's program "trailblazing." But Hrabowski also drew significantly on his own experience studying math at Hampton University, an HBCU.[31] Indeed, I wouldn't be surprised if many of these early scholars' programs at HWCUs relied on the vision, experience, and expertise of HBCU alums who had learned firsthand that a supportive environment nurtures collective brilliance.

With this successful HBCU model in mind, Hrabowski and his team went about constructing a rigorous STEM program that relies on fourteen principles. Some should sound familiar: an application process that includes in-person interviews with potential candidates; robust financial support for scholars; impressive institutional and public financial support for the program itself; a mandatory summer bridge program for incoming scholars, one offering courses in math, science, and African American studies; study groups; tutoring; mentorship; regular academic advising; and reliable faculty involvement. In addition, starting their sophomore year, scholars are expected to get research lab experience with faculty. Thanks to the close relationships they develop with faculty, they may even cowrite and publish an article or two. Indeed, faculty advising is a mainstay of the program.[32]

While much of the above are standard features of high-performing STEM programs, other aspects are perhaps less common. The emphasis on community stands out in this regard. The Meyerhoff Program creates a "family-like" environment that contributes to student belonging. For example, scholars live in a residential learning community during their first year. They have continuous supportive contact with program staff and administrators, who often serve as "surrogate parents." They attend frequent "family meetings" with other Meyerhoff scholars, upper-class mentors, and staff. Scholars also meet and build relationships with program alumni who serve as all-important role models, and they are encouraged to get involved with the local community, especially underserved youth in Baltimore. Finally, program staff involve students' families in their learning, keeping them apprised of their children's progress. This latter practice is not a way to preemptively deal with meddlesome helicopter parents but a way to recognize that for some college students, going to college is a collective experience, and that guaranteeing student success requires bringing families and communities into the education process.[33]

While these fourteen principles structure the Meyerhoff Program, Hrabowski emphasizes the importance of the broader underlying values, what he sometimes calls "the four pillars" of the program: first, high expectations, not just for the scholars but also for faculty and staff; second, a learning community focused on teamwork and collaboration as opposed to conflict and competition; third, faculty engagement throughout the four years; and fourth, constant evaluation and assessment.[34]

What exactly does faculty involvement in this program look like? For starters, it means faculty partners are willing to go beyond inclusive teaching and engage in fundamental course redesign, especially when it comes to those critical introductory STEM courses. The number-one priority when it comes to course redesign is eliminating the weeding-out mentality that, as Hrabowski and Peter Henderson argue, hurts all students, including women, people with disabilities, white students, and students of color. Rather than focus on weeding out, these courses should instead support problem-focused learning and group- or team-based learning. Some faculty use the flipped-classroom model, in which students learn information before class through reading or watching recorded lectures and then use class time for activities that require them to process and make sense of what they've learned. A few faculty have even made their lesson plans widely available to other STEM faculty.[35] Not only does a major reorientation like this benefit students, but it also benefits the academy in general by encouraging and strengthening a sense of scholarly community among faculty that can so often be lacking.

Indeed, community is at the center of all things Meyerhoff, and that includes assessment practices. In the summer math course, all Meyerhoff scholars receive the same score as the lowest-scoring students on certain assignments. As Hrabowski explains, "The purpose is to motivate all students to help the least-prepared students perform at their best."[36] In other words, Meyerhoff fosters a learning environment in which scholars pursue academic excellence through community as opposed to competition. In so doing, scholars' program leaders and their faculty partners can work together to reimagine STEM curriculum and practice altogether.

How do we know these approaches work? Simple: all the evidence suggests so. As early as 1996, the Meyerhoff Program received the National Science Foundation's Presidential Award for Excellence in Science. Just a few years later, program leaders noted that Meyerhoff students had begun to achieve science GPAs slightly higher than those of their white and Asian peers.[37] Thirty years on, the program still guarantees stellar results. According to NSF data, UMBC is the number-one baccalaureate institution for African American undergraduates who go on to earn PhDs in the natural sciences and engineering as well as doctorates in the life sciences, mathematics, and computer science.[38] In 2019, Meyerhoff boasted undergraduate STEM retention rates of more than 90 percent.[39] Indeed, a 2019 article in the journal *Science* concluded that "no other major university has achieved similar outcomes" in retaining diverse students in STEM fields.[40] It's no wonder that the Meyerhoff Program was featured in Barack Obama's President's Council of Advisors on Science and Technology.[41]

Unsurprisingly, the program's alumni are quickly becoming leaders in their fields. Meyerhoff scholar Kizzmekia Corbett helped create one of the COVID-19 vaccines and was included in *Time* magazine's 100 Next list of innovators in 2021. Anthony Fauci himself penned the article about her.[42] Moreover, the Meyerhoff model has already been exported successfully to other universities, including Penn State and the University of North Carolina at Chapel Hill. In 2019, Priscilla Chan Zuckerberg gave nearly $7 million to find ways to replicate and adapt the Meyerhoff model to UC Berkeley and UC San Diego.[43]

In spite of Hrabowski's having envisioned and implemented a highly successful and dynamic STEM program model that promises excellent results, I would argue that this model is not nearly as widespread as it should be. Why? According to Hrabowski and Henderson, the answer is staring us in the face: university leaders are "guilty of a lack of imagination at best or a lack of commitment at worst."[44] And there are real-world consequences. Women and people of color are far less represented in STEM professions than white and Asian men. If Black and Latinx people make their way into the profession, their salaries tend to be lower than those of their white and Asian peers.[45] Rethinking STEM curricula and pedagogy, then, has the potential to address systemic income inequality and reduce the gender pay gap in those fields.[46]

Scholars' programs also offer other opportunities to enhance institutional collaborations—for example, between HWCUs and the world of industry. Rather than one-off diversity recruitment events that occur only in the fall of senior year, real corporate partnerships should consist of long-term corporate investment in student success and potential. As Thomas Angel, a former racial affinity center leader and now Career Services director at a prestigious HBCU, put it, "Don't just poach our students. Invest in us in a nontokenizing way." Angel suggests that if corporations are serious about diversity, equity, and inclusion, they need to take a long look at themselves in the mirror. "If you want access to our students," said Angel, "tell me how many women and people of color work at your company and actually stay at your company." He added, "Students aren't here to meet your [corporate] goals."[47] The same could be said of students of color at HWCUs.

Of course, the exact mission, design, and organization of scholars' programs will differ from one institution to the next for a number of reasons, not least of all funding. But when done well, they have a proven track record of success. In the end, if HWCUs are committed to bringing racially, ethnically, and socioeconomically diverse students into their communities, the least they can do is provide those students and the faculty who teach them with the tools they need to succeed and thrive.

Chapter 7

HWCUs and Restorative Justice

Today's practitioners have an embarrassment of riches when it comes to DEI best practices. Professional organizations, guides, toolkits, and other materials provide effective strategies for maneuvering HWCUs to support historically marginalized students.[1] I have no desire to replicate those efforts. Instead I've opted to assemble lesser-known initiatives that create opportunities for high-impact change and that will require us to stretch our imaginations. While the previous chapter focused on relatively low-hanging fruit that capitalizes on preexisting infrastructure at HWCUs, this chapter draws from the vibrant world of social activism and builds on an exciting wave of new scholarship on reparations and the modern university by scholars such as Ariana González Stokas.[2] In this final chapter, I introduce the framework of restorative justice, which centers relationship and community building and was developed by people of color in the United States. The philosophy of restorative justice revolves around reducing harm, which requires acknowledgment, repair, and a plan for restoration and accountability.[3]

The framework of restorative justice has the potential to revolutionize how HWCUs do business. It offers an opportunity to be truthful about the past and begin the process of making amends. It suggests ways that we can work to be in right relationship with one another on our various college campuses and in our local communities. It is, in short, a paradigm shift that, while challenging, is eminently possible. As the prominent abolitionist thinker, organizer, and leader Mariame Kaba has written, "Changing everything might sound daunting, but it also means there are many places to start, infinite opportunities to collaborate, and endless imaginative interventions and experiments to create."[4] Indeed, Kaba encourages us to engage in creative experimentation by reimagining a world without police and with more community support. As she puts it, she's open to failure. What matters is that we learn and keep trying.[5]

In that spirit, I want to draw our attention to several successful experiments in higher education that aim to uncover the past, address harm, repair broken relationships with communities of color, and truly center equity and justice at HWCUs. It is not an exhaustive list, but it is a thought-provoking and, I hope, inspiring one. In the end, this chapter asks: If we take histories of oppression into account, and if we apply social justice frameworks like restorative justice, what could higher education look like?

Acknowledge

Over time, we've seen a greater willingness in the United States to offer public acknowledgments and apologies for past wrongs perpetrated by the US government. In 1997, President Bill Clinton apologized for the forty-year Tuskegee Experiment, an unsavory episode in which the US Public Health Service lured hundreds of Black American men to participate in a study about the untreated effects of syphilis by lying to them, hiding their syphilis diagnoses, and pretending to offer medical care. This is but one example. In 2000, on the 175th anniversary of the founding of the Bureau of Indian Affairs, the assistant secretary of Indian Affairs issued an apology to Native Americans for the office's role in "the ethnic cleansing and cultural annihilation" of Indigenous people.[6] This is a striking admission for a government agency.

The turn toward public reckonings extends beyond the federal government. We're seeing a growing wave of voluntary disclosures from companies, churches, newspapers, and other organizations throughout the United States. According to Leslie M. Harris, James T. Campbell, and Alfred L. Brophy, these historical reckonings have paved the way for a number of creative reparative experiments, including "truth commissions, monetary reparations programs, collective apologies, days of remembrance, and the erection (or removal) of public memorials."[7] In short, US society is on the precipice of something big.

HWCUs are no exception to this wider national trend. Indeed, most HWCUs currently find themselves at a crossroads: senior leaders can either acknowledge their universities' role in histories of violence, dispossession, and disenfranchisement or they can continue to engage in the collective national delusion. Though there are still holdouts, more and more HWCUs are rising to the challenge. Prompted by renewed student activism, several HWCUs have begun to investigate their institutions' ties to Indigenous dispossession, to the trade in enslaved persons, and to the promotion of racist ideologies, and doing so has led to all kinds of creative experiments in the name of restoration and justice.

The push to form veritable "truth commissions" at HWCUs came in the early 2000s. The movement began at Yale, Brown, and William and Mary. Princeton soon followed suit.[8] Today, nearly fifty universities have launched similar initiatives. As Harris writes, "We may be entering an era in which publicly disclosing historical ties to slavery and the slave trade will not seem outlandish at all but rather a basic institutional responsibility."[9]

Higher-education institutions increasingly support research-driven projects that recuperate forgotten histories. Often historians take the lead, scouring university archives for information, poring over dusty documents, and generally trying to fit the crooked pieces of the past into a cohesive narrative. Brown University is one pioneer in this regard. The university's efforts to uncover institutional ties to slavery began with the arrival of Ruth Simmons as university president in 2001. Of note, Simmons was the first African American woman to hold the office throughout Brown's two and a half centuries of existence. At the dawn of the twenty-first century, she was also the first African American president of an Ivy League university.[10]

The year 2003 marked the 250th anniversary of the institution. On that occasion, Simmons formed a scholarly commission to investigate Brown's ties to the trade in enslaved persons. Three years later, in 2006, Brown released a report that included many of the troubling findings discussed in chapter 1. The report spawned a number of institutional initiatives, including the establishment of racial affinity spaces for students of color, the formation of academic research centers dedicated to the study of race and ethnicity, and the creation of living learning communities for students interested in the history of African and African American politics, history, and culture.

Brown's faculty and researchers also found ways to both build on their research and transform it into accessible teaching material for the broader public. In 2021, Brown released an expanded edition of the report along with a "digital teaching" resource for use in student orientations and academic courses at the university. The materials are also available to folks beyond the university. The project's expansion is exemplary for at least two reasons: first, it is an elegant way to meld research and scholarship with student affairs engagement and community education; and second, it is precisely this kind of innovative, outside-the-box thinking that will push us further forward on the path toward social justice in higher education.[11]

Brown's Slavery and Justice Initiative garnered national and international attention because it offered and continues to offer an excellent model of what recuperative historical projects in higher education can look like and what change they can lead to. Other HWCUs took note. It is believed that Brown inspired some eighty colleges and universities in the United States, Canada, United Kingdom, and Ireland to undertake similar efforts. Indeed, the 2013 president's commission at the University of Virginia explicitly cited Brown, as well as Emory University and the University of North Carolina at Chapel Hill, as the impetus for its own investigative project. According to the project's website, "The University of Virginia will join other premier institutions in exploring and commemorating its relationship with slavery, as well as the lives of the enslaved people who were an integral part of early life at Jefferson's University."[12]

Brown also gave rise to the Harvard and the Legacy of Slavery initiative, which began in 2007 as a research project entitled "Harvard and Slavery: Seeking a Forgotten History." Sven Beckert, a history professor, appears to have directed the initial project. It would take some time for the project to garner a level of institutional attention comparable to Brown's project, but in 2019, Harvard's president formally established the program. The university team associated with the initiative was charged with compiling what researchers had learned over the previous decade about Harvard's ties to slavery and formulating recommendations for addressing those misdeeds.[13]

As HWCUs have begun to shine a light on their pasts, the names of campus buildings and other iconography have also come under close scrutiny. Take, for example, Kroeber Hall at UC Berkeley, named after Alfred Kroeber—widely considered the founder of anthropology in the American West. Kroeber was also cofounder and president of the

American Anthropological Association and founder of the Linguistic Society of America, and he played significant roles in the establishment of other professional anthropological organizations in the first half of the twentieth century. In 2021, Kroeber's name was stripped from Berkeley's campus building. The movement in favor of the renaming had been brewing for some time. It was common knowledge that Kroeber had a penchant for collecting and archiving Native American remains, twentieth-century behavior that recalls the actions of his eighteenth- and nineteenth-century higher-education predecessors. But Kroeber did other very peculiar things. According to the university's account, he "took custody" of a Native man named Ishi and made him into "a living exhibit for museum visitors" who watched as Ishi made Native crafts and stone tools. When Ishi died of tuberculosis in 1916, Kroeber ignored Ishi's wishes to be cremated. Instead, Kroeber autopsied Ishi's body, once again recalling the macabre experiments to which early surgeons subjected the stolen bodies of nonwhite peoples in the nineteenth century.[14]

While many supported the move to rename the building, others strongly disagreed. They argued that proponents of the renaming were doing an injustice to a man who contributed so much to the field of anthropology. But as Berkeley professor Paul Fine, chair of the Building Name Review Committee, attested, the renaming wasn't about breeding discomfort and shame. According to Fine, the decision "was less about passing judgment on Alfred Kroeber and more about the university forging better relationships with Native Americans."[15] In other words, the drive to rename campus buildings is about imagining new ways to be in authentic, meaningful community with those whom universities and their representatives have harmed in the past.

We might also consider the case of the University of California, Hastings College of the Law, a law school named after the first chief justice of the California Supreme Court, Serranus Clinton Hastings. Hastings participated rather enthusiastically in the mass murder and displacement of Yuki Indians in the 1850s and 1860s. After years of legal battle pursued by descendants of the Yuki tribe, the name of California's first law school was finally thrown into question in 2021. In 2023, the law school was officially renamed the University of California College of the Law, San Francisco.[16]

Stripping campus buildings of the names of those who contributed to violence and oppression is, in many ways, just the first step, and it raises the question: What next? For some, the removal of names like

FIGURE 11.   Alfred Kroeber (center) flanked by the Yahi Indian Ishi (right) and the Yahi translator Sam Batwai (left), 1911.
Source: UCSF History Collection, UC San Francisco, Library, University Archives.

Kroeber and Hastings offers an opportunity to remember a different past, one that pays homage to historically marginalized figures who have long been overlooked. We've seen some examples of this already. In 2017, Yale's president changed the name of Calhoun College, named after the notorious enslaver and white supremacist John C. Calhoun, to Grace Hopper College, honoring a Yale grad who studied science, joined the army, and participated in World War II. In 2017, Montana State University in Billings rethought the name of its main administrative building, McMullen Hall, a building named after the university's first president who openly praised Hitler's adoption of eugenics policies, including forced sterilizations. In 2020, the University of Texas at Austin renamed the Robert L. Moore Building the Physics, Math and Astronomy Building, severing the college's association with a math professor who refused to teach Black students at the university. The list goes on and on.[17]

The impulse behind these efforts is eminently understandable, and I deeply appreciate these renamings as one creative response to the new questions that we are asking ourselves in this moment. But I can't help but worry that in removing one history and replacing it with another, we may unintentionally whitewash history once again. That is, in renaming buildings and universities after women, queer folks, and people of color, we risk pretending that their erasure never took place to begin with. We also risk obscuring the oppressive forces that sought to deny their existence, to marginalize and exclude them from HWCUs as well as from US society more largely. In trying to recuperate and pay homage to a new history, we risk concealing the old history. The challenge is to hold both truths at once. Princeton, for example, erected an "anti-monument" to former US president and university alumnus Woodrow Wilson, after whom the School of Public and International Affairs was named, to acknowledge the white supremacist's "complex legacy."[18] The lesson here is that there are ways to remove names without erasing history in the process.

The furor over renaming universities and buildings is part of a larger national and even global debate about which past we choose to remember and how its narratives have been written onto the physical campus. Think, for example, of the statues and memorials that came tumbling down in the wake of the global protests of summer 2020. In Bristol, England, protesters toppled a bronze statue of the enslaver Edward Colston and chucked it into a nearby harbor. That same year, protesters in the former French colony of Martinique tore down a statue of Marie Antoinette as well as a statue of the seventeenth-century trader Pierre Bélain d'Esnambuc, who established Martinique as France's first Caribbean colony. Across the United States, protesters or local removal projects took down two hundred statues and memorials in 2020. Most of these incidents occurred in the South, but not all. Oklahoma and Missouri saw similar developments. Indeed, in the last several years, the wave of statue removals has given rise to a veritable industry charged with bringing down these remnants of a sordid past.[19]

The state of Virginia has emerged as one of the most bitter ideological battlegrounds over how we as a people will choose to remember our nation's past. One of the most well-known episodes took place in 2017 in Charlottesville, where protesters sought the removal of a statue of Robert E. Lee. In response, a number of Far Right white-nationalist extremists converged on Charlottesville in what became known as the Unite the Right rally. The rally turned deadly when James Alex Fields Jr.

deliberately plowed his car into protesters who supported the statue's removal, claiming the life of one young woman in the process. The episode is a stark reminder of just how violent the fight over national memory has become in the twenty-first century.

Many who oppose the removal of statues and memorials argue that they are innocent vestiges of a distant past. Certainly, some monuments to historical figures who engaged in egregious behaviors date to the eighteenth and nineteenth centuries. But others were erected decades later as tributes. Take, for instance, the fact that many Confederate monuments were erected between 1900 and 1920, decades after the end of the Civil War. The construction of these monuments coincided with the enactment of Jim Crow laws in the South as well as the revival of the Ku Klux Klan throughout the United States. Their construction coincided, then, with a resurgence of vicious anti-Blackness across the nation.

The United Daughters of the Confederacy (UDC) played an outsized role in the erection of Confederate memorials decades after the end of the Civil War. The association, founded in 1894, brought together white Southern women who claimed to be descendants of Confederate soldiers. They were fiercely committed to propagating the famed "Lost Cause" narrative that emerged in the post–Civil War South. The Lost Cause narrative posited—and continues to posit—that the South fought nobly during the Civil War, and that its soldiers and citizens were fighting not over slavery but for the preservation of states' rights. The "War of Northern Aggression," as some Southerners still call the Civil War, jeopardized the South's way of life, leaving them with no choice but to take up arms to defend themselves.

The United Daughters of the Confederacy were instrumental in perpetuating this false, self-aggrandizing narrative of Southern victimhood. Decades after the Civil War had ended, these white Southern women threw themselves into fundraising for statues and memorials of Confederate soldiers. They even bankrolled the erection of memorials to the Ku Klux Klan, an organization that some UDC members much admired. They were remarkably successful in their efforts, building hundreds of memorials across the South. Silent Sam, a monument erected in 1913 to celebrate heroic University of North Carolina alumni who fought for the Confederacy, is but one example of a UDC passion project. In 2018, it, too, was brought down by protesters.

Following this first building craze from the 1890s through the 1920s, a second flurry of Confederate construction activities in the mid-1950s lasted through the 1960s—a period coinciding almost too perfectly with the rise of the civil rights movement. According to James M. Thomas, "Both spikes suggest they were a part of a larger response among white Southerners to reclaim power and control over an African American population that was no longer bound to the system of slavery."[20] The timing of their construction, then, is a critical part of why these monuments are so vile. The motives behind the construction of memorials and statues that pay tribute to enslavers, Confederate soldiers, the KKK, and other white-supremacist figures add insult to the original injury. It's like celebrating white supremacy not once but twice.

Although we often tell ourselves that these events took place long ago, in fact these histories are uncomfortably recent. As with the renaming of universities, schools, and buildings, they pose new sets of questions: What do we do with the torn-down remains of these statues and memorials? Should they be destroyed? Personally I think not, and I'm in good company. As R. Owen Williams writes, "Until we have truly extirpated racism from our culture and society, we need these reminders. Slavery, the Confederacy, and postemancipation racism are all embarrassingly real elements of our nation's past; it is essential that we not forget any of it."[21] Williams puts it even more poignantly: "In erasing the evidence of these twentieth-century acts, do we leave ourselves open to twenty-first century forgetting?"[22]

How do we square our aversion to the past with the need to remember it still? Here, again, we can draw from creative experiments unfolding throughout the country. The dismantled pieces of a large Robert E. Lee statue in Richmond, for instance, are headed to the Black History Museum and Cultural Center of Virginia. Some plans are even more inventive. There was talk of melting down a statue of Lee in Charlottesville and creating new iconography from the remains. These moves reflect a desire to not destroy once-venerated white-supremacist symbols, but rather to transform them for use in educating the public about the nation's past. In this approach, the past is not hidden away or destroyed but put on display for critical thought and reflection.[23]

HWCUs offer other models. The construction of commemorative memorials such as the Memorial to Enslaved Laborers at the University of Virginia is one excellent example. Two granite semicircles carve out a quiet space on the campus for visitors to learn and contemplate. Within the semicircles, visitors find a historical record describing the daily lives of the more than four hundred enslaved African and African-descended men and women who labored at the university throughout the nineteenth century. These brief histories are engraved on granite plaques. A gentle stream of water runs over their etched words. The Memorial to Enslaved Laborers is a model for how we can reckon with the past by transforming campus landscapes without erasing histories of oppression in the process.[24]

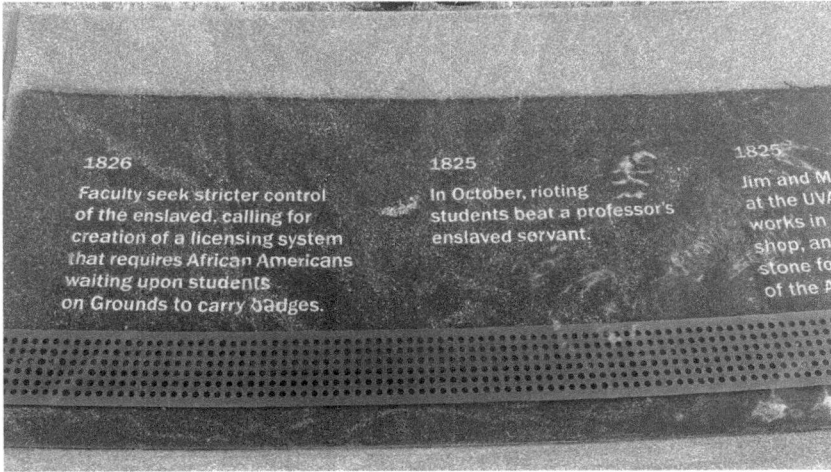

FIGURE 12. Engraved histories at the University of Virginia's Memorial to Enslaved Laborers.
Source: Photo by the author.

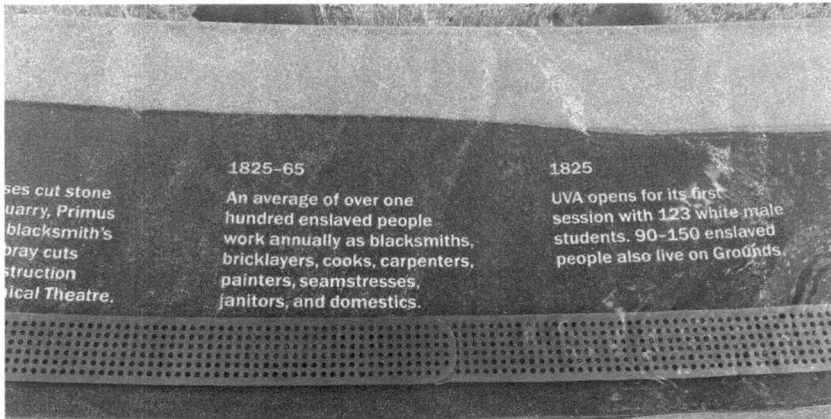

FIGURE 13. Engraved histories at the University of Virginia's Memorial to Enslaved Laborers.
Source: Photo by the author.

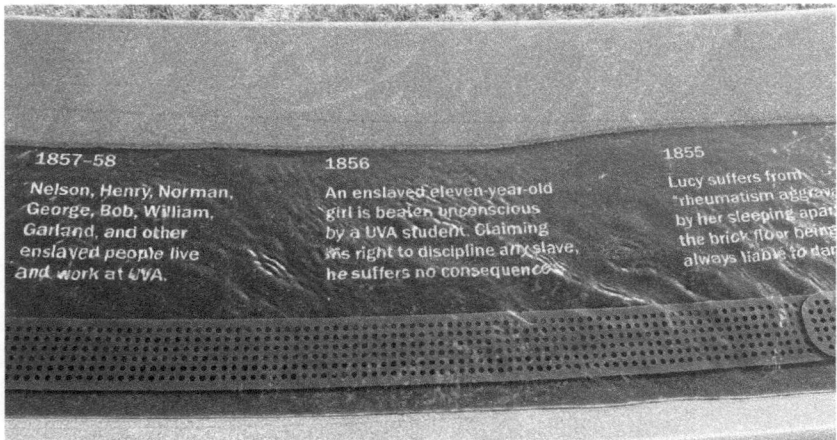

FIGURE 14. Engraved histories at the University of Virginia's Memorial to Enslaved Laborers.
Source: Photo by the author.

While slavery projects are often front and center in present-day higher-education initiatives to uncover institutions' ties to histories of oppression, there have also been significant efforts to address histories of Indigenous dispossession. For example, many universities have adopted the practice of issuing land acknowledgments. At minimum, land acknowledgments are a statement of recognition that colleges and universities, and especially HWCUs, sit on Indigenous land. More robust land acknowledgments are very specific about exactly which Native tribes were dispossessed and via what means or acts during the establishment of land-grant universities.

Increasingly, HWCUs' land acknowledgments stress the key role that local tribes played in stewarding the land. They also emphasize that Native descendants retain a connection to said land, and that Indigenous peoples are still very much a part of our society. It's not uncommon for faculty and administrative leaders to include these land acknowledgments in their email signatures or to begin talks, lectures, conferences, and other university events at their home institutions with these statements.

Though there is great variation in the genre of land acknowledgments, some institutions seem more willing than others to highlight not only that universities sit on Indigenous land but that they sit on *stolen* Indigenous land. Take, for example, Colorado State University's land acknowledgment, crafted by Indigenous faculty, staff, and administrators. The CSU website states, "Our founding came at a dire cost to native nations and peoples whose land this university was built upon."[25] Similarly, Michigan State University's statement acknowledges that the university occupies the "ancestral, traditional, and contemporary lands of the Anishinaabeg" and cites the 1819 Treaty of Saginaw that forced the cession of the land. The statement ends, "By offering this Land Acknowledgement, we affirm Indigenous sovereignty and will work to hold Michigan State University more accountable to the needs of American Indian and Indigenous peoples."[26]

While land acknowledgments are certainly a step in the right direction, they are an imperfect solution. As one campus administrator pointed out to me, typically the tribes that institutions acknowledge have a formal association with the federal government, which gives them access to coveted state resources.[27] And since the US government determines which tribes meet federally defined criteria for recognition and which tribes don't, institutional land acknowledgments risk inadvertently reproducing federal colonizing practices. It's a challenge, to be sure, but it's not an insurmountable one.

A harsher critique is that land acknowledgments don't go far enough. For many Native activists, real reconciliation requires returning the land to its original Indigenous stewards. This is a core feature of what is called the Land Back movement. There, too, higher education already has its first model. In September 2022, California State University, Chico, became the first university to return land to a local Indigenous tribe, the Mechoopda, who had lived there for thousands of years. That territory encompasses ninety-three acres of land known as Butte Creek Ecological Preserve.[28] As far as I am aware, no other HWCUs to date have formally ceded territory back to Native tribes. In the face of such a monumental task, acknowledgments look paltry indeed, and, perhaps worse, they seem performative.

I'll be the first to admit that land acknowledgments are a far cry from the restitution of land to Indigenous people. But again, I can't help but see them as a step in the right direction. For the vast majority of Americans, histories of Indigenous dispossession—and, indeed, the ongoing existence of Indigenous people—are little known and even more rarely discussed. In the national consciousness, the myth of the vanishing Indian—that is, the belief that Native populations no longer exist—remains very much intact. In that sense, land acknowledgments may be a practical place to start. That position is commensurate with moving beyond acknowledgment to action. The critical question is really: What flows from such reckonings with the past? In short, then what? To answer that question, we must turn to the fraught projects of reparation.

Repair

Since the end of World War II, significant advances in global movements for reparations have occurred. In the postwar decades, there was a growing public emphasis on the rights of victims and the importance of recognizing and safeguarding human rights. During the civil rights movement, we also saw the rise of movements that made claims to rights on the part of collectives of people, not just individuals.[29] The years since the 1950s, then, have created prime circumstances for the modern-day appearance of the struggle for reparations on the part of communities harmed by state-sanctioned violence.

For many Americans, the notion of reparations may seem foreign, impractical, or downright ludicrous. But reparation experiments have numerous precedents. From 1952 through 1966, West Germany paid the State of Israel more than 3 billion marks as a means of restoring wealth stolen during the Holocaust from Jewish people, many of whom found themselves impoverished at the end of the war, if they survived the Holocaust at all. In 2004, Haiti, the former French slave colony and the world's first independent Black nation, claimed $22 billion in reparations from France. In short, reparations are not just theoretically possible; they're eminently doable.

Even in the United States, reparations efforts have occasionally gained some traction. In 1980, by order of the US Supreme Court, the federal government paid Sioux Indians $122 million for land appropriated in 1877. Japanese Americans also successfully fought for recognition from the US government for their forced incarceration in internment camps during World War II. Not only did they receive a formal apology from the United States, but the government allocated $20,000 to each surviving internment victim. Of note, this was in 1988, in Reagan's America.

In the United States, African Americans first articulated reparations demands in the 1960s, and the campaign for reparations made a resurgence in the 1990s when Representative John Conyers Jr. put it squarely on the congressional agenda. As one might expect, support for reparations fell along racial lines. In the 1990s and early 2000s, more than half of African Americans supported reparations, while upward of 95 percent of white Americans opposed reparations.[30] By 2014, those numbers had shifted slightly. Approximately 79 percent of white Americans rejected the notion of cash payments, while that figure was closer to 19 percent among Black Americans. By 2021, 72 percent of white Americans opposed financial reparations, compared to just 14 percent of African Americans.[31] While that's not a huge shift, it is something.

In 2014, Ta-Nehisi Coates offered perhaps the most compelling argument for reparations in recent decades. In "A Case for Reparations," which was published in *The Atlantic*, Coates walked readers through the historical justification for how and why issuing reparations for Black Americans was a worthy and necessary endeavor. He focused specifically on the ways that Black Americans had been systematically disenfranchised, oppressed, and impoverished by US state and society and why, as a result, they have been largely unable to accumulate wealth. For many moderates and liberals, the article functioned as a wake-up call regarding the economic injustice that the past has wrought in our present.[32]

What exactly are US advocates of the reparations movement asking for? At the most basic level, reparations are material gestures that both acknowledge harm done by the US government and seek to hold the state accountable for those harms. In 2019, the Movement for Black Lives offered a clear list of US-sanctioned harms for which the federal government must atone:

1. Reparations for the systemic denial of access to high quality educational opportunities in the form of full and free access for all Black people (including undocumented and currently and formerly incarcerated people) to lifetime education including: free access and open admissions to public community colleges and universities, technical education (technology, trade and agricultural), educational support programs, retroactive forgiveness of student loans, and support for lifetime learning programs.

2. Reparations for the continued divestment from, discrimination toward and exploitation of our communities in the form of a guaranteed minimum livable income for all Black people, with clearly articulated corporate regulations.

3. Reparations for the wealth extracted from our communities through environmental racism, slavery, food apartheid,

housing discrimination and racialized capitalism in the
form of corporate and government reparations focused on
healing ongoing physical and mental trauma, and ensuring
our access and control of food sources, housing and land.

4. Reparations for the cultural and educational exploitation,
erasure, and extraction of our communities in the form of
mandated public school curriculums that critically examine
the political, economic, and social impacts of colonialism
and slavery, and funding to support, build, preserve, and
restore cultural assets and sacred sites to ensure the recognition and honoring of our collective struggles and triumphs.

5. Legislation at the federal and state level that requires the
United States to acknowledge the lasting impacts of slavery, [and] establish and execute a plan to address those
impacts. This includes the immediate passage of H.R.40, the
"Commission to Study Reparation Proposals for African-
Americans Act" or subsequent versions which call for reparations remedies.[33]

These are just a few possibilities among many. For instance, in 2020,
William Darity and A. Kirsten Mullen put forth their own very detailed
plan for what US reparations to Black Americans could look like, ultimately arriving at a figure close to $14 trillion.[34] At the end of the day,
there are plenty of ways to approach reparations. As Black Lives Matter
cofounder Patrisse Cullors writes, reparations could include everything
from financial restitution and land redistribution to culturally relevant
education programs and language recuperation programs. And she is
keen to point out that such efforts require commitment at the local,
state, and federal levels.[35]

In fact, in the United States, federal, state, and local efforts have
explored the possibility of reparations, though success has thus far
been limited. Since Conyers first submitted a proposal for reparations
to Congress in 1989, the bill, known as H.R. 40 in reference to the forty
acres the US government promised to Black Americans after the Civil
War, has been routinely voted down. Of note, the proposed legislation
does not actually call for reparations. Rather, it asks for the creation
of a congressional commission to study the possibility of reparations
and offer potential recommendations. In many ways, then, it is a fairly
humble request that has nevertheless been stymied at every turn for
more than three decades. And though there have been some positive

signs since 2019 that H.R. 40 may be gaining traction, as of this writing, the bill has yet to make it past Congress.

Reparations movements have gained a bit more traction at the local level. In 2021, Evanston, Illinois, became the first US city to adopt a reparations motion, which created a restorative housing program for Black Americans to address and compensate for years of state-sanctioned housing segregation.[36] A year later, in 2022, California became the first state to form a reparations task force charged with undertaking research and drawing up recommendations for restitution to African American descendants of slavery. Among the recommendations suggested was the provision of free college tuition, an acknowledgment that in depriving African Americans access to higher education for hundreds of years, US state and society contributed to present-day impoverishment in many communities of color.[37]

How might we apply the struggle for reparations to the world of higher education? Again, we can draw on successful experiments pursued by HWCUs since the 2010s. Virginia Theological Seminary in Alexandria was among the first HWCUs to pilot reparations programs to acknowledge and atone for the institution's use of enslaved labor. In 2019, the seminary established a $1.7 million reparations fund earmarked for the descendants of enslaved persons whose labor was used to establish and maintain the school. These annual cash payments are also distributed to Black members of the local community whom the seminary discriminated against during the early decades of the twentieth century. To identify those individuals, members of the seminary community work closely with genealogists. During the initial year of the program, twelve descendants received about $2,100 each.[38]

Other institutions have followed suit. Princeton Theological Seminary and Georgetown University, a Jesuit school, have both pledged funds to atone for their involvement in the system of enslavement. In 2022, Harvard University, too, released a 134-page report detailing its ties to slavery and pledged $100 million to address what then president Lawrence Bacow called "Harvard's extensive entanglements with slavery." In addition to allocating money to descendants of enslaved laborers tied to the university, Harvard leadership earmarked funds for the construction of memorials to the enslaved on campus, the augmentation of African American history curricula, and investments in schools in the US South and the West Indies, where many Harvard men originally made their fortunes through slavery.[39] The report also spurred on the establishment of exchange programs with historically Black colleges and universities (HBCUs) and some tribal colleges in recognition of how Harvard University presidents, administrators, and faculty engaged in the trade of African and African-descended people as well as Indigenous peoples.[40]

Indeed, in spite of the prevalent belief that HBCUs are plagued by chronic dysfunction and poor leadership, these institutions pioneer efforts that leverage higher-education institutions as a force to disrupt structural racism and oppression.[41] Howard University offers a Prison-to-Professionals (P2P) program for formerly incarcerated individuals seeking to obtain a college degree. Howard and other HBCUs also work closely with community-based organizations. In 2021, the Tennessee Higher Education in Prison Initiative (THEI) partnered with community colleges to provide incarcerated folks with a college education. These efforts have cut recidivism by 47 percent. Since then, THEI has formed partnerships with other HBCUs, including Lane College in Tennessee and Claflin College in South Carolina. These initiatives aim to build "a new prison-to-college pipeline" that could positively impact the lives of thousands of people, especially people of color, who are disproportionately incarcerated. HWCUs can and should look to HBCUs for such inspiration and guidance.[42]

Public universities, too, are at the forefront of transformative efforts. Take, for example, the University of California system, which in 2022 began to waive tuition and fees for Native American students residing in-state to address the fact that its universities were founded on stolen Native land.[43] So, too, have Metropolitan State University of Denver, the University of Minnesota system, and the State of Oregon.[44] Of course, institutions will confront the issue of how to refrain from inadvertently reproducing colonial practices by offering benefits only to federally recognized tribes. But where there's a will, there's a way. When the UC system introduced tuition waivers for Native students from federally recognized tribes, the Federated Indians of Graton Rancheria stepped in, assembling $2.5 million for Native California students from non-federally-recognized tribes to attend college. It's a stopgap measure, to be sure, but it's a reminder that resource-rich HWCUs can and should try to tackle these challenges head-on rather than shy away from them.[45]

All of these initiatives have something in common: they move beyond recognition to the all-important *redistribution* of ill-gotten resources. Like the research-driven truth commissions that seek to surface their institutions' ties to slavery, HWCUs could similarly fund research projects that identify all land seizure and treaties made with the original Indigenous caretakers of what has become university land, pinpointing the acres bought and sold. HWCUs could then identify university endowments rooted in the profits gained from Indigenous dispossession. South Dakota State University, for example, redirected income from remaining Morrill Act acres into programming and support for Native students.[46] While returning land to its original stewards is of course the ultimate goal, these steps move us in the right direction.

As many scholars and activists have pointed out, HWCUs can also work harder to repair relationships with local tribal communities. At minimum, they should audit all university departments and programs for Native artifacts, cultural objects, and human remains, and return them to Indigenous groups without delay. In December 2021, the University of California Office of the President issued precisely such a policy through the Native American Cultural Affiliation and Repatriation Policy.[47] HWCUs might also find ways to help local K–12 schools integrate more Native history into their classes or expand educational programs in the local community surrounding or near the university. The newly named University of California College of the Law, San Francisco, for example, has built institutional partnerships with Yuki Indians to benefit the descendants of those who experienced genocide. In 2020, the university also founded an Indigenous Law Center to create and identify more spaces where students can learn about Indigenous law through curriculum.

Other HWCUs could similarly integrate more Native history into college curricula, offer support services to Native students, or appoint administrative liaisons who work to mend relationships with local tribal communities. This is precisely what UCLA has done by hiring an adviser to the chancellor on Native American affairs. And HWCUs can venture even further, imagining ways they might support local tribally controlled colleges. Partnerships between state and community colleges could also be enhanced to support students who attend tribal colleges, helping them adjust to four-year institutions.

Initiatives on this scale are a reminder that one-off solutions aren't enough. In January 2022, the Lumina Foundation, a nonprofit foundation that supports postsecondary educational access and success, partnered with Equal Measure, a social change nonprofit, to examine inequities in higher education. The organizations issued a three-part series on advancing equity in education that provides a framework for how to suss out problems and generate strategies to address inequities. Overall, the series pushes higher-education leaders to identify "root causes" of inequities that exist off campus (what it calls "elevating social determinants") and histories of oppression in our country (or "unearthing historic injustice"). According to the report, "Without examining root causes, solutions are more likely to be short-term, programmatic 'band aids' that will not resolve the underlying issues facing students today and in the future."[48] This approach is useful because it reminds us that there are rarely one-size-fits-all solutions, that strategies must be tailored to specific institutions.

The report provides the example of North State Together, a regional umbrella organization located in Northern California that brings together the work of five collectives focused on educational equity. Their institutional partnership with Shasta College began with recognizing links between health outcomes and education for Shasta residents. Using disaggregated data, researchers determined that Indigenous communities suffered from the greatest educational disparities in the area. They turned to historical injustices that posed significant hurdles for Indigenous youth, including the difficulty many faced accessing postsecondary education. These discoveries led to significant reorientations in policies, curricula, and practices. Among other things, school leaders started to make the connection that chronic absence among Indigenous students often mapped onto tribal holidays that went unrecognized at the state or federal level. From there, they were able to engage in focused strategies, including adjustments to the school calendar to reflect tribal ceremonies. These discoveries also prompted the development of a "cradle to career" vision that North State Together crafted to interrupt inequities at every stage of education through college graduation.[49]

As we've seen, reparations projects are rich and varied. They include a wide variety of initiatives that seek to address and repair harm, primarily through the redistribution of resources. There are, of course, plenty of kinks to work out. Should reparations be limited only to the descendants of the enslaved or to all folks who identify as Black and have experienced discrimination in the United States that has similarly hampered their social mobility? I don't have the answer to this question. These complications reflect the historical reality of racism in the US. The point is that we mustn't walk away just because things seem too complicated. We can and must accept the messiness of history and strive to make things right any way we can.[50]

Restore

Universities would also benefit from a more robust adoption of restorative justice values, systems, policies, and practices. What is restorative justice? Restorative justice is a counter to judicial and legalistic processes that focus on punishment and retribution. Instead it is an approach that is relationship centered. It focuses on the harm done and its impact on relationships and the wider community, and it asks what action can be taken to repair said harm. As Mariame Kaba writes, "It's very much a framework and an ideology and a way of living that is interested in making sure that we remain in right relationship with each other, with the land, with the environment."[51] In many ways, then, we might consider restorative justice a form of reparations at the interpersonal level.

The model of retributive justice in the United States, and elsewhere, focuses on rules and laws. It asks: What law was broken, who broke it, and what punishment is warranted? Instead, restorative justice asks: Who was harmed, what do they need, and whose obligation is it to meet those needs? Rather than punitive, it is restorative; instead of sending a "tough on crime" message, it encourages individual and community transformation.[52]

Restorative justice as a way of approaching relationship, harm, and communities is hardly new. Restorative practices are living traditions, and they offer significant wisdom. There is wide consensus that restorative justice traces its lineage to Indigenous practices and cultures in the South Pacific and the Americas, and that similar philosophies undergirded many African cultures and societies.[53] The same goes for Indigenous forms of justice in the United States. As James Kilgore has written, "Pre-1824 tribal courts embodied a restorative approach that greatly differed from the punitive, adversarial systems of the United Stated."[54] As Mariame Kaba also observes, the United States deemed Native justice "insufficiently punitive, and therefore uncivilized." Consequently, the US government eventually replaced Native justice with US law on reservations.[55] In fact, the problems and limitations of the punitive Western legal and educational system have prompted many modern-day movements for restorative justice.

Since the 1980s, we have seen successful experiments in restorative justice in criminal justice systems around the world. Some of the earliest experiments unfolded in the late 1980s and early 1990s in Australia and New Zealand to address the historical oppression of Maori

Indigenous populations. Eventually, these experiments made their way to the UK, Canada, and most recently the United States.[56] In fact, by July 2020, some form of restorative justice practices have become standard features in legal systems across the US. The only states that defy this trend are North Dakota, Rhode Island, South Dakota, South Carolina, and Wyoming.[57]

It probably comes as no surprise that historically marginalized populations are typically at the forefront of restorative justice movements. They are, after all, most impacted by systems of injustice in Western societies, especially those founded on settler colonialism. The focus on restorative justice practices began in criminal justice as a response to mass incarceration, but since then, it's become a philosophy and set of practices that have entered a number of other fields, including social work, education, workplaces, and local communities.[58]

Though still a fairly recent phenomenon in the United States, restorative justice has found fertile ground in K–12 education systems, primarily because of the all-too-real school-to-prison pipeline. The school-to-prison pipeline is the product of racial disparities in student punishment; zero-tolerance policies that push out students, especially students of color; and the introduction of police presence in K–12 schools, especially in urban schools composed largely of minority students.[59] The proper implementation of restorative justice in K–12 schools offers a means to interrupt the school-to-prison pipeline. Study after study shows that restorative justice practices in K–12 schools reduce racial disparities in school punishment among students. Restorative justice also improves the wider school climate, primarily by enhancing student relationships with teachers.[60]

In education settings, restorative justice has yet to really migrate beyond the K–12 school system. But there are many reasons we should consider implementing restorative justice practices on colleges campuses. I'm hardly the first person to point this out. Higher education culture is steeped in retributive justice. According to David Karp and Olivia Frank, "Colonial colleges made use of fines, suspension, expulsion, and various restrictions, but flogging and boxing (receiving blows to the head) were the most common sanctions."[61] These legacies persist today. Modern-day colleges implement a model of "progressive exclusion," moving from probation to suspension to expulsion.[62] In this manner, violations of campus codes of conduct lead to legalistic proceedings that hew closely to how the wider US criminal justice system operates.

But restorative justice practices are a better alternative. First, restorative justice processes are a good philosophical fit. These processes contribute to the development of emotional maturity and thus are in line with the wider approach to student development that student affairs officers have adopted.[63] Restorative justice bypasses the issue of unfair application of rules due to administrator bias, avoiding discriminatory punishments. It also enlists students who have caused harm into a process where they have responsibility for drafting their own accountability and repair processes, as opposed to abiding by some decision meted out from on high.

What might the adoption of restorative justice look like in practice on college campuses? David Karp, a leader in the field, has spent a significant amount of time considering precisely that. At the most basic level, he argues, it would change our approach to handling certain campus incidents. Restorative justice practices are particularly effective for minor and nonviolent infractions, including noise violations, theft, vandalism, alcohol-related disruptions, and cheating. Instead of punitive responses, it would lead to the implementation of circles and restorative conferencing, which allow the person(s) harmed to explain the impact of that harm on them, and provide a structure by which the person(s) who harmed the individual in question participate in drafting their own modes of accountability. For Karp, accountability measures rooted in restorative justice would include monetary reparation for damage done, drafting agreements that outline how to ensure the behavior doesn't happen again, writing apology letters, and writing papers that demonstrate learning about the issue.[64] These responses provide a path by which individuals who have caused harm in the community can take ownership, make amends, and eventually be reintegrated into the community as transformed individuals. These are the most obvious ways to implement restorative justice. But there are weightier issues to consider.

Previous chapters have cited instances of identity-based violence on college campuses, from swastikas sprayed on buildings to nooses hung in campus dorms. Is restorative justice appropriate in addressing these incidents?

Many HWCUs have instituted bias reporting protocols to address identity-based harm. Often born out of student protests, these protocols signify an institutional recognition that microaggressions—and worse—thoroughly imbue many campus cultures. In terms of process, students who have experienced or witnessed identity-based bias incidents can report them anonymously online. From there, an investigative process of some sort usually follows. If the student who was reported on is found culpable, they may experience punitive measures. In other instances, they may be asked to issue a formal apology to the party, or parties, harmed. In the best-case scenario, at least in my opinion, they may be asked to undertake, and even be guided through, an educational process that encourages them to learn and reflect on the histories that enable their behaviors.

At minimum, bias reporting systems represent an institutional acknowledgment that interpersonal identity-based harm happens on college campuses. They thus demonstrate institutional commitment to intervene in and disrupt cultures of oppression that we know thrive on their campuses. From that angle, it is hard not to appreciate the development of these bias reporting systems, as they may very well reflect a genuine desire to respond to the concerns of historically marginalized students.

Increasingly, though, folks have begun to question this discipline-and-punish model that reflects US society's own preference for carceral solutions. Once again, abolitionism offers us a useful framework that challenges us to question our worldviews and imagine new ways of being in relationship with one another. According to abolitionist thought, if we are working to thwart the application of a punitive system against some, then we must work to thwart punitive systems against all. This doesn't mean refusing to hold people accountable, but it does mean moving away from the revenge paradigm. It also requires asking different questions and devising different solutions from those most often used—suspension, expulsion, and so on.

These approaches have yielded results beyond higher education. In 2016, in Ashburn, Virginia, youths sprayed swastikas on a schoolhouse that had been built in the nineteenth century to educate Black children in a segregated educational system. When the teenagers were eventually hauled into court for vandalism, Judge Avelina Jacob opted for a restorative approach rather than a punitive one. The commonwealth attorney asked, "Is it going to change their perspective on swastikas if you put them in the juvenile center and locked them up?" Instead the judge assigned the group of teens a reading list that included books like *12 Years a Slave* by Solomon Northup, *To Kill a Mockingbird* by Harper Lee, and *Night* by Elie Wiesel. The youths had the summer to select books, read them, and thus educate themselves about everything from the US system of enslavement, anti-Blackness, and Jim Crow racism to

World War II, antisemitism, and the Holocaust. Later, the teens reported learning information they'd never been exposed to in school beyond a few hours in this or that history class. Based on their reactions, reading and education had a tremendous impact on them.[65]

The question of how to approach racist incidents on campus has dogged administrators ever since the student protest movements of the 1960s and 1970s. As more and more Black students arrived on predominantly white campuses, they faced whitelash and institutional opposition. Reflecting back on his role as ombudsman for a small college in the Northeast, Greg Collins explained the quandary in which he sometimes found himself. When white students engaged in overtly racist behavior on campus, students of color wanted to see major punishment, especially expulsion. But he was always reluctant to exact what was called for. From Collins's perspective, ostracizing white students and removing them permanently from the community prevented their racial learning and their ability to take ownership of their mistakes, to take accountability in a way that would transform them and the wider campus community. Instead he asked offending students to take courses on race and racism and to complete all assignments to the instructor's satisfaction. He didn't mandate that they take those courses for credit, but he did ensure that they showed personal growth over time.[66]

There are hints that these restorative justice approaches are already making inroads in some corners of the higher-education world. More and more nonprofit organizations offer training and coaching in restorative justice practices for college and university staff. And some HWCUs offer services for educators. The University of San Diego does so through its own Center for Restorative Justice, located in the School of Leadership and Education Sciences.[67] Other HWCUs provide restorative justice practices in-house, usually via the Office of Student Conduct or its equivalent. Some consider the University of Michigan, which launched restorative justice efforts in 2008, a pioneer in this regard.[68] Other colleges and universities have followed suit, instituting restorative circles, conferencing, and conflict-resolution processes for students.[69]

This is not to say that the implementation of restorative justice doesn't come with its own set of challenges. It very much does. This accounts for the fact that only very few campuses use restorative practices. In 2009, just 8 percent of campus communities used such practices.[70] Part of the reason why so few HWCUs use restorative justice is because, like any other university initiative, it requires time, money, and manpower that a lot of places just don't have. Others, echoing nineteenth-century US officials, argue that it's impractical. One article from the Right-leaning Real Clear Investigations derided restorative justice as "a softer approach [in the] higher-stakes experiment in student safety." In fact, that is a pretty common misconception.[71]

Restorative justice processes are also challenging to implement because they presume there is something to restore in the first place. That requires a deep sense of mutual trust and belonging on campus communities, which, as we've seen throughout this book, many modern colleges and universities fail to build with historically marginalized students, staff, and faculty. Consequently, if and when harm occurs, higher-education institutions are hamstrung by the lack of a solid relational foundation. Once again, equity practitioners on the ground who work closely with students typically fill this gap, lending credibility to institutions as they seek to reconcile with historically marginalized students. It's just another way that equity practitioners bridge institutional gaps.

But the more challenging barrier to creating restorative campus cultures is, quite simply, us. As one administrator from James Madison University observed, the use of restorative justice requires a paradigm shift in the way we think about the social good. It demands that we decenter our desire for revenge and instead recenter the values of relationship and community building.[72] It's true; restorative justice is nowhere near as cut and dried as traditional models of discipline, which translate a transgression into a punishment. Instead, as we've seen above, restorative justice requires creative tailoring in order to produce different solutions to redress different harms. It defies easy regulation and implementation. It is, in a word, messy.

To be fair, the unwillingness to shift toward a restorative mindset is not just on the part of university staff, faculty, and leaders. As Greg Collins's story above indicates, students, too, may crave retributive justice. Personally, I understand this sentiment. I myself grew up in a household that placed a premium on traditional discipline rather than restorative discipline. But there is a singular tension here that we can't avoid. How can we hold the fact that colleges and universities are by definition sites of learning, while recognizing that some kinds of learning will inevitably come at the expense of others? How do we hold two truths that seem to pull in opposite directions at once?

Again, I want to acknowledge that I know from personal experience that pursuing restorative rather than retributive justice is a tough mindset shift. I myself have taken years to come around, and I still struggle. In addition to basic socialization, one of the hardest things for me to wrap my mind around is how restorative justice could ever possibly be enough to address Title IX violations. Not only have I experienced sexual assault on a college campus myself, but far too many of my close friends have too. For a long time, and sometimes still, my own personal experience and what I consider my feminist politics prevented me from wanting anything other than retributive justice.

If you're anything like me, restorative justice applied to sexual assault cases might feel like a bridge too far. But there are reasons to reconsider our positions. The turn to police and incarceration to handle gender and sexual violence is known as carceral feminism. A term coined by the Barnard sociologist Elizabeth Bernstein, carceral feminism describes a feminist response to gender and sexual violence that emerged during the 1970s, 1980s, and 1990s, a response that relies on the police state and mass incarceration to punish perpetrators. It also happens to center white feminism, which effectively sidelines women-of-color feminisms that historically attend also to racial justice.[73]

In higher-education settings, carceral feminism would look like, well, precisely my idea of justice for the harmed party. It would culminate with punitive disciplinary measures like suspension and expulsion and, if I had my way, perhaps worse. But, as in the United States more broadly, carceral solutions have gotten us nowhere. According to researchers, students who have experienced sexual harm on campus are rarely served well by the existing Title IX process, which includes monthslong investigations that exclude and disempower the victim.[74] Moreover, through the lens of racial equity, Title IX practices pose obstacles to communities of color. Research suggests that Black women are less likely to report sexual assault and that women of color are less likely to pursue Title IX resources after an attack. Rather, many Black women and other women of color who have been assaulted place importance on the processes of healing and accountability within the context of their respective cultures and politics. For example, Black students who experienced sexual assault at UCLA experienced it not only as gender- and sex-based violence but also through the prism of the Black Lives Matter struggle.[75] That is, they experienced it through the prism of both their gender and racial identities.

In the face of mounting evidence that existing Title IX processes do not serve all students well, is it time to question the status quo? I won't claim to be an expert, and I've already transparently shared that this is an area I struggle with, on a personal, professional, and political level. But in the spirit of asking other folks to open themselves up to new possibilities, I'll demand the same of myself.

There are, in fact, precedents for restorative approaches to Title IX cases. Take, for instance, PRISM, or Promoting Restorative Initiatives for Sexual Misconduct on College Campuses. PRISM is a project run out of the aforementioned School of Leadership and Education Sciences at the University of San Diego. It brings together academics and restorative justice practitioners to envision restorative approaches to gender-based and sexual violence on college campuses. Its goal is to promote accountability through relationship-based processes. PRISM embraces a "whole campus" response, including restorative circles for sexual assault prevention efforts, restorative conferencing in response to misconduct, and reentry circles for students returning from suspension.[76]

What do students do in these circles? According to David Karp, one of the primary authors of the program and a leading researcher in restorative justice approaches in higher education, "The approach is really about gathering students in smaller circles to have dialogues about Title IX topics in a way that's not just lecturing to them about what the rules are." He adds, "It's more focused on their understanding of consent, setting their own sexual standards with each other around sexual communication, around alcohol and sex, around hookup culture, all of these issues that all converge to create an unsafe environment for students."[77] There's evidence to suggest that a restorative approach may actually be as effective for victims of harm as current Title IX practices, perhaps even more so.[78]

Other responses to gender- and sex-based violence are possible, including community-based and community-led interventions. In *Becoming Abolitionists*, Derecka Purnell cites the Chicago organization Assata's Daughters. Volunteers at Assata's Daughters began by focusing their efforts on women, femme, and gender-nonconforming individuals. Before long, however, organizational leaders realized that, because gender-based and sexual violence are rooted in widespread patriarchy and misogyny, the organization needed to expand programming to boys and men. As Purnell writes, efforts like these were part of a larger process of social transformation that requires us *all* to unlearn violence as the only solution to the violence we ourselves have experienced.[79]

In spite of the many challenges of restorative approaches, HWCUs have already begun to translate the framework of acknowledge-repair-restore into concrete actions, with the aim of making amends with communities of color harmed by these universities' founding, maintenance, and expansion. We have entered a period in which reparative actions have become a core institutional expectation. The consensus is clear; those who refuse to get on board will be left behind.

Epilogue
Higher Education and Transformative Justice

This book has traced the evolution of HWCUs and shined a light on how this nation's oldest colleges and universities were built on white-supremacist ideologies. Throughout the centuries, HWCUs have produced and reproduced a variety of exclusions based on class, gender, ability, and especially race. These exclusionary systems, cultures, policies, and practices calcified over the centuries, and we contend with them still. Although the radical student movements of the 1960s and 1970s introduced sweeping changes, the progressive moment was ultimately short lived. Though diversity practitioners at HWCUs have certainly made headway over the years, their wins remain partial because they operate within institutions that employ a power-blind diversity-and-inclusion framework that obscures structural inequality, masks institutional whiteness, and more often than not bows under the immense pressure of whitelash.

Without a doubt, the rebirth of liberatory social movements and renewed student activism since the mid-2010s have forced equity and justice back onto the institutional agenda of most HWCUs. With the high-profile murders of Black Americans, and the viral video of George Floyd's murder in particular, students and faculty once again sounded the alarm, drawing the public's attention back to persistent legacies of racism, anti-Blackness, and myriad other forms of oppression that endure on college campuses still. HWCUs responded accordingly, but, as of this writing, many have already begun to renege on the promises so ardently made in summer 2020.[1] Until we are willing to face the truth of the past with courage and conviction, we are condemned to repeat this frustratingly predictable historical pattern, and it will always be to the detriment of historically marginalized students and communities.

This book has asked: What might it look like if we stayed the course rather than fall back into the same old patterns? What if we recognized the furious eruption of anti-DEI and anti-critical-race-theory fervor for what it is: the phenomenon of whitelash that has always followed fast on the heels of bursts of social progress in this country? And what if we dared to take seriously COVID-19's brutal lesson that institutions can, in fact, change rapidly if and when their hand is forced?

Plenty of books offer DEI best practices to improve diversity, inclusion, and belonging at HWCUs, but I've endeavored to take a different tack. By taking as my starting point histories of power and oppression rooted in white supremacy, I've invited us to rethink our current DEI approaches. In addition to revealing how ongoing legacies of institutional whiteness hinder diversity practitioners, I've offered some paths forward, above all recognizing that DEI is an academic *and* student life issue, and encouraging faculty and diversity practitioners to work together more closely, as they did in the sixties and seventies to excellent effect. I've discussed successful scholars' programs that have long produced tried-and-true results primarily because they recenter the college classroom in the student experience. I've also suggested that one reason why such programs are so successful is that they involve faculty who are willing to strive beyond inclusive teaching, to experiment with more liberatory pedagogies, and to engage in more radical innovation that truly transforms learning environments. Most significantly, I've argued that restorative justice models offer HWCUs blueprints for how to address past harms, repair broken relationships, and restore a sense of community on their campuses and beyond campus walls.

The frameworks I've applied throughout this book come to us from generations of abolitionists and activists of color invested in imagining new responses to state-sanctioned violence against the public that do not depend on policing, surveillance, and incarceration. The aims of this book are of course far more modest. But I've nevertheless drawn on abolitionist thinking when possible because it offers us insight and spurs the imagination. With that in mind, I'd like to close by suggesting that, while change at the institutional level is important, in the end, it is systems-level change that will truly transform higher education and society more largely.

What would structural transformation in higher ed look like? Rethinking admissions processes is one critical step toward acknowledging and reversing centuries of exclusion. Removing barriers to college access would include, for instance, the elimination of the SATs or at the very least going test optional, a policy that rose in popularity during the pandemic.[2] Those institutions with the resources to do so should work toward the introduction of need-blind admission. As we saw in the previous chapter, a handful of public institutions have already committed to waiving tuition for Native students and descendants of the formerly enslaved. Now that the Supreme Court has struck down race-based affirmative action in college admissions, these reparative measures are that much more important. Indeed, education scholars and DEI practitioners are actively at work developing new policy approaches in our post-affirmative-action climate.[3]

Any discussion of college admissions necessarily brings us to the vexed question of legacy preferences. In *What Universities Owe Democracy*, Johns Hopkins University president Ronald Daniels describes legacy preferences as "a naked form of hereditary advantage."[4] Indeed, one study found that 43 percent of white students at Harvard were legacies, athletes, or the relatives of donors or staff members, and that almost 70 percent of all legacy students are white.[5] "Legacy preference is immobility written as policy," Daniels contends, "preserving for children the same advantages enjoyed by their parents."[6] He argues passionately for the abolition of legacy preferences, which lie in direct contrast with modern democratic values—namely, access and opportunity for all. And while, once again, there are pitfalls to avoid, top-notch universities such as MIT and Cal Tech have already ended the centuries-old practice.[7]

While this book focuses on selective HWCUs, public institutions including community colleges serve the vast majority of first-generation, low-income students in this country. The same could be said of many HBCUs.[8] Public universities, community colleges, regional institutions—they've all learned how to do more with less, but they shouldn't be working with so little to begin with. For years, scholars have advocated for the reversal of decades of federal education policy that stripped public institutions of precious resources. They call for government reinvestment in public education, and especially in the federal Pell Grant program, which would dramatically improve the prospects of first-generation, low-income students of color. That step alone would go a long way toward reducing the crisis in student debt that assails today's college goers and making it more affordable for students from "nontraditional" backgrounds to obtain a college degree.

Federal policy could support the rehabilitation of the public-education sector in other ways too. I'm hardly the first to point out a fundamental contradiction at the heart of the modern university: the corporatization of higher-education institutions allows some to amass huge amounts of wealth, which is entirely at odds with their ongoing tax-exempt status as so-called nonprofit organizations.[9] In 2017, the government introduced legislation to tax the university endowments of a small number of private colleges and universities, which, in the words of Jennifer Bird-Pollan, allowed us to "treat university endowments more like the private equity funds they increasingly resemble."[10] That's especially the case for elite institutions that possess the most endowment assets. As dozens of education policy experts have argued, that wealth could—and should—be productively distributed to less resourced postsecondary institutions and the lower-income students whom they serve.[11] Relatedly, the leaders of public institutions must depart from privatization models, which, as Christopher Newfield has written, encourage "market-oriented, cost-focused managerialism."[12] For Newfield and a host of others, the use of corporate practices from the private sector destroys "the public university's unique product—low-cost, no-debt, high-quality university learning on a mass scale, or *mass quality*."[13] The redistribution of resources from wealthy HWCUs to public institutions would make that possible.

Other initiatives will require institutions to address their specific histories with local communities. For example, it's well known that, in the name of clearing out Black "slums" and hastening gentrification, HWCUs displaced low-income communities of color. This history has long haunted the University of Chicago, which, since the 1930s and 1940s, used restrictive covenants to push out low-income communities of color, mostly Black residents from the South Side. For years, there has been bad blood between local residents and the university. Some have called for the university to make amends for those harms by investing in affordable housing for historically displaced low-income communities. Other universities with similar track records might consider such steps too.[14]

American studies professor Christina Heatherton once wrote, "Show me the boundary between a school and a local community, and I will tell you what the students there are being taught about themselves and their place in the world."[15] That is, if HWCUs are cut off from their local communities, what does that signal to undergraduates about their relationship with and responsibility to one another? Along these lines, we must reimagine what was once called "community service."[16] Today, we are more likely to speak in the vernacular of service learning or engaged learning, which brings us back to the college classroom. There are many ways that institutions define engaged learning, but I would put it this way: in engaged learning models, faculty create learning objectives that require students to work collaboratively with community partners. The emphasis is on developing and applying research, writing, and communication skills to real-world problems with real-world impact.

As Daniels writes, "Today, service learning is a centerpiece of civic and community engagement at colleges and universities."[17] In keeping with the general thrust of his argument, he contends that service learning prepares students for the responsibilities of democratic citizenship. Not only am I in full agreement, but I would take it a step further. Engaged learning offers an opportunity for institutions to root out colonialist legacies that still shape their community-oriented initiatives. In much of Europe, aristocratic notions of noblesse oblige long shaped how the wealthy imagined their civic responsibilities to the lower orders. Theirs was a duty to uplift and civilize benighted peasants. In many ways, these domestic attitudes and ideologies were later magnified and applied globally. It was, after all, the white man's burden that drove colonial expansion and empire building.

HWCUs are products of their histories and still reflect these traditions. Remember that the earliest colonial colleges were founded with the explicit mission to uplift so-called savage heathens through a European education. Unfortunately, some universities unthinkingly reproduce those condescending and paternalistic practices, socializing many college students into an at best ignorant, and at worst arrogant, way of being in community with others. In other words, when not done carefully and intentionally, community service masquerading as engaged learning risks reproducing classist, racist, and colonialist mindsets that are at odds with meaningful community building.

What would it look like to depart from a community service model? In 2022, the Lumina Foundation, an education nonprofit, published a report that offers a valuable guiding framework.[18] In the first place, it would mean that institutions work with community partners that "hold power, authority, and resources over local systems" and that "serve a wider geographic footprint than their campuses."[19] This alone would ensure that resulting initiatives address specific concerns of the community and would thus be relevant.

After identifying partners, universities should enter into power-conscious conversations with local communities, recognizing community members and organizations as equals that have the indisputable right to determine priorities affecting their day-to-day lives. At minimum, such an approach communicates respect and humility, which on its own goes a long way. It also denotes a shift from a power-hoarding to a power-sharing mentality, examples of which our society so painfully lacks at the moment.[20]

I hasten to point out that accounting for the needs and wishes of a community also means accepting that not all folks will welcome such partnerships, at least not at first. And why would they? Time and again, we've seen how low-income communities of color have suffered from the capitalist expansion of the higher-education-industrial complex. More specifically, urban "renewal" and real estate "development" projects mask naked attempts at empire building in US cities that push longtime residents out of their homes to make room for idyllic, tourist-friendly college towns.[21] Overcoming mistrust is no easy thing. But once trust is built, colleges and universities have the precious opportunity to work in partnership with community organizations to alleviate systemic inequalities at the local level.

As we've seen throughout, faculty-led research projects are a great entry point into engaged learning. Recall that what began as small-scale investigations into institutional ties to slavery often grew into full-blown research projects involving students, many of which prompted additional initiatives at the institutional level. They offer a fantastic example of the real transformative potential of research and scholarship. How might we extend that model? Educational researchers have been at the forefront when it comes to asking this question. Thanks to them, we know more than ever. We understand well the benefits of "diversity" in higher education. We know now how to better prepare historically marginalized students for college. In addition to expanding college access, we also know how to support students' college success. Above all, we know that a college degree promotes socioeconomic mobility and the broader social good.

While this strand of faculty research has been invaluable in shaping equity-and-inclusion efforts in colleges and universities, there are other ways still that we might focus, or refocus, the purpose of academic research in the service of creating a more just world. Take the "Mapping Pollution" project at UC Irvine, wherein scholars worked closely with local environmental activists to examine the history and public health effects of soil-lead contamination in Santa Ana, a historically low-income Latinx city neighboring Irvine. The interdisciplinary project required the participation of scientists as well as historians and public health experts, and was in fact initiated by a PhD candidate in the History Department, Juan Manuel Rubio.[22]

"Mapping Pollution" offers many insights and reflects the new process I've outlined above. Unlike in the traditional academic research model, scholars didn't necessarily pursue research according to their own interests. Rather, they worked with local communities to define a public health problem, effectively decentering the academic model whereby a researcher enters their project assuming that they alone define the contours of the project. Rather, in this model, the project is to be defined collectively through community input and collaboration, from research question formulation to data collection, analysis, and recommendations. A model like this requires researchers to rethink their research processes, to create equal space for others in the room. It also requires trust, commitment, engagement, and relationship building with local communities. And it's yet another way to actualize the idea that universities have obligations to their communities, that they can and should use their resources to benefit the wider public good.

In a book inspired by the intellectual thought and labor of abolitionists, I would be remiss if I did not broach the fraught issue of police on college campuses. The American studies professor Davarian Baldwin addresses this question head-on in his book *In the Shadow of the Ivory Tower*. Baldwin focuses specifically on the University of Chicago, which has amassed a police force so large that it's rivaled only by that of the Vatican.[23] In addition to policing the college campus, starting in 2011, UCPD officers were permitted to make arrests off campus too, extending their purview into local communities. In short, theirs is a private police force endowed with public law-enforcement privileges. It is, to say the least, a danger to democracy and the just rule of law.

The consequences have been devastating. Since 2011, UCPD officers have issued citations to Black people at far higher rates than anyone else. In 2018, three in four drivers stopped by University of Chicago campus police were Black. Campus officers have shot and killed Black residents over simple traffic violations.[24] Worse yet, this model of policing has become one that other prestigious universities located in lower-income communities of color, including Johns Hopkins, have sought to emulate.[25] The result? As Baldwin writes in an article published in the *Chronicle of Higher Education*, "Colleges have become one of the primary policing agents in big cities and small towns across the country."[26]

Baldwin insists that college campuses should be "ground zero" for the movement to abolish the police. He cites Justice Department statistics that show that in 2012, 92 percent of public colleges and 38 percent of private colleges employed police officers, some of whom were armed. Baldwin echoes the argument of many abolitionists who point out that police officers are simply not trained to handle the majority of the cases they're called in for, and that those resources would be better directed toward trained medical professionals and social workers. As evidence, Baldwin cites the fact that officers aren't trained for the kind of work that they're asked to do nine out of ten times. In the face of such damning evidence, he asks, "Why couldn't colleges serve as a model for a new vision of public safety? Why couldn't institutions supply teams of trauma and health-care workers instead of armed police units to the residents of their cities? Why couldn't we replace campus-police facilities with neighborhood kitchens that turn unused supplies from dining halls into healthy meals for communities in need? That is what abolition could look like."[27]

The idea is not as outlandish as it is often portrayed. Even before 2020, we saw increasing numbers of police reform efforts on college campuses, often spurred on by racial profiling incidents involving students of color.[28] Since 2020, successful abolitionist experiments have cropped up at HWCUs around the country—for instance, at the University of Pennsylvania and UCLA.[29] In summer 2020, abolitionist students, educators, and college town residents even established the Cops Off Campus Coalition to think through alternatives to policing.[30]

Other institutions have faced even bolder calls for police abolition following all-too-familiar tragedies. Two years after Portland State University cops shot navy veteran Jason Washington seventeen times, the movement to get cops off PSU's campus caught on.[31] In September 2021, PSU's student newspaper reported that the Campus Public Safety Office indeed implemented a policy of unarmed patrols, but it was quick to point out that the policy stopped just short of full disarmament, which students had demanded the previous year.[32] As it turns out, that omission foreshadowed what was to come. As of May 2023, PSU has retreated from the abolitionist promises made in summer

2020, and many other HWCUs are following suit.[33] For all the promise of 2020, the window of opportunity is already closing, and we're losing our way once more.

These are merely a handful of ways that we can get closer to achieving structural transformation in higher education. By no means is it an exhaustive list; no such thing exists. But it offers a few possibilities about how we might go about disrupting and reversing legacies of exclusion that continue to shape higher education. Along the way, these ideas give us a little glimpse into what it could look like if we pushed the limits of our imagination.

I won't pretend that what I'm proposing is easy. It's absolutely not. Transformative efforts in higher education require significant paradigm shifts and new ways of thinking. Painful as it was, the early COVID-19 era got us closer to just that. A terrible public health crisis disrupted centuries of higher ed tradition and hastened rapid institutional change. My hope is that this book prompts us to take those lessons to heart, to embrace the possibility that we have more power to change things than we are often told. All we need to do is ask ourselves new questions, imagine a different future, then move closer to that vision.

Few of us are likely to see this scale of transformation in our lifetimes. But just because we won't be there to see it doesn't mean we don't owe it to future generations to at least try. After all, we stand atop the shoulders of those who came before us. Where would we be without them?

We're not responsible for the decisions made by people who existed long, long before us. But we are responsible for the society we inherit, riddled as it is with inequalities forged in another era. Let's not squander all the hard work of generations past. Let's not lose momentum as we so often have. Let's use our resources, our creativity, and our energy to imagine new ways that higher education can serve us—all of us.

NOTES

Introduction

1. Levin, "No Home, No Wi-Fi"; Casey, "College Made Them Feel Equal."
2. Wilder, *Ebony & Ivy*; Harris, Campbell, and Brophy, *Slavery and the University*; Stein, *Unsettling the University*. For a regularly updated list of the top ten HWCUs, see the online appendix on my website at https://drnimishabarton.com/just-future.
3. See also racialized organization theory, in Ray, *On Critical Race Theory*, chap. 8. For examples of how institutional whiteness shapes school cultures and policies, see Chandler-Ward and Denevi, *Learning and Teaching While White*, chap. 3.
4. Anderson, *White Rage*; Lippard, Carter, and Embrick, *Protecting Whiteness*; Joseph, *Third Reconstruction*, chap. 3.
5. Eve Tuck and K. Wayne Yang describe the multiplicity of today's social justice struggles as the product of "diverse dreaming that has happened under [the] rising sun [of social justice]" and acknowledge "that those dreams are not so far apart, even while they may be incommensurable in their goals." Tuck and Yang, "Introduction," 1.
6. I owe a particular debt to the following works by scholars and activists who have shaped my thinking: Kelley, *Freedom Dreams*; Davis, *Abolition Democracy*; Cullors, "Abolition and Reparations"; Kaba, *We Do This 'til We Free Us*; Purnell, *Becoming Abolitionists*; Davis et al., *Abolition. Feminism. Now.*
7. Bell and Hartmann, "Diversity in Everyday Discourse"; Ahmed, *On Being Included*, 10.
8. Castagno, *Educated in Whiteness*; Thomas, *Diversity Regimes*.

1. Origins

1. Dunbar-Ortiz, *Indigenous Peoples' History*, 199.
2. For rigorous analyses of higher education through the interrelated frameworks of settler colonial studies, decolonization, decoloniality, and /or the postcolonial, see Grande, "Refusing the University"; Stein, *Unsettling the University*; Stokas, *Reparative Universities*.
3. Wilder, *Ebony & Ivy*, 17.
4. Dunbar-Ortiz, *Indigenous Peoples' History*, chap. 1.
5. Quoted in Dunbar-Ortiz, *Indigenous Peoples' History*, 28.
6. Lowman and Barker, *Settler*.
7. Wolfe, "Settler Colonialism," 388.

8. Dunbar-Ortiz, *Indigenous Peoples' History*, 38–39.

9. Wilder, *Ebony & Ivy*, 36.

10. Wilder, *Ebony & Ivy*, 21.

11. Quoted in Wilder, *Ebony & Ivy*, 21.

12. Gasman, Nguyen, and Conrad, "Lives Intertwined," 121–22.

13. Thelin, *History of American Higher Education*, 30, 39, 162.

14. Thelin, *History of American Higher Education*, 39.

15. Wilder, *Ebony & Ivy*, 26.

16. Reyhner and Eder, *American Indian Education*, 36.

17. Fox, Lowe, and McClellan, "Where We Have Been," 8.

18. Bohan, "Islands of Hope."

19. Wilder, *Ebony & Ivy*, 26–28.

20. Beck, "American Indians Higher Education," 14.

21. Wilder, *Ebony & Ivy*, 41–42.

22. Wilder, *Ebony & Ivy*, 33–36.

23. Quoted in Wilder, *Ebony & Ivy*, 160.

24. Thelin, *History of American Higher Education*, 25.

25. Thelin, *History of American Higher Education*, 36.

26. Wilder, *Ebony & Ivy*, 193–94.

27. Beckert et al., "Harvard and Slavery," 229; Wilder, *Ebony & Ivy*, 193.

28. Merrell, "Declarations of Independence."

29. Dunbar-Ortiz, *Indigenous Peoples' History*, 142.

30. Nash, "Entangled Pasts."

31. Nash, "Entangled Pasts," 437–41.

32. Lee and Ahtone, "Land-Grab Universities."

33. Lee and Ahtone, "Land-Grab Universities."

34. Nash, "Entangled Pasts," 451–52.

35. Nash, "Entangled Pasts," 452.

36. Nash, "Entangled Pasts," 457–62.

37. Lee and Ahtone, "Land-Grab Universities."

38. Nash, "Entangled Pasts," 456.

39. Lee and Ahtone, "Land-Grab Universities."

40. Wilder, *Ebony & Ivy*, 70, 114–15.

41. Wilder, *Ebony & Ivy*, 139.

42. Harris, Campbell, and Brophy, *Slavery and the University*, 5.

43. Thomas, "Hidden Links."

44. Wilder, *Ebony & Ivy*, 109.

45. Wilder, *Ebony & Ivy*, 243.

46. Zamudio-Suarez, "5 Colleges."

47. Wilder, *Ebony & Ivy*, 122.

48. Wilder, *Ebony & Ivy*, 120–28.

49. Wilder, *Ebony & Ivy*, 134.

50. Harris, Campbell, and Brophy, *Slavery and the University*, 6.

51. Wilder, *Ebony & Ivy*, 199.

52. Wilder, *Ebony & Ivy*, 42.

53. Wilder, *Ebony & Ivy*, 137.

54. Williams, "Forgetting Slavery," 326.

55. Wilder, *Ebony & Ivy*, 120.

56. Washington and Lee University, *A Difficult, Yet Undeniable, History*, pamphlet, n.d.

57. Harris, Campbell, and Brophy, *Slavery and the University*, 4.

58. Wilder, "'Sons from the Southward,'" 33.

59. Wilder, *Ebony & Ivy*, 67.

60. Wilder, *Ebony & Ivy*, 109.

61. Wilder, *Ebony & Ivy*, 48–49.

62. Thelin, *History of American Higher Education*, 24.

63. Thelin, *History of American Higher Education*, 165.

64. Oast, "Negotiating the Honor Culture," 86–87.

65. Oast, "Negotiating the Honor Culture," 89.

66. Wilder, *Ebony & Ivy*, 140–43.

67. Oast, "Negotiating the Honor Culture," 88.

68. Wilder, *Ebony & Ivy*, 90.

69. Wilder, *Ebony & Ivy*, 85–86.

70. Wilder, *Ebony & Ivy*, 187–88, 209.

71. Beckert et al., "Harvard and Slavery," 224.

72. Wilder, *Ebony & Ivy*, 196.

73. Lovejoy, "Meet Grandison Harris."

74. Wilder, *Ebony & Ivy*, 199–201.

75. Renschler and Monge, "Samuel George Morton Cranial Collection," 33–34.

76. Quoted in Renschler and Monge, "Samuel George Morton Cranial Collection," 34.

77. Brophy, "Proslavery Political Theory," 78.

78. Brophy, "Proslavery Political Theory," 76.

79. Brophy, "Proslavery Political Theory," 65.

80. Jamieson, "Making Their Case."

81. Wilder, *Ebony & Ivy*, 221.

82. Wilder, *Ebony & Ivy*, chap. 7.

83. Brophy, "Proslavery Political Theory," 70.

84. Brophy, "Proslavery Political Theory," 70. See also Stovall, *White Freedom*.

85. Wilder, *Ebony & Ivy*, chap. 8.

86. Beckert et al., "Harvard and Slavery," 235.

87. Wilder, *Ebony & Ivy*, 267.

88. Wilder, *Ebony & Ivy*, 265.

89. Wilder, *Ebony & Ivy*, 271.

90. Hollander and Sandweiss, "Princeton and Slavery."

91. Chung, "Harvard Museum"; Tryens-Fernandes, "University of Alabama"; Kunze, "University of Kansas"; Smith and Bosman, "Congress Told Colleges."

92. Ngu and Suozzo, "Local Museum or University."

93. Kassutto, "Remains of Children"; Pilkington, "Bones of Black Children"; Princeton University Office of Communications, "Princeton Receives Report."

2. Whitelash

1. For a regularly updated table showing the years when the top ten HWCUs officially admitted women and Black Americans, see the online appendix on my website at https://drnimishabarton.com/just-future.

2. Anderson, *White Rage*; Lippard, Carter, and Embrick, eds., *Protecting Whiteness*; Joseph, *Third Reconstruction*, chap. 3.

3. Wilder, *Ebony & Ivy*, 111.

4. Nash, *Women's Education*, 5.

5. Thelin, *History of American Higher Education*, 55.

6. Nash, *Women's Education*, 115.

7. Nash, *Women's Education*, chap. 4.

8. Thelin, *History of American Higher Education*, 180-82.

9. Malkiel, *"Keep the Damned Women Out."*

10. Morris, "'I Have at Last Found My Sphere,'" 198-99; Malkiel, *"Keep the Damned Women Out,"* chap. 1.

11. Morris, "'I Have at Last Found My Sphere,'" 199-200.

12. Thelin, *History of American Higher Education*, 185-86, 231.

13. Nash, *Women's Education*, 115; Malkiel, *"Keep the Damned Women Out,"* chap. 1.

14. Thelin, *History of American Higher Education*, 98, 143, 182-83.

15. Evans, *Black Women in the Ivory Tower*, 21.

16. Evans, *Black Women in the Ivory Tower*, 21-23.

17. Evans, *Black Women in the Ivory Tower*, 111-13.

18. Evans, *Black Women in the Ivory Tower*, 24-25.

19. Evans, *Black Women in the Ivory Tower*, 58.

20. Evans, *Black Women in the Ivory Tower*, 48.

21. Thelin, *History of American Higher Education*, 227-28; Evans, *Black Women in the Ivory Tower*, 48.

22. Evans, *Black Women in the Ivory Tower*, 55.

23. Nash, *Women's Education*, 116.

24. Karabel, *Chosen*, 96.

25. Karabel, *Chosen*, 21.

26. Karabel, *Chosen*, 116.

27. Karabel, *Chosen*, 4.

28. Hammond, "SAT and Systemic Racism."

29. Hirt, "Columbia for Jews?"

30. Thelin, *History of American Higher Education*, 227.

31. Karabel, *Chosen*, 128-31.

32. Karabel, *Chosen*, 45-52; Levien, "Crimson Klan."

33. Karabel, *Chosen*, 60-61.

34. Karabel, *Chosen*, 79.

35. Karabel, *Chosen*, 82-83.

36. Fox, Lowe, and McClellan, "Where We Have Been," 9.

37. Beck, "American Indians Higher Education."

38. Reyhner and Eder, *American Indian Education*, chap. 5.

39. Reyhner and Eder, *American Indian Education*, chap. 11.

40. Bohan, "Islands of Hope," 8.

41. Gasman, Nguyen, and Conrad, "Lives Intertwined."

42. Fox, Lowe, and McClellan, "Where We Have Been," 10.

43. Fox, Lowe, and McClellan, "Where We Have Been," 9–10.

44. Bohan, "Islands of Hope," 9.

45. Beck, "American Indians Higher Education."

46. Beck, "American Indians Higher Education," 17.

47. Reyhner, "1819–2013."

48. Evans, *Black Women in the Ivory Tower*, 33.

49. Harper and Patton, "Access and Equity," 393.

50. Baumgartner, "Towers of Intellect."

51. Harper and Patton, "Access and Equity," 393.

52. For a list of HBCUs in the United States, see the online appendix on my website at https://drnimishabarton.com/just-future.

53. Kendi, *Black Campus Movement*, 13–15.

54. Gasman, Nguyen, and Conrad, "Lives Intertwined," 124; Kendi, *Black Campus Movement*, 17.

55. Thelin, *History of American Higher Education*, 102.

56. Harper and Patton, "Access and Equity," 394.

57. Harper and Patton, "Access and Equity," 394.

58. Geiger, *American Higher Education*, 32.

59. Thelin, *History of American Higher Education*, 136.

60. Thelin, *History of American Higher Education*, 103.

61. Thelin, *History of American Higher Education*, 187.

62. Evans, *Black Women in the Ivory Tower*, 67–68.

63. Kendi, *Black Campus Movement*, 21.

64. Thelin, *History of American Higher Education*, 176, 186, 233.

65. Rooks, *White Money/Black Power*, 14.

66. Kendi, *Black Campus Movement*, 18.

67. Levien, "Crimson Klan."

68. Kendi, *Black Campus Movement*, 18–19.

69. Thelin, *History of American Higher Education*, 233.

70. Kendi, *Black Campus Movement*, 19.

71. Kendi, *Black Campus Movement*, 21.

72. Geiger, *American Higher Education*, chap. 3.

73. Mettler, *Soldiers to Citizens*.

74. Thelin, *History of American Higher Education*, 263.

75. Geiger, *American Higher Education*, chap. 2.

76. Thelin, *History of American Higher Education*, 267.

77. Geiger, *American Higher Education*, 71.

78. Reginald Thomas, interview by the author, July 15, 2021.

79. Bohan, "Islands of Hope," 9.

80. Beck, "American Indians Higher Education," 17.

81. Bohan, "Islands of Hope," 7.

82. Kendi, *Black Campus Movement*, 24–25.

83. Thelin, *History of American Higher Education*, 304.

84. Thelin, *History of American Higher Education*, 304.
85. Kendi, *Black Campus Movement*, 27.
86. Kendi, *Black Campus Movement*, 26–27.
87. Geiger, *American Higher Education*, 155.
88. Kendi, *Black Campus Movement*, 64.
89. Thomas, *Diversity Regimes*, 36.
90. Kendi, *Black Campus Movement*, 27.
91. Thelin, *History of American Higher Education*, 196–99.

3. Turning Points

1. Kendi, *Black Campus Movement*, 99.
2. Ahmed, *On Being Included*, chap. 2.
3. Fox, Lowe, and McClellan, "Where We Have Been," 11.
4. Gasman, Nguyen, and Conrad, "Lives Intertwined," 127.
5. Beck, "American Indians Higher Education," 18.
6. Beck, "American Indians Higher Education," 18.
7. Beck, "American Indians Higher Education," 18.
8. Fox, Lowe, and McClellan, "Where We Have Been," 11.
9. Bohan, "Islands of Hope," 9.
10. For a list of tribal colleges in the United States, see the online appendix on my website at https://drnimishabarton.com/just-future.
11. Gasman, Nguyen, and Conrad, "Lives Intertwined," 130.
12. Beck, "American Indians Higher Education"; Reyhner and Eder, *American Indian Education*, chap. 11.
13. Kendi, *Black Campus Movement*, 27; Lopez, Passel, and Rohal, *Modern Immigration Wave*.
14. Kendi, *Black Campus Movement*, 123.
15. Ferguson, *Reorder of Things*, 5.
16. University of Michigan Center for Social Solutions, "History of Diversity."
17. Kendi, *Black Campus Movement*, 85–86.
18. Ferguson, *Reorder of Things*, 77.
19. Schrecker, "50-Year War."
20. Yamane, *Student Movements for Multiculturalism*, 207–8.
21. Kendi, *Black Campus Movement*, 109–10.
22. Kendi, *Black Campus Movement*, 82–83.
23. Kendi, *Black Campus Movement*, 114–15; Ferguson, *Reorder of Things*, 33.
24. Kendi, *Black Campus Movement*, 118–19.
25. Baldwin, *Shadow of the Ivory Tower*, chap. 1.
26. Baldwin, *Shadow of the Ivory Tower*, chap. 4.
27. Rojas, *Black Power to Black Studies*, chaps. 1–3.
28. Kendi, *Black Campus Movement*, 93–97.
29. Yamane, *Student Movements for Multiculturalism*, 12.
30. University of Michigan Center for Social Solutions, "History of Diversity."

31. Vassar College, "History of Africana Studies."

32. Ferguson, *Reorder of Things*, 43.

33. Loss, *Between Citizens and the State*, chap. 6.

34. Byrd, Brunn-Bevel, and Ovink, *Intersectionality and Higher Education*, 13.

35. Princeton University, "History—Carl A. Fields Center"; Brown University, "TWC History at Brown."

36. Yale University, Afro-American Cultural Center, "History"; Yale University, La Casa Cultural: Latino Cultural Center, "History."

37. Bennet, "USC's Black Cultural Center"; University of Southern California, La CASA, "Nuestra Historia & Our Name."

38. Wolf-Wendel, *Reflecting Back, Looking Forward*, xiv.

39. Oregon State University, Diversity & Cultural Engagement, "Lonnie B. Harris Black Cultural Center."

40. San Francisco State University, Equity & Community Inclusion Unit, "Brief History of Black Student Centers."

41. Swarthmore College Black Cultural Center, "Our History"; University of Illinois Urbana-Champaign, Bruce D. Nesbitt African American Cultural Center, "History."

42. Colorado State University, "History of B/AACC."

43. Boise State University Student Equity Center, "History of Student Equity"; Ernest Thomas Cooper, interview by the author, August 17, 2021.

44. Elena Gonzalez, interview by the author, August 9, 2021.

45. University of Tennessee, Knoxville, Multicultural Student Life, "History of the Black Cultural Center."

46. University of Wisconsin–Madison, Multicultural Student Center, "Black Cultural Center."

47. California State University, Long Beach, "Office of Multicultural Affairs."

48. Garner, "Opening the Doors."

49. Hailu and Scott, "Half-Century Fight."

50. University of Wisconsin–Madison, Multicultural Student Center, "Black Cultural Center."

51. Pittman, "Why I Came Back."

52. Wolf-Wendel, *Reflecting Back, Looking Forward*, vi.

53. Oakland University, "Ambassador Dr. Augustine Pounds."

54. Veronica Cade, interview by the author, August 27, 2021. For the locations of sundown towns in the United States, see "Geographical Map of Historical Sundown Towns."

55. Rothstein, *Color of Law*.

56. Cade, interview.

57. Cade, interview.

58. Maines, "Trail-Blazing KU Professor Dies at 86."

59. Hanner, "Sense of Belonging."

60. Reginald Thomas, interview by the author, July 15, 2021.

61. Thomas Angel, interview by the author, August 10, 2021.

62. Wolf-Wendel, *Reflecting Back, Looking Forward*, xiv.

63. Quoted in Wolf-Wendel, *Reflecting Back, Looking Forward*, 117.

64. Cooper, interview; Thomas, interview; Geoffrey B. King, interview by the author, July 27, 2021.

65. Thomas, interview; Hanner, "Sense of Belonging."

66. Johnson, *Undermining Racial Justice*, 110.

67. Cooper, interview.

68. Oakland University, "Black Alumni Association"; *Oakland University Magazine*, "Up Front"; Oakland University, "Ambassador Dr. Augustine Pounds."

69. Shepherd, *Resistance from the Right*.

70. Loss, *Between Citizens and the State*, 215; Geiger, *American Higher Education*, chap. 6.

71. Loss, *Between Citizens and the State*, chap. 7.

72. Okechukwu, *To Fulfill These Rights*, chaps. 1–2.

73. Ford, "Affirmative Action Was Derailed."

74. Castagno, *Educated in Whiteness*, introduction.

75. Bonilla-Silva, *Racism without Racists*, 3, 7.

76. Newkirk, *Diversity, Inc.*, 119–20; Thelin, *History of American Higher Education*, chap. 8; Johnson, *Undermining Racial Justice*.

77. Bok, Shulman, and Bowen, *Shape of the River*, 9.

78. Dudziak, *Cold War Civil Rights*.

79. Harvey, *Brief History of Neoliberalism*; Newfield, *Unmaking the Public University*; Fabricant and Brier, *Austerity Blues*; Fergus, *Land of the Fee*.

80. Bianca Hutchins, interview by the author, July 26, 2021.

81. Ferguson, *Reorder of Things*, chap. 4.

82. Newkirk, *Diversity, Inc.*, 15.

83. Fox, Lowe, and McClellan, "Where We Have Been," 11.

84. Quoted in Newkirk, *Diversity, Inc.*, 117.

85. Hutchins, interview.

86. Hutchins, interview.

87. Loss, *Between Citizens and the State*, 223.

88. Cole, *Campus Color Line*.

89. Hailu and Scott, "Half-Century Fight."

90. University of Tennessee, Knoxville, Multicultural Student Life, "History of the Black Cultural Center."

91. Texas State University, "History, Student Initiatives"; Wake Forest University Intercultural Center, "Diversity @ Wake"; Wanda Rutherford, interview by the author, August 20, 2021.

92. Hutchins, interview.

93. University of Kansas, Office of Multicultural Affairs, "Our Story."

94. Lopez, Passel, and Rohal, *Modern Immigration Wave*, 118.

95. Schrecker, "50-Year War."

96. Graff and Cain, "Peace Plan."

97. See for example, Roger Kimball's *Tenured Radicals* (1990) and Dinesh D'Souza's *Illiberal Education* (1991). Donadio, "Revisiting the Canon Wars."

98. Graff and Cain, "Peace Plan," 7.

99. Elena Gonzalez, interview by the author, August 9, 2021; Charlotte Walker, interview by the author, August 9, 2021.

100. Walker, interview.

101. Walker, interview.

102. Yamane, *Student Movements for Multiculturalism*, 16; Kendi, *Black Campus Movement*, 70–71.

103. Rojas, *Black Power to Black Studies*, 94.

104. Rooks, *White Money/Black Power*.

105. University of Michigan Center for Social Solutions, "History of Diversity."

106. Mangan, "Enrolling Diverse Students."

107. Ali Taylor, interview by the author, September 24, 2021.

108. Taylor, interview.

109. Platt, "End Game," 103.

110. Walker, interview.

111. Ahmed, *On Being Included*, 65.

112. Thomas, interview; Hutchins, interview; Rutherford, interview..

113. Ahmed, *On Being Included*, 52–54.

114. Ahmed, *On Being Included*, 58.

4. Diversity Practitioners and Institutional Whiteness

1. Thomas, *Diversity Regimes*.

2. Kymlicka, *Multicultural Odysseys*, 130–31.

3. Ahmed, *On Being Included*, chap. 5.

4. Keeanga-Yamahtta Taylor has expressed this opinion as part of a reconceptualization of Black politics in the twenty-first-century United States.

5. See, for example, Pittman, "Why I Came Back."

6. Elena Gonzalez, interview by the author, August 9, 2021.

7. Greg Collins, interview by the author, November 2, 2021.

8. Greg Collins, interview by the author, November 4, 2021.

9. Flannery, "Mental Health Crisis."

10. Byrd, Brunn-Bevel, and Ovink, *Intersectionality and Higher Education*, 181; Nixon, "Women of Color University Chief Diversity Officers."

11. Nixon, "Women of Color University Chief Diversity Officers."

12. Charlotte Walker, interview by the author, August 9, 2021.

13. Byrd, Brunn-Bevel, and Ovink, *Intersectionality and Higher Education*, 181; Nixon, "Women of Color University Chief Diversity Officers."

14. Cameron Rogers, interview by the author, August 30, 2021.

15. Elsie Beaty, interview by the author, October 19, 2021.

16. Rogers, interview.

17. Walker, interview.

18. Gonzalez, interview.

19. Walker, interview.

20. Equal Measure and the Lumina Foundation, *Transforming Mindsets, Powering Change: Advancing Equity*, 13–14.

21. Walker, interview.

22. Gardner, "Truth about Strategic Plans."

23. Ali Taylor, interview by the author, September 24, 2021.

24. Wanda Rutherford, interview by the author, August 20, 2021.

25. Walker, interview.

26. Rutherford, interview.

27. Equal Measure and the Lumina Foundation, *Transforming Mindsets, Powering Change: Advancing Equity*, 9, 24, 25.

28. National Center for Education Statistics, "Fast Facts"; Baker and Koedel, "Trends in Faculty Diversity." For a regularly updated dataset on faculty racial and ethnic diversity, see the online appendix on my website at https://drnimishabarton.com/just-future.

29. Subbaraman, "#BlackInTheIvory"; Flaherty, "Scholars Talk about Being Black."

30. June and O'Leary, "How Many Black Women."

31. For just a handful of examples, see Johnson-Bailey and Lee, "Women of Color in the Academy"; Monzó and SooHoo, "Translating the Academy"; Gutiérrez y Muhs, *Presumed Incompetent*; Gibson, "Far-Reaching Effects"; Dennie, "Assault on Black Academics"; García Peña, *Community as Rebellion*.

32. Donaldson, "Higher Ed's Great Resignation."

33. Gasman, Abiola, and Travers, "Diversity and Senior Leadership."

34. Gasman, Abiola, and Travers, "Diversity and Senior Leadership," 3; Nixon, "Women of Color University Chief Diversity Officers"; Adedoyin, "Colleges' Presidential Searches."

35. Ahmed, *On Being Included*, 34.

36. Ahmed, *On Being Included*, 147.

37. Mary Elizabeth Brown, interview by the author, October 11, 2021.

38. Brown, interview.

39. Newkirk, *Diversity, Inc.*, 5.

40. Ernest Cooper, interview by the author, August 17, 2021.

41. Reginald Thomas, interview by the author, July 15, 2021.

42. Rutherford, interview.

43. Thomas, interview.

44. Knox, "'Shouting Down an Empty Hallway.'"

5. The Classroom and the Culture Wars

1. Sawchuk, "Critical Race Theory." For additional information about the history, origins, and purpose of critical race theory, see Ray, *On Critical Race Theory*.

2. Imadali, "CRT MAP."

3. James Loewen explores this subject in his classic *Lies My Teacher Told Me*.

4. Levine, "Time for an Overhaul." For a broader history of how the concept of academic freedom came to be defined, see Levine, *Allies and Rivals*, chap. 7.

5. AAUP, "FAQs on Academic Freedom."

6. Levine, "Time for an Overhaul."

7. Gannon, *Radical Hope*, 127.

8. Lukianoff and Haidt, *Coddling of the American Mind*, 8.

9. Ahmed, "Against Students."

10. Gannon, *Radical Hope*, 115.

11. Ahmed, "Against Students."

12. See also Barton, "What's Missing."

13. For a regularly updated statistical overview of faculty demographics, see the online appendix on my website at https://drnimishabarton.com/just-future.

14. Gabbatt, "Rightwing Group Targets Academics."

15. Johnson, *Undermining Racial Justice*, 9.

16. For a regularly updated statistical overview of undergraduate demographics, see the online appendix on my website at https://drnimishabarton.com/just-future.

17. Denial, *Pedagogy of Kindness*, chap. 3.

18. Pryal, "When 'Rigor' Targets Disabled Students."

19. Denial, "Pedagogy of Kindness."

20. Denial, *Pedagogy of Kindness,* chap. 2.

21. Richtel, "'It's Life or Death.'"

22. Supiano, "Redefinition of Rigor."

23. Duckworth, *Grit*. Duckworth's definition of grit is also the title of a number of articles previously published by Duckworth and coauthors. See, for example, Duckworth et al., "Grit: Perseverance and Passion for Long-Term Goals."

24. Love, *We Want to Do More Than Survive*, 70.

25. Love, "'Grit Is in Our DNA.'"

26. CDC, "Categories of Essential Workers."

27. Jack and Sathy, "Cancel the Word 'Rigor.'"

28. Hines and Fallace, "Pedagogical Progressivism," 19.

29. On critical consciousness, see Freire, *Pedagogy of the Oppressed*, chap. 3.

30. Banks, "Construction and Historical Development," 74.

31. Banks, "Construction and Historical Development," 74.

32. Ladson-Billings, "Culturally Relevant Pedagogy"; Ladson-Billings, "But That's Just Good Teaching!"

33. Gay, "Coming of Age Ethnically"; Gay, "Preparing for Culturally Responsive Teaching"; Gay, *Culturally Responsive Teaching*.

34. hooks, *Teaching to Transgress*, 37.

35. hooks, *Teaching to Transgress*, 4.

36. hooks, *Teaching to Transgress*, 5.

37. hooks, *Teaching to Transgress*, 148.

38. Judith DeGroat, interview by the author, October 13, 2021.

39. One excellent example is Gannon, *Radical Hope.*

40. Ahmed, "Against Students."

41. Quoted in Holley and Steiner, "Safe Space," 51.

42. Hess and McAvoy, *Political Classroom.*

43. Hess and McAvoy, *Political Classroom*, 4–5.

44. See, for example, Renihan, Spilker, and Wright, *Sound Pedagogy.*

45. Kishimoto, "Anti-racist Pedagogy."

46. Hammond, *Culturally Responsive Teaching.*

47. Kishimoto, "Anti-racist Pedagogy," 545.
48. Tuck and Yang, "Decolonization Is Not a Metaphor," 2.
49. Tuck and Yang, "Decolonization Is Not a Metaphor."
50. hooks, *Teaching to Transgress*, 40.
51. For a fuller discussion of this subject, see Barton, "Lessons."
52. Sathy and Hogan, "How to Make Your Teaching More Inclusive."
53. Krukowski, Carr, and Arigo, "Pandemic-Related Tenure Timeline Extensions." For additional guidance on how to establish equity in pandemic-era tenure processes, see Gannon, "Faculty Evaluation."

6. Programs and Pedagogical Innovation

1. Ladson-Billings, "Achievement Gap to the Education Debt."
2. Keels, *Campus Counterspaces*.
3. The scholarship is voluminous. See the special issue of *American Behavioral Scientist* titled "Supporting First-Generation, Low-Income, and Underrepresented Students' Transitions to College through Comprehensive and Integrated Programs," published in March 2020, edited by Adrianna Kezar and Joseph A. Kitchen.
4. Lopez, Passel, and Rohal, *Modern Immigration Wave*, 118.
5. US Census Bureau, "2014 National Population Projections Tables."
6. Krogstad, "Reflecting a Demographic Shift."
7. Abrams, *Our Time Is Now*, 36.
8. National Center for Education Statistics, "Digest of Education Statistics, 2018."
9. Newfield, *Great Mistake*, 4.
10. Aries, *Race and Class Matters*.
11. Whitley, Benson, and Wesaw, *Landscape Analysis*, 17.
12. US Department of Education, "Percent of Undergraduate Students."
13. Postsecondary National Policy Institute, "Factsheets: First-Generation Students."
14. Postsecondary National Policy Institute, "Factsheets: First-Generation Students."
15. Stephens et al., "Unseen Disadvantage."
16. Keels, *Campus Counterspaces*, 2.
17. Ali Taylor, interview by the author, September 24, 2021.
18. US Department of Education, "Federal TRIO Programs."
19. See, for example, Winograd et al., "Educational Opportunity Program."
20. Malcom Washington, interview by the author, November 10, 2021.
21. Elsie Beaty, interview by the author, October 19, 2021.
22. Washington, interview.
23. Draxler et al., "Inclusive Sentence-Level Writing Support."
24. Inoue, *Labor-Based Grading Contracts*.
25. Carillo, *Hidden Inequities*.
26. Stommel, "Ungrading." See also Denial, *Pedagogy of Kindness*.
27. Denial, *Pedagogy of Kindness*.

28. Hrabowski and Henderson, "How to Actually Promote Diversity."
29. Hrabowski and Henderson, "Nothing Succeeds like Success."
30. Hrabowski and Henderson, "More Diverse Research Community."
31. Hrabowski and Henderson, "More Diverse Research Community."
32. Hrabowski and Henderson, "More Diverse Research Community."
33. Hrabowski et al., *Overcoming the Odds*, 164–66, 220–21.
34. Young, "How to Diversify STEM Fields."
35. Hrabowski and Henderson, "Nothing Succeeds like Success."
36. Suran, "Keeping Black Students in STEM."
37. Hrabowski et al., *Overcoming the Odds*, 164, 167.
38. Hrabowski and Henderson, "Nothing Succeeds like Success."
39. Suran, "Keeping Black Students in STEM."
40. Sto. Domingo et al., "Replicating Meyerhoff," 335.
41. President's Council of Advisors on Science and Technology, *Engage to Excel*.
42. Fauci, "2021 TIME100 Next."
43. Hrabowski and Henderson, "Nothing Succeeds like Success."
44. Hrabowski and Henderson, "How to Actually Promote Diversity."
45. Sanders, "Chan Zuckerberg Initiative."
46. *New York Times*, "Missing From Science Class."
47. Thomas Angel, interview by the author, August 10, 2021.

7. HWCUs and Restorative Justice

1. See, for example, Pickett et al., *Anti-racism Strategy on Campus*.
2. Stokas, *Reparative Universities*.
3. Davis, *Race and Restorative Justice*.
4. Kaba, *We Do This 'til We Free Us*, 5.
5. Kaba, *We Do This 'til We Free Us*, 167.
6. Harris, Campbell, and Brophy, *Slavery and the University*, 9; US Department of the Interior, Indian Affairs. "Gover Apologizes."
7. Harris, Campbell, and Brophy, *Slavery and the University*, 7.
8. Harris, Campbell, and Brophy, *Slavery and the University*, 4–5.
9. Harris, Campbell, and Brophy, *Slavery and the University*, 13.
10. Simmons, "Slavery and Justice at Brown."
11. Brown University, "Brown & Slavery & Justice."
12. University of Virginia, "President's Commission."
13. Levien, "Crimson Klan."
14. Kell, "Kroeber Hall."
15. Kell, "Kroeber Hall."
16. Fuller, "New Name."
17. YaleNews, "Calhoun College's Name"; Oxner, "'The Eyes of Texas'"; Spitalniak, "Colleges Seek Better Ways."
18. Valenti, "University Dedicates Marker."
19. Burch, "National Movement."
20. Thomas, *Diversity Regimes*, 28.

21. Williams, "Forgetting Slavery," 328.

22. Williams, "Forgetting Slavery," 331.

23. Gershon, "Robert E. Lee Statue."

24. Cotter, "Grief for a Hidden Past."

25. Colorado State University, "Land Acknowledgment."

26. Michigan State University, American Indian and Indigenous Studies, "Land Acknowledgement."

27. Elena Gonzalez, interview by the author, August 9, 2021.

28. Staples, "Ancestral Land."

29. Kymlicka, *Multicultural Odysseys*, 88, 91, 110–11.

30. Harris, Campbell, and Brophy, *Slavery and the University*, 11.

31. Reichelmann and Hunt, "How We Repair It."

32. Coates, "Case for Reparations."

33. Movement for Black Lives, "Reparations."

34. Darity and Mullen, *From Here to Equality*.

35. Cullors, "Abolition and Reparations," 1686–87.

36. "Evanston Local Reparations."

37. Luna, "California Task Force."

38. Swarns, "Seminary Flourished on Slave Labor"; Forson, "Enslaved Labor Built These Universities"; Wright, "Seminary Built on Slavery."

39. Hartocollis, "Harvard Details Its Ties to Slavery."

40. Mangan, "'Disturbing and Even Shocking.'"

41. Adedoyin, "Black Colleges Have Been Portrayed as Deficient."

42. Carrillo, "New Prison-to-College Pipeline."

43. Ross, "Native American Students."

44. Zamudio-Suarez, "Colleges Are Waiving Tuition."

45. Adedoyin, "Who Is Native American Enough?"

46. Lee and Ahtone, "Land-Grab Universities."

47. Haynes, "Native American Graves Protection and Repatriation Act (NAGPRA) Survey."

48. Equal Measure and the Lumina Foundation, *Transforming Mindsets, Powering Change: Getting to the Root*, 5.

49. Equal Measure and the Lumina Foundation, *Transforming Mindsets, Powering Change: Getting to the Root*, 16.

50. Swarns, "Seminary Flourished on Slave Labor"; Wright, "Seminary Built on Slavery."

51. Kaba, *We Do This 'til We Free Us*, 148.

52. Zehr, *Little Book of Restorative Justice*.

53. Fronius et al., *Restorative Justice in U.S. Schools*, 5; Davis, *Race and Restorative Justice*, chap. 2.

54. Quoted in Kaba, *We Do This 'til We Free Us*, 62.

55. Kaba, *We Do This 'til We Free Us*, 62.

56. Fronius et al., *Restorative Justice in U.S. Schools*, 8.

57. González, "State of Restorative Justice," 51.

58. Davis, *Race and Restorative Justice*.

59. Hirschfield and Celinska, "Beyond Fear."

60. Fronius et al., *Restorative Justice in U.S. Schools.*

61. Karp and Frank, "Restorative Justice and Student Development," 142.

62. Karp and Frank, "Restorative Justice and Student Development," 143.

63. Clark, "Call for Restorative Justice."

64. Karp, *Little Book of Restorative Justice.*

65. Hauser, "Teenage Vandals."

66. Greg Collins, interview by the author, November 2, 2021.

67. University of San Diego, "Center for Restorative Justice."

68. Knott, "One University Went All-In."

69. These have included Loyola University Maryland, the College of New Jersey, and Skidmore College. See Loyola University Maryland, "Restorative Practices—Student Conduct"; Mangan, "More Colleges Are Trying Restorative Justice"; Skidmore College, "College Launches Restorative Justice Project."

70. Clark, "Call for Restorative Justice."

71. Bielski, "Racially Sensitive 'Restorative' School Discipline."

72. Clark, "Call for Restorative Justice."

73. Bernstein, "Sexual Politics.'" See also Gruber, *Feminist War on Crime*; Davis et al., *Abolition. Feminism. Now.*

74. Koss and Chisholm, "Time Is Now."

75. Bellows, "Sexual-Assault Survivors of Color."

76. Karp, "Restorative Justice."

77. Mangan, "More Colleges Are Trying Restorative Justice."

78. Koss and Chisholm, "Time Is Now."

79. Purnell, *Becoming Abolitionists*, chap. 5.

Epilogue

1. Mangan, "'More Cowardly Than Cautious'"; Bellows, "Colleges Acted."

2. Elias, "Test-Optional Policies."

3. Brown-Nagin et al., "How to Fix."

4. Daniels, *What Universities Owe Democracy*, 79.

5. Silva, "43 Percent of Harvard's White Students."

6. Daniels, *What Universities Owe Democracy*, 78.

7. Hill, "Ending Legacy Admissions."

8. Adedoyin, "Black Colleges Have Been Portrayed as Deficient."

9. See, for example, Bok, *Universities in the Marketplace*; Slaughter and Rhoades, *Academic Capitalism*; Selingo, *College (Un)Bound.*

10. Bird-Pollan, "Taxing the Ivory Tower," 1055.

11. See, for example, Baum, "Endowments and Federal Tax Policy."

12. Newfield, *Great Mistake*, 5.

13. Newfield, *Great Mistake*, 16.

14. O'Brien, "It's Complicated"; Cole, *Campus Color Line*, chap. 2; Baldwin, *Shadow of the Ivory Tower*, chap. 4.

15. Quoted in Lichtenbaum, "Corporate Bodies."

16. I want to thank Stephanie Reyes-Tuccio for having extensive, eye-opening conversations on this topic with me.

17. Daniels, *What Universities Owe Democracy*, 115.

18. Equal Measure and the Lumina Foundation, *Transforming Mindsets, Powering Change: Advancing Equity*, 22.

19. Equal Measure and the Lumina Foundation, *Transforming Mindsets, Powering Change: Advancing Equity*, 11.

20. Equal Measure and the Lumina Foundation, *Transforming Mindsets, Powering Change: Advancing Equity*, 20–21.

21. Baldwin, *Shadow of the Ivory Tower*.

22. Cole, "Mapping Pollution."

23. Baldwin, *Shadow of the Ivory Tower*, 118.

24. Baldwin, *Shadow of the Ivory Tower*, 120–22.

25. Baldwin, *Shadow of the Ivory Tower*, 122–24.

26. Baldwin, "Abolish the Campus Police."

27. Baldwin, "Abolish the Campus Police."

28. Mangan, "Students Demand"; Gluckman, "Can Colleges Reform?"

29. Baldwin, *Shadow of the Ivory Tower*, 124.

30. Cops Off Campus Coalition (website); Abolition University, "Cops Off Campus Research Collective."

31. Bellows, "Portland State U."

32. Bascom, "CPSO Begins 'Unarmed' Patrols."

33. Bellows, "Colleges Acted."

BIBLIOGRAPHY

AAUP (American Association of University Professors). "FAQs on Academic Freedom." July 14, 2021. https://www.aaup.org/programs/academic-freedom/faqs-academic-freedom.

Abolition University. "Cops Off Campus Research Collective." Accessed November 18, 2020. https://abolition.university/cops-off-campus-research-collective/.

Abrams, Stacey. *Our Time Is Now: Power, Purpose, and the Fight for a Fair America.* New York: Henry Holt, 2020.

Adedoyin, Oyin. "For Decades, Black Colleges Have Been Portrayed as Deficient. What Changed?" *Chronicle of Higher Education*, November 15, 2022. https://www.chronicle.com/article/good-news-for-hbcus.

——. "How Colleges' Presidential Searches Weed Out Candidates of Color and Women." *Chronicle of Higher Education*, November 2, 2022. https://www.chronicle.com/article/how-colleges-presidential-searches-weed-out-candidates-of-color-and-women.

——. "Who Is Native American Enough?" *Chronicle of Higher Education*, September 14, 2022. https://www.chronicle.com/article/who-is-native-enough.

Ahmed, Sara. "Against Students." *New Inquiry*, June 29, 2015. https://thenewinquiry.com/against-students/.

——. *On Being Included: Racism and Diversity in Institutional Life.* Durham, NC: Duke University Press, 2012.

Anderson, Carol. *White Rage: The Unspoken Truth of Our Racial Divide.* New York: Bloomsbury, 2016.

Aries, Elizabeth. *Race and Class Matters at an Elite College.* Philadelphia: Temple University Press, 2008.

Baker, Sofia P., and Cory Koedel. "Trends in Faculty Diversity at Selective Public Universities in the 21st Century." EdWorkingPaper: 23-827. Annenberg Institute at Brown University. August 2023. https://doi.org/10.26300/0h0x-m546.

Baldwin, Davarian L. *In the Shadow of the Ivory Tower: How Universities Are Plundering Our Cities.* New York: Bold Type Books, 2021.

——. "Why We Should Abolish the Campus Police." *Chronicle of Higher Education*, May 19, 2021. https://www.chronicle.com/article/why-we-should-abolish-campus-police.

Banks, James A. "The Construction and Historical Development of Multicultural Education, 1962–2012." *Theory into Practice* 52, no. 1 (July 25, 2013): 73–82.

Barshay, Jill. "Black College Enrollment Sharply Down during Covid Summer of 2020." Hechinger Report, September 8, 2020. https://hechingerre port.org/proof-points-black-college-enrollment-sharply-down-during-covid-summer-of-2020/.

Barton, Nimisha. "Lessons: On Dialogue, Monologue, and Academic Performance." *Nimisha Barton, PhD* (blog), January 14, 2019. https://www.drnimishabarton.com/redacted/lessons-on-dialogue-monologue-and-performance.

——. "What's Missing from the Discourse on 'Harm.'" Inside Higher Ed, August 17, 2023. https://www.insidehighered.com/opinion/views/2023/08/17/whats-missing-harm-and-trauma-discourse-opinion.

Bascom, Sean. "CPSO Begins 'Unarmed' Patrols, Keeps Guns." *PSU Vanguard*, October 19, 2021. https://psuvanguard.com/cpso-begins-unarmed-patrols-keeps-guns/.

Baum, Sandy. "Endowments and Federal Tax Policy." Urban Institute, Center on Education and Data Policy. July 2019. https://www.urban.org/sites/default/files/publication/100535/endowments_and_federal_tax_policy.pdf.

Baumgartner, Kabria. "Towers of Intellect: The Struggle for African American Education in Antebellum New England." In Harris, Campbell, and Brophy, *Slavery and the University*, 179–96.

Beck, David R. M. "American Indians Higher Education before 1974: From Colonization to Self-Determination." *Australian Journal of Indigenous Studies* 27, no. 2 (1999): 12–23.

Beckert, Sven, Balraj Gill, Jim Henle, and Katherine May Stevens. "Harvard and Slavery: A Short History." In Harris, Campbell, and Brophy, *Slavery and the University*, 224–50.

Bell, Joyce M., and Douglas Hartmann. "Diversity in Everyday Discourse." *American Sociological Review* 72, no. 6 (2007): 895–914.

Bellows, Kate Hidalgo. "Colleges Acted to Rein In Their Police. Then They Backtracked." *Chronicle of Higher Education*, May 23, 2023. https://www.chronicle.com/article/why-colleges-didnt-rein-in-their-police.

——. "Portland State U. Is Disarming Its Campus Police. Activists Say It's a 'Media Stunt.'" *Chronicle of Higher Education*, June 17, 2021. https://www.chronicle.com/article/portland-state-u-is-disarming-its-campus-police-activists-say-its-a-media-stunt.

——. "Sexual-Assault Survivors of Color Seek Healing Outside the Title IX Office." *Chronicle of Higher Education*, September 6, 2022. https://www.chronicle.com/newsletter/race-on-campus/2022-09-06.

Bennet, Andrea. "USC's Black Cultural Center Marks 40 Years as a Valued Venue for Candid Conversation." USC News, December 20, 2017. https://news.usc.edu/132841/uscs-black-cultural-center-marks-40-years-as-a-valued-venue-for-real-talk/.

Bernstein, Elizabeth. "The Sexual Politics of the 'New Abolitionism.'" *Differences* 18, no. 3 (December 1, 2007): 128–51. https://doi.org/10.1215/10407391-2007-013.

Bielski, Vince. "Racially Sensitive 'Restorative' School Discipline Isn't Behaving Very Well." Real Clear Investigations, February 2, 2022. https://www.real

clearinvestigations.com/articles/2022/02/02/racially_sensitive_restorative_school_discipline_isnt_behaving_very_well_814382.html.

Bird-Pollan, Jennifer. "Taxing the Ivory Tower: Evaluating the Excise Tax on University Endowments." *Pepperdine Law Review* 48, no. 4 (September 15, 2021): 1055–84.

Bohan, Claire H. "Islands of Hope: A History of American Indians and Higher Education." *Curriculum History*, 1996, 5–14.

Boise State University Student Equity Center. "History of the Student Equity Center." Accessed June 27, 2021. http://www.boisestate.edu/student-equity/about-us/history-of-student-equity/.

Bok, Derek. *Universities in the Marketplace: The Commercialization of Higher Education*. Princeton, NJ: Princeton University Press, 2003.

Bok, Derek, James Lawrence Shulman, and William G. Bowen. *The Shape of the River: Long-Term Consequences of Considering Race in College and University Admissions*. Princeton, NJ: Princeton University Press, 1998.

Bonilla-Silva, Eduardo. *Racism without Racists: Color-Blind Racism and the Persistence of Racial Inequality in America*. 5th ed. Lanham, MD: Rowman & Littlefield, 2018.

Brophy, Alfred L. "Proslavery Political Theory in the Southern Academy, 1832–1861." In Harris, Campbell, and Brophy, *Slavery and the University*, 65–83.

Brown, Sarah. "How to Win Hispanic Students Back." *Chronicle of Higher Education*, February 22, 2022. https://www.chronicle.com/newsletter/race-on-campus/2022-02-22.

Brown University. "Brown & Slavery & Justice." Accessed July 12, 2022. https://slaveryandjustice.brown.edu/.

——. "TWC History at Brown, Brown Center for Students of Color." Accessed August 6, 2021. https://www.brown.edu/campus-life/support/students-of-color/history.

Brown-Nagin, Tomiko, Natasha Warikoo, Richard D. Kahlenberg, Roland Fryer, Demond Drummer, Darrick Hamilton, and Olufemi Ogundele. "How to Fix College Admissions Now." *New York Times*, July 5, 2023. https://www.nytimes.com/interactive/2023/07/05/opinion/affirmative-action-college-admissions.html.

Brunsma, David L., Eric S. Brown, and Peggy Placier. "Teaching Race at Historically White Colleges and Universities: Identifying and Dismantling the Walls of Whiteness." *Critical Sociology* 39, no. 5 (2013): 717–38.

Burch, Audra D. S. "How a National Movement Toppled Hundreds of Confederate Symbols." *New York Times*, February 28, 2022. https://www.nytimes.com/interactive/2022/02/28/us/confederate-statue-removal.html.

Byrd, W. Carson, Rachelle J. Brunn-Bevel, and Sarah M. Ovink. *Intersectionality and Higher Education: Identity and Inequality on College Campuses*. New Brunswick, NJ: Rutgers University Press, 2019.

California State University, Long Beach. "Office of Multicultural Affairs: About." Accessed June 19, 2021. https://web.csulb.edu/divisions/students/oma/mcc/about.html.

Carillo, Ellen C. *The Hidden Inequities in Labor-Based Contract Grading*. Current Arguments in Composition. Logan: Utah State University Press, 2021.

Carrillo, Sequoia. "HBCUs Are Building a New Prison-to-College Pipeline." NPR, August 17, 2022. https://www.npr.org/2022/08/17/1117523697/hbcus-are-building-a-new-prison-to-college-pipeline.

Casey, Nicholas. "College Made Them Feel Equal. The Virus Exposed How Unequal Their Lives Are." *New York Times,* May 5, 2020. https://www.nytimes.com/2020/04/04/us/politics/coronavirus-zoom-college-classes.html.

Castagno, Angelina E. *Educated in Whiteness.* Minneapolis: University of Minnesota Press, 2014.

CDC (Centers for Disease Control and Prevention). "Categories of Essential Workers: COVID-19 Vaccination." October 1, 2021. https://www.cdc.gov/vaccines/covid-19/categories-essential-workers.html.

Chandler-Ward, Jenna, and Elizabeth Denevi. *Learning and Teaching While White: Antiracist Strategies for School Communities.* New York: W. W. Norton.

Chung, Christine. "Harvard Museum Will Return Hundreds of Native American Hair Samples." *New York Times,* November 10, 2022. https://www.nytimes.com/2022/11/10/us/harvard-museum-native-american-hair.html.

Clark, Karen L. "A Call for Restorative Justice in Higher Education Judicial Affairs." *College Student Journal* 48, no. 4 (December 1, 2014): 705–13.

Coates, Ta-Nehisi. "The Case for Reparations." *The Atlantic,* May 22, 2014. https://www.theatlantic.com/magazine/archive/2014/06/the-case-for-reparations/361631/.

Cole, Eddie R. *The Campus Color Line: College Presidents and the Struggle for Black Freedom.* Princeton, NJ: Princeton University Press, 2020.

Cole, Megan. "Mapping Pollution." UCI School of Humanities News, April 22, 2021. https://www.humanities.uci.edu/news/mapping-pollution.

Colorado State University. "History of B/AACC, Black/African American Cultural Center." Accessed June 27, 2021. https://baacc.colostate.edu/about/history-of-b-aacc/.

——. "Land Acknowledgment." Accessed July 12, 2022. https://landacknowledgment.colostate.edu/.

Cops Off Campus Coalition (website). Accessed December 4, 2022. https://copsoffcampuscoalition.com/.

Cotter, Holland. "Turning Grief for a Hidden Past into a Healing Space." *New York Times,* August 16, 2020. https://www.nytimes.com/2020/08/16/arts/design/university-of-virginia-enslaved-laborers-memorial.html.

Cullors, Patrisse. "Abolition and Reparations: Histories of Resistance, Transformative Justice, and Accountability." "Prison Abolition," special issue, *Harvard Law Review* 132 (April 10, 2019): 1684–94.

Daniels, Ronald J. *What Universities Owe Democracy.* Baltimore: Johns Hopkins University Press, 2021.

Darity, William A., and A. Kirsten Mullen. *From Here to Equality: Reparations for Black Americans in the Twenty-First Century.* Chapel Hill: University of North Carolina Press, 2020.

Davis, Angela Y. *Abolition Democracy: Beyond Empire, Prisons, and Torture.* New York: Seven Stories, 2005.

Davis, Angela Y., Gina Dent, Erica R. Meiners, and Beth E. Richie. *Abolition. Feminism. Now.* Chicago: Haymarket Books, 2022.

Davis, Fania E. *The Little Book of Race and Restorative Justice: Black Lives, Healing, and US Social Transformation.* New York: Good Books, 2019.

Denial, Cate. "A Pedagogy of Kindness." *Hybrid Pedagogy* (blog), August 15, 2019. https://hybridpedagogy.org/pedagogy-of-kindness/.

———. *A Pedagogy of Kindness.* Tulsa: University of Oklahoma Press, forthcoming.

Dennie, Nneka. "The Assault on Black Academics." *Chronicle of Higher Education,* June 18, 2021. https://www.chronicle.com/article/the-assault-on-black-academics.

Donadio, Rachel. "Revisiting the Canon Wars." *New York Times,* September 16, 2007. https://www.nytimes.com/2007/09/16/books/review/Donadio-t.html.

Donaldson, Sahalie. "How Higher Ed's Great Resignation Falls along Race and Gender Lines." *Chronicle of Higher Education,* March 15, 2022. https://www.chronicle.com/newsletter/race-on-campus/2022-03-15.

Draxler, Bridget, Anne Berry, Manuela Novoa Villada, and Victoria Gutierrez. "Inclusive Sentence-Level Writing Support." *Praxis* 19, no. 3 (2022): 59–71.

Duckworth, Angela. *Grit: The Power of Passion and Perseverance.* New York: Scribner, 2018.

Duckworth, Angela L., Christopher Peterson, Michael D. Matthews, and Dennis R. Kelly. "Grit: Perseverance and Passion for Long-Term Goals." *Journal of Personality and Social Psychology* 92, no. 6 (2007): 1087–101.

Dudziak, Mary L. *Cold War Civil Rights: Race and the Image of American Democracy.* Politics and Society in Twentieth-Century America. Princeton, NJ: Princeton University Press, 2011.

Dunbar-Ortiz, Roxanne. *An Indigenous Peoples' History of the United States.* Boston: Beacon, 2014.

Elias, Jacquelyn. "Test-Optional Policies Now Dominate Higher Ed." *Chronicle of Higher Education,* November 16, 2022. https://www.chronicle.com/article/test-optional-policies-now-dominate-higher-ed.

Equal Measure and the Lumina Foundation. *Transforming Mindsets, Powering Change: Advancing Equity through Postsecondary Education Policy and Practice.* January 2022. https://static.equalmeasure.org/uploads/2022/01/Jan_LuminaTalentHub_Advancing_Equity0122-2.pdf.

———. *Transforming Mindsets, Powering Change: Getting to the Root.* January 2022. https://static.equalmeasure.org/uploads/2022/01/Jan_LuminaTalentHub-GettingtotheRoot-0122.pdf.

Evans, Stephanie Y. *Black Women in the Ivory Tower, 1850–1954: An Intellectual History.* Gainesville: University Press of Florida, 2007.

"Evanston Local Reparations." City of Evanston, IL. Accessed July 9, 2022. https://www.cityofevanston.org/government/city-council/reparations.

Fabricant, Michael, and Stephen Brier. *Austerity Blues: Fighting for the Soul of Public Higher Education.* Baltimore: Johns Hopkins University Press, 2016.

Fauci, Anthony. "2021 TIME100 Next: Kizzmekia Corbett." *Time*, February 17, 2021. https://time.com/collection/time100-next-2021/5937718/kizzmekia-corbett/.

Fergus, Devin. *Land of the Fee: Hidden Costs and the Decline of the American Middle Class*. New York: Oxford University Press, 2018.

Ferguson, Roderick A. *The Reorder of Things: The University and Its Pedagogies of Minority Difference*. Minneapolis: University of Minnesota Press, 2012.

Flaherty, Colleen. "The Souls of Black Professors." Inside Higher Ed, October 20, 2020. https://www.insidehighered.com/news/2020/10/21/scholars-talk-about-being-black-campus-2020.

Flannery, Mary Ellen. "The Mental Health Crisis on College Campuses." NEA-Today, March 29, 2023. https://www.nea.org/advocating-for-change/new-from-nea/mental-health-crisis-college-campuses.

Ford, Richard Thompson. "How Affirmative Action Was Derailed by Diversity." *Chronicle of Higher Education*, September 16, 2022. https://www.chronicle.com/article/derailed-by-diversity.

Forson, Tracy Scott. "Enslaved Labor Built These Universities. Now They Are Starting to Repay the Debt." *USA TODAY*, February 12, 2020. https://www.usatoday.com/story/news/education/2020/02/12/colleges-slavery-offering-atonement-reparations/2612821001/.

Fox, Mary Jo Tippeconnic (Comanche), Shelly C. Lowe (Navajo), and George S. McClellan. "Where We Have Been: A History of Native American Higher Education." *New Directions for Student Services* 2005, no. 109 (2005): 7–15.

Freire, Paolo. *Pedagogy of the Oppressed*. Translated by Myra Bergman Ramos. New York: Penguin Books, 2017.

Fronius, Trevor, Hannah Persson, Sarah Guckenburg, Nancy Hurley, and Anthony Petrosino. *Restorative Justice in U.S. Schools: A Research Review*. WestEd Justice and Prevention Research Center, February 2016.

Fuller, Thomas. "A New Name for California's Oldest Law School? It's Not Easy." *New York Times*, March 17, 2022. https://www.nytimes.com/2022/03/17/us/new-name-california-law-school.html.

Gabbatt, Adam. "US Rightwing Group Targets Academics with Professor Watchlist." *The Guardian*, September 17, 2021. https://www.theguardian.com/education/2021/sep/17/turning-point-usa-professor-watchlist.

Gannon, Kevin M. "Faculty Evaluation after the Pandemic." *Chronicle of Higher Education*, June 9, 2021. https://www.chronicle.com/article/faculty-evaluation-after-the-pandemic.

——. *Radical Hope: A Teaching Manifesto*. Teaching and Learning in Higher Education. Morgantown: West Virginia University Press, 2020.

García Peña, Lorgia. *Community as Rebellion: A Syllabus for Surviving Academia as a Woman of Color*. Chicago: Haymarket Books, 2022.

Gardner, Lee. "The Truth about Strategic Plans." *Chronicle of Higher Education*, September 29, 2021. https://www.chronicle.com/article/the-truth-about-strategic-plans.

Garner, Julie. "Opening the Doors." *Viewpoints: The Face of Diversity at the University of Washington*, Spring 2008. https://issuu.com/uwalumni/docs/viewpoints_2008spring.

Gasman, Marybeth, Ufuoma Abiola, and Christopher Travers. "Diversity and Senior Leadership at Elite Institutions of Higher Education." *Journal of Diversity in Higher Education* 8, no. 1 (March 2015): 1–14.

Gasman, Marybeth, Thai-Huy Nguyen, and Clifton F. Conrad. "Lives Intertwined: A Primer on the History and Emergence of Minority Serving Institutions." *Journal of Diversity in Higher Education* 8, no. 2 (2015): 120–38.

Gay, Geneva. "Coming of Age Ethnically: Teaching Young Adolescents of Color." *Theory into Practice* 33, no. 3 (1994): 149–55.

——. *Culturally Responsive Teaching: Theory, Research, and Practice.* New York: Teachers College Press, 2018.

——. "Preparing for Culturally Responsive Teaching." *Journal of Teacher Education* 53, no. 2 (March 2002): 106–16. https://doi.org/10.1177/002248710 2053002003.

Geiger, Roger L. *American Higher Education since World War II: A History.* Princeton, NJ: Princeton University Press, 2019.

"Geographical Map of Historical Sundown Towns." History and Social Justice. Accessed September 24, 2023. https://justice.tougaloo.edu/map/.

Gershon, Livia. "Richmond's Robert E. Lee Statue Is Headed to a Black History Museum." *Smithsonian Magazine*, January 5, 2022. https://www.smith sonianmag.com/smart-news/richmond-confederate-monuments-headed-to-black-history-museum-180979319/.

Gibson, Amelia. "The Far-Reaching Effects of How Campuses Treat Senior Faculty of Color." Inside Higher Ed, February 15, 2019. https://www.insidehighered.com/advice/2019/02/15/far-reaching-effects-how-campuses-treat-senior-faculty-color-opinion.

Gluckman, Nell. "Can Colleges Reform Their Police Departments? One Says Yes, and Here's How." *Chronicle of Higher Education*, September 21, 2021. https://www.chronicle.com/article/can-colleges-reform-their-police-depart ments-one-says-yes-and-heres-how.

González, Thalia. "The State of Restorative Justice in American Criminal Law." *Wisconsin Law Review*, no. 6 (2020): 1147–97.

Graff, Gerald, and William E. Cain. "Peace Plan for the Canon Wars." *National Forum* 69, no. 3 (Summer 1989): 7–9.

Grande, Sandy. "Refusing the University." In Tuck and Wang, *Toward What Justice?*, 47–65.

Gruber, Aya. *The Feminist War on Crime: The Unexpected Role of Women's Liberation in Mass Incarceration.* Oakland: University of California Press, 2021.

Gutiérrez y Muhs, Gabriella. *Presumed Incompetent: The Intersections of Race and Class for Women in Academia.* Boulder: University Press of Colorado, 2012.

Hailu, Ruth A., and Olivia C. Scott. "The Half-Century Fight for a Multicultural Center." *Harvard Crimson*, February 15, 2018. https://www.thecrim son.com/article/2018/2/15/fight-for-multicultural-center/.

Hammond, Bruce G. "The SAT and Systemic Racism." Inside Higher Ed, August 17, 2020. https://www.insidehighered.com/admissions/views/2020/08/17/history-sat-reflects-systemic-racism-opinion.

Hammond, Zaretta. *Culturally Responsive Teaching and the Brain: Promoting Authentic Engagement and Rigor among Culturally and Linguistically Diverse Students.* Thousand Oaks, CA: Corwin, 2015.

Hanner, Carol L. "A Sense of Belonging." *Wake Forest Magazine*, October 3, 2018. https://magazine.wfu.edu/2018/10/03/a-sense-of-belonging/.

Harper, Shaun R., and Lori D. Patton. "Access and Equity for African American Students in Higher Education: A Critical Race Historical Analysis of Policy Efforts." *Journal of Higher Education* 80, no. 4 (July–August 2009): 389–414.

Harris, Leslie M., James T. Campbell, and Alfred L. Brophy, eds. *Slavery and the University: Histories and Legacies.* Athens: University of Georgia Press, 2019.

Hartocollis, Anemona. "Harvard Details Its Ties to Slavery and Its Plans for Redress." *New York Times*, April 26, 2022. https://www.nytimes.com/2022/04/26/us/harvard-slavery-redress-fund.html.

Harvey, David. *A Brief History of Neoliberalism.* Oxford: Oxford University Press, 2007.

Hauser, Christine. "Teenage Vandals Were Sentenced to Read Books. Here's What One Learned." *New York Times*, April 5, 2018. https://www.nytimes.com/2018/04/05/books/racist-graffiti-sentenced-read.html.

Haynes, Douglas. "Native American Graves Protection and Repatriation Act (NAGPRA) Survey." Email from University of California, Irvine, August 29, 2022.

Hess, Diana E., and Paula McAvoy. *The Political Classroom: Evidence and Ethics in Democratic Education.* Critical Social Thought. New York: Routledge, 2015.

Hill, Catherine B. "Ending Legacy Admissions Won't End Inequity." *Chronicle of Higher Education*, October 20, 2021. https://www.chronicle.com/article/ending-legacy-admissions-wont-end-inequity.

Hines, Michael, and Thomas Fallace. "Pedagogical Progressivism and Black Education: A Historiographical Review, 1880–1957." *Review of Educational Research* 93, no. 3 (2023): 1–33.

Hirschfield, Paul J., and Katarzyna Celinska. "Beyond Fear: Sociological Perspectives on the Criminalization of School Discipline." *Sociology Compass* 5, no. 1 (January 2011): 1–12.

Hirt, Leeza. "Columbia for Jews? The Untold Story of Seth Low Junior College." *The Current*, Fall 2016. http://www.columbia-current.org/seth_low_junior_college.html.

Hollander, Craig B., and Martha A. Sandweiss. "Princeton and Slavery: Holding the Center." In Harris, Campbell, and Brophy, *Slavery and the University*, 46–64.

Holley, Lynn C., and Sue Steiner. "Safe Space: Student Perspectives on Classroom Environment." *Journal of Social Work Education* 41, no. 1 (January 2005): 49–64.

hooks, bell. *Teaching to Transgress: Education as the Practice of Freedom.* New York: Routledge, 1994.

Hrabowski, Freeman A., III, and Peter H. Henderson. "How to Actually Promote Diversity in STEM." *The Atlantic*, November 29, 2019. https://

www.theatlantic.com/ideas/archive/2019/11/how-umbc-got-minority-stu
dents-stick-stem/602635/.

——. "Nothing Succeeds like Success." *Issues in Science and Technology* (blog),
July 29, 2021. https://issues.org/nothing-succeeds-like-success-underre
presented-minorities-stem/.

——. "Toward a More Diverse Research Community: Models of Success."
Issues in Science and Technology (blog), April 24, 2017. https://issues.org/
toward-a-more-diverse-research-community-models-of-success/.

Hrabowski, Freeman A, Kenneth I. Maton, Monica L. Greene, and Geoffrey L.
Greif. *Overcoming the Odds: Raising Academically Successful African American
Young Women*. Oxford: Oxford University Press, 2002.

Imadali, Eli. "CRT MAP: Critical Race Theory Legislation and Schools."
Chalkbeat, February 1, 2022. https://www.chalkbeat.org/22525983/
map-critical-race-theory-legislation-teaching-racism.

Inoue, Asao B. *Labor-Based Grading Contracts: Building Equity and Inclusion in the
Compassionate Writing Classroom*. Perspectives on Writing. Fort Collins,
CO: WAC Clearinghouse, 2019.

Jack, Jordynn, and Viji Sathy. "It's Time to Cancel the Word 'Rigor.'" *Chronicle
of Higher Education*, September 24, 2021. https://www.chronicle.com/
article/its-time-to-cancel-the-word-rigor.

Jamieson, Patrick C. "Making Their Case: Religion, Pedagogy, and the Slavery
Question at Antebellum Emory College." In Harris, Campbell, and Brophy, *Slavery and the University*, 99–113.

Johnson, Matthew. *Undermining Racial Justice: How One University Embraced Inclusion and Inequality*. Histories of American Education. Ithaca, NY: Cornell
University Press, 2020.

Johnson-Bailey, Juanita, and Ming-Yeh Lee. "Women of Color in the Academy:
Where's Our Authority in the Classroom?" *Feminist Teacher* 15, no. 2
(2005): 111–22.

Joseph, Peniel E. *The Third Reconstruction: America's Struggle for Racial Justice in the
Twenty-First Century*. New York: Basic Books, 2022.

June, Audrey Williams, and Brian O'Leary. "How Many Black Women Have Tenure on Your Campus? Search Here." *Chronicle of Higher Education*, May 27,
2021. https://www.chronicle.com/article/how-many-black-women-have-
tenure-on-your-campus-search-here.

Kaba, Mariame. *We Do This 'til We Free Us: Abolitionist Organizing and Transforming Justice*. Abolitionist Papers Series. Chicago: Haymarket Books, 2021.

Karabel, Jerome. *The Chosen: The Hidden History of Admission and Exclusion at Harvard, Yale, and Princeton*. Boston: Houghton Mifflin, 2005.

Karp, David R. *The Little Book of Restorative Justice for Colleges and Universities:
Repairing Harm and Rebuilding Trust in Response to Student Misconduct*. Inter-
course, PA: Good Books, 2013.

——. "Restorative Justice and Responsive Regulation in Higher Education:
The Complex Web of Campus Sexual Assault Policy in the United States
and a Restorative Alternative." In *Restorative and Responsive Human Services*, edited by Gale Burford, John Braithewaite, and Valerie Braithwaite,
143–64. New York: Routledge, 2019.

Karp, David, and Olivia Frank. "Restorative Justice and Student Development in Higher Education: Expanding 'Offender' Horizons beyond Punishment and Rehabilitation to Community Engagement and Personal Growth." In *Offenders No More: An Interdisciplinary Restorative Justice Dialogue*, edited by Theo Gavrielides, 141–64. New York: Nova Science, 2015.

Kassutto, Maya. "Remains of Children Killed in MOVE Bombing Sat in a Box at Penn Museum for Decades." Billy Penn, April 21, 2021. https://billypenn.com/2021/04/21/move-bombing-penn-museum-bones-remains-princeton-africa/.

Keels, Micere. *Campus Counterspaces: Black and Latinx Students' Search for Community at Historically White Universities*. Ithaca, NY: Cornell University Press, 2019.

Kell, Gretchen. "Kroeber Hall, Honoring Anthropologist Who Symbolizes Exclusion, Is Unnamed." Berkeley News, January 26, 2021. https://news.berkeley.edu/2021/01/26/kroeber-hall-unnamed/.

Kelley, Robin D. G. *Freedom Dreams: The Black Radical Imagination*. Boston: Beacon, 2002.

Kendi, Ibram X. *The Black Campus Movement: Black Students and the Racial Reconstitution of Higher Education, 1965–1972*. New York: Palgrave Macmillan, 2012..

Kishimoto, Kyoko. "Anti-racist Pedagogy: From Faculty's Self-Reflection to Organizing within and beyond the Classroom." *Race Ethnicity and Education* 21, no. 4 (2018): 540–54.

Knott, Katherine. "How One University Went All-In on Restorative Justice." *Chronicle of Higher Education*, October 18, 2016. https://www.chronicle.com/article/how-one-university-went-all-in-on-restorative-justice/.

Knox, Liam. "'Shouting Down an Empty Hallway.'" Inside Higher Ed, February 2, 2023. https://www.insidehighered.com/news/2023/02/03/frustrated-dei-staff-are-leaving-their-jobs.

Koss, Mary P., and Kate Chisholm. "The Time Is Now: Restorative Justice for Sexual Misconduct." *Chronicle of Higher Education*, February 16, 2020. https://www.chronicle.com/article/the-time-is-now-restorative-justice-for-sexual-misconduct/.

Krogstad, Jens Manuel. "Reflecting a Demographic Shift, 109 U.S. Counties Have Become Majority Nonwhite since 2000." Pew Research Center, August 21, 2019. https://www.pewresearch.org/fact-tank/2019/08/21/u-s-counties-majority-nonwhite/.

Krukowski, Rebecca A., Loneke T. Blackman Carr, and Danielle Arigo. "Pandemic-Related Tenure Timeline Extensions in Higher Education in the United States: Prevalence and Associated Characteristics." *Challenges* 13, no. 2 (July 28, 2022): 1–11.

Kunze, Jenna. "University of Kansas Says It Has Native American Remains in Museum Collection." Native News Online, September 21, 2022. https://nativenewsonline.net/sovereignty/university-of-kansas-says-its-has-native-american-remains-in-museum-collection.

Kymlicka, Will. *Multicultural Odysseys: Navigating the New International Politics of Diversity*. Oxford: Oxford University Press, 2007.

Ladson-Billings, Gloria. "But That's Just Good Teaching! The Case for Culturally Relevant Pedagogy." *Theory Into Practice* 34, no. 3 (Summer 1995): 159–65.

———. "From the Achievement Gap to the Education Debt: Understanding Achievement in U.S. Schools." *Educational Researcher* 35, no. 7 (October 1, 2006): 3–12.

———. "Toward a Theory of Culturally Relevant Pedagogy." *American Educational Research Journal* 32, no. 3 (Autumn 1995): 465–91.

Lassabe Shepherd, Lauren. *Resistance from the Right: Conservatives and the Campus Wars in Modern America.* Chapel Hill: University of North Carolina Press, 2023.

Lee, Robert, and Tristan Ahtone. "Land-Grab Universities." *High Country News*, March 30, 2020. https://www.hcn.org/issues/52.4/indigenous-affairs-education-land-grab-universities.

Levien, Simon. "The Crimson Klan." *Harvard Crimson*, March 28, 2021. https://www.thecrimson.com/article/2021/3/25/harvard-klan-scrut/.

Levin, Dan. "No Home, No Wi-Fi: Pandemic Adds to Strain on Poor College Students." *New York Times*, October 22, 2020. https://www.nytimes.com/2020/10/12/us/covid-poor-college-students.html.

Levine, Emily J. *Allies and Rivals: German-American Exchange and the Rise of the Modern Research University.* Chicago: University of Chicago Press, 2021.

———. "It's Time for an Overhaul of Academic Freedom." *Washington Post*, June 9, 2021. https://www.washingtonpost.com/outlook/2021/06/09/its-time-an-overhaul-academic-freedom/.

Lichtenbaum, Rosie. "Corporate Bodies, Disdainful and Aloof: Columbia Fraternities and White Supremacy." 2019. https://columbiaandslavery.colum bia.edu/content/dam/cuandslavery/seminars/hist-3518/2019-projects/Lichtenbaum%202019%20-%20Corporate%20Bodies,%20Disdainful%20and%20Aloof.pdf.

Lippard, Cameron D., J. Scott Carter, and David G. Embrick, eds. *Protecting Whiteness: Whitelash and the Rejection of Racial Equality.* Seattle: University of Washington Press, 2020.

Loewen, James W. *Lies My Teacher Told Me: Everything Your American History Textbook Got Wrong.* New York: New Press, 2018.

Long, Heather, and Danielle Douglas-Gabriel. "The Latest Crisis: Low-Income Students Are Dropping Out of College This Fall in Alarming Numbers." *Washington Post*, September 16, 2020. https://www.washingtonpost.com/business/2020/09/16/college-enrollment-down/.

Lopez, Mark Hugo, Jeffrey Passel, and Molly Rohal. *Modern Immigration Wave Brings 59 Million to U.S., Driving Population Growth and Change through 2065.* Pew Research Center, September 28, 2015. https://www.pewresearch.org/hispanic/wp-content/uploads/sites/5/2015/09/2015-09-28_modern-immigration-wave_REPORT.pdf.

Loss, Christopher P. *Between Citizens and the State: The Politics of American Higher Education in the 20th Century.* Politics and Society in Modern America. Princeton, NJ: Princeton University Press, 2012.

Love, Bettina L. "'Grit Is in Our DNA': Why Teaching Grit Is Inherently Anti-Black." *Education Week*, February 13, 2019. https://www.edweek.org/

leadership/opinion-grit-is-in-our-dna-why-teaching-grit-is-inherently-anti-black/2019/02.

——. *We Want to Do More Than Survive: Abolitionist Teaching and the Pursuit of Educational Freedom*. Boston: Beacon, 2019.

Lovejoy, Bess. "Meet Grandison Harris, the Grave Robber Enslaved (and Then Employed) by the Georgia Medical College." *Smithsonian Magazine*, May 6, 2014. https://www.smithsonianmag.com/history/meet-grandi son-harris-grave-robber-enslaved-and-then-employed-georgia-college-medi cine-180951344/.

Lowman, Emma Battell, and Adam J. Barker. *Settler: Identity and Colonialism in 21st Century Canada*. Halifax: Fernwood, 2015.

Loyola University Maryland. "Restorative Practices—Student Conduct." Accessed July 13, 2022. https://www.loyola.edu/department/student-conduct/restorative-practices (page discontinued).

Lukianoff, Greg, and Jonathan Haidt. *The Coddling of the American Mind: How Good Intentions and Bad Ideas Are Setting Up a Generation for Failure*. New York: Penguin Books, 2018.

Luna, Taryn. "California Task Force Suggests Reparations in Report Detailing Lasting Harms of Slavery." *Los Angeles Times*, June 1, 2022. https://www.latimes.com/california/story/2022-06-01/california-to-unveil-groundbreaking-slavery-reparations-report.

Maines, Sophia. "Trail-Blazing KU Professor Dies at 86." *Lawrence Journal World*, April 27, 2006.

Malkiel, Nancy Weiss. *"Keep the Damned Women Out": The Struggle for Coeducation*. Princeton, NJ: Princeton University Press, 2016.

Mangan, Katherine. "'Disturbing and Even Shocking': Harvard to Spend $100 Million to Atone for 'Immoral' Ties to Slavery." *Chronicle of Higher Education*, April 26, 2022. https://www.chronicle.com/article/disturb ing-and-even-shocking-harvard-to-spend-100-million-to-atone-for-immoral-ties-to-slavery.

——. "Enrolling Diverse Students When Race Is Off the Table." *Chronicle of Higher Education*, September 2, 2022. https://www.chronicle.com/article/after-affirmative-action.

——. "'More Cowardly Than Cautious': Faculty Decry College Leaders' Silence on DEI Attacks." *Chronicle of Higher Education*, May 25, 2023. https://www.chronicle.com/article/more-cowardly-than-cautious-faculty-decry-college-leaders-silence-on-dei-attacks.

——. "Students Demand That More Colleges Break Ties with the Local Police." *Chronicle of Higher Education*, June 2, 2020. https://www.chronicle.com/article/students-demand-that-more-colleges-break-ties-with-the-local-police.

——. "Why More Colleges Are Trying Restorative Justice in Sex-Assault Cases." *Chronicle of Higher Education*, September 17, 2018. https://www.chronicle.com/article/why-more-colleges-are-trying-restorative-jus tice-in-sex-assault-cases/.

Merrell, James H. "Declarations of Independence: Indian-White Relations in the New World." In *The American Revolution: Its Character and Limit*,

edited by Jack P. Green, 197–223. New York: New York University Press, 1989.

Mettler, Suzanne. *Soldiers to Citizens: The G.I. Bill and the Making of the Greatest Generation.* Oxford: Oxford University Press, 2005.

Michigan State University, American Indian and Indigenous Studies. "Land Acknowledgement." Accessed July 12, 2022. https://aiis.msu.edu/land/.

Monzó, Lilia D., and Suzanne SooHoo. "Translating the Academy: Learning the Racialized Languages of Academia." *Journal of Diversity in Higher Education* 7, no. 3 (2014): 147–65.

Morris, J. Brent. " 'I Have at Last Found My Sphere': The Unintentional Development of a Female Abolitionist Stronghold in Antebellum New England." In Harris, Campbell, and Brophy, *Slavery and The University*, 197–214.

Movement for Black Lives. "Reparations." February 21, 2019. https://perma.cc/G6KU-GKC5.

Nash, Margaret A. "Entangled Pasts: Land-Grant Colleges and American Indian Dispossession." *History of Education Quarterly* 59, no. 4 (November 2019): 437–67. https://doi.org/10.1017/heq.2019.31.

——. *Women's Education in the United States, 1780–1840.* New York: Palgrave Macmillan, 2005.

National Center for Education Statistics. "Digest of Education Statistics, 2018." October 2018. https://nces.ed.gov/programs/digest/d18/tables/dt18_306.10.asp.

——. "Fast Facts: Race/Ethnicity of College Faculty, Fall 2021." 2023. https://nces.ed.gov/fastfacts/display.asp?id=61.

National Student Clearinghouse Research Center. *Current Term Enrollment Estimates, Spring 2022.* June 14, 2022. https://nscresearchcenter.org/wp-content/uploads/CTEE_Report_Spring_2022.pdf.

New York Times. "Missing From Science Class." Editorial, December 10, 2013. https://www.nytimes.com/2013/12/11/opinion/too-few-girls-and-minorities-study-tech-subjects.html.

——. "Some Colleges Have More Students from the Top 1 Percent Than the Bottom 60. Find Yours." January 18, 2017. https://www.nytimes.com/interactive/2017/01/18/upshot/some-colleges-have-more-students-from-the-top-1-percent-than-the-bottom-60.html.

Newfield, Christopher. *The Great Mistake: How We Wrecked Public Universities and How We Can Fix Them.* Critical University Studies. Baltimore: Johns Hopkins University Press, 2016.

——. *Unmaking the Public University: The Forty-Year Assault on the Middle Class.* Cambridge, MA: Harvard University Press, 2008.

Newkirk, Pamela. *Diversity, Inc.* New York: Hachette, 2019.

Ngu, Ash, and Andrea Suozzo. "Does Your Local Museum or University Still Have Native American Remains?" ProPublica, January 11, 2023. https://projects.propublica.org/repatriation-nagpra-database/.

Nixon, Monica L. "Experiences of Women of Color University Chief Diversity Officers." *Journal of Diversity in Higher Education* 10, no. 4 (December 2017): 301–17.

Oakland University. "Ambassador Dr. Augustine Pounds Connects with Her Roots." March 5, 2010. https://ucmapps.oakland.edu/NewsArchive/Data/20100305-Ambassador-Dr-Augustine-Pounds-connects-with-her-roots.html.

——. "The Black Alumni Association." Accessed August 6, 2021. https://library.oakland.edu/archives/baa/index.php.

Oakland University Magazine. "Up Front." Summer 1985.

Oast, Jennifer Bridges. "Negotiating the Honor Culture: Students and Slaves at Three Virginia Colleges." In Harris, Campbell, and Brophy, *Slavery and the University*, 84–98.

O'Brien, Katie. "It's Complicated: The University of Chicago's Relationship with Its Neighbors." WBEZ Chicago, April 20, 2019. https://www.wbez.org/stories/its-complicated-the-university-of-chicagos-relationship-with-its-neighbors/4882b290-40d8-4730-bb68-2eaea92be0bc.

Okechukwu, Amaka. *To Fulfill These Rights: Political Struggle over Affirmative Action and Open Admissions.* New York: Columbia University Press, 2019.

Oregon State University, Diversity & Cultural Engagement. "Lonnie B. Harris Black Cultural Center." November 2, 2016. https://dce.oregonstate.edu/bcc.

Oxner, Reese. "UT-Austin Says It Will Keep 'The Eyes of Texas' as School Song, but Will Rename Buildings as Black Students Call for Change." *Texas Tribune,* July 13, 2020. https://www.texastribune.org/2020/07/13/university-texas-austin-eyes-texas/.

Pickett, Clyde Wilson, Elizabeth F. Ortiz, Vernese Edghill-Walden, James A. Felton III, David H. Garcia, Amoaba Gooden, Donald A. Outing, et al. *A Framework for Advancing an Anti-racism Strategy on Campus.* National Association of Diversity Officers in Higher Education (NADOHE), 2021.

Pilkington, Ed. "Bones of Black Children Killed in Police Bombing Used in Ivy League Anthropology Course." *The Guardian,* April 23, 2021. http://www.theguardian.com/us-news/2021/apr/22/move-bombing-black-children-bones-philadelphia-princeton-pennsylvania.

Pittman, Edward. "Why I Came Back: An Alumni Perspective." *Diverse: Issues in Higher Education,* June 8, 2021. https://www.diverseeducation.com/demographics/african-american/article/15109397/why-i-came-back-an-alumni-perspective.

Platt, Anthony M. "End Game: The Rise and Fall of Affirmative Action in Higher Education." *Social Justice* 24, no. 2 (68) (1997): 103–18.

Postsecondary National Policy Institute. "Factsheets: First-Generation Students." November 2021. https://pnpi.org/first-generation-students/.

President's Council of Advisors on Science and Technology. *Engage to Excel: Producing One Million Additional College Graduates with Degrees in Science, Technology, Engineering, and Mathematics.* February 2012. https://obamawhitehouse.archives.gov/sites/default/files/microsites/ostp/pcast-engage-to-excel-final_2-25-12.pdf.

Princeton University. "History—Carl A. Fields Center for Equality + Cultural Understanding." Accessed August 6, 2021. http://fieldscenter.princeton.edu/history.

Princeton University Office of Communications. "Princeton Receives Report Detailing Inquiry into University's Role in Handling of MOVE Bombing Remains." August 31, 2021. https://www.princeton.edu/news/2021/08/31/princeton-receives-report-detailing-inquiry-universitys-role-handling-move-bombing.

Pryal, Katie Rose Guest. "When 'Rigor' Targets Disabled Students." *Chronicle of Higher Education*, October 6, 2022. https://www.chronicle.com/article/when-rigor-targets-disabled-students.

Purnell, Derecka. *Becoming Abolitionists: Police, Protests, and the Pursuit of Freedom.* London: Verso, 2021.

Ray, Victor. *On Critical Race Theory: Why It Matters & Why You Should Care.* New York: Random House, 2022.

Reichelmann, Ashley V., and Matthew O. Hunt. "How We Repair It: White Americans' Attitudes toward Reparations." Brookings Institution, December 8, 2021. https://www.brookings.edu/blog/how-we-rise/2021/12/08/how-we-repair-it-white-americans-attitudes-toward-reparations/.

Renihan, Colleen, John Spilker, and Trudi Wright, eds. *Sound Pedagogy: Radical Care in Music.* Urbana: University of Illinois Press, forthcoming.

Renschler, Emily S., and Janet Monge. "The Samuel George Morton Cranial Collection." *Expedition Magazine* 50, no. 3 (November 2008): 30–38.

Reyhner, John. "1819–2013: A History of American Indian Education." *Education Week*, December 3, 2013. https://www.edweek.org/leadership/1819-2013-a-history-of-american-indian-education/2013/12.

Reyhner, Jon, and Jeanne Eder. *American Indian Education: A History.* 2nd ed. Norman: University of Oklahoma Press, 2017.

Richtel, Matt. " 'It's Life or Death': The Mental Health Crisis among U.S. Teens." *New York Times*, April 23, 2022. https://www.nytimes.com/2022/04/23/health/mental-health-crisis-teens.html.

Rojas, Fabio. *From Black Power to Black Studies: How a Radical Social Movement Became an Academic Discipline.* Baltimore: Johns Hopkins University Press, 2007.

Rooks, Noliwe. *White Money/Black Power: The Surprising History of African American Studies and the Crisis of Race in Higher Education.* Boston: Beacon, 2006.

Ross, Abbi. "Native American Students Can Now Attend U. of California Tuition-Free." *Chronicle of Higher Education*, April 27, 2022. https://www.chronicle.com/article/native-american-students-can-now-attend-u-of-california-tuition-free.

Rothstein, Richard. *The Color of Law: A Forgotten History of How Our Government Segregated America.* New York: Liveright, 2017.

San Francisco State University, Equity & Community Inclusion Unit. "Brief History of Black Student Centers." Accessed June 27, 2021. https://equity.sfsu.edu/center-history.

Sanders, Robert. "Chan Zuckerberg Initiative Launches Effort to Increase Diversity of STEM Students." Berkeley News, April 9, 2019. https://news.berkeley.edu/2019/04/09/chan-zuckerberg-initiative-launches-effort-to-increase-diversity-of-stem-students/.

Sathy, Viji, and Kelly A. Hogan. "How to Make Your Teaching More Inclusive." *Chronicle of Higher Education*, July 22, 2019. https://www.chronicle.com/article/how-to-make-your-teaching-more-inclusive/.

Sawchuk, Stephen. "What Is Critical Race Theory, and Why Is It under Attack?" *Education Week*, May 18, 2021. https://www.edweek.org/leadership/what-is-critical-race-theory-and-why-is-it-under-attack/2021/05.

Schrecker, Ellen. "The 50-Year War on Higher Education." *Chronicle of Higher Education*, October 14, 2022. https://www.chronicle.com/article/the-50-year-war-on-higher-education.

Selingo, Jeffrey J. *College (Un)Bound: The Future of Higher Education and What It Means for Students*. Boston: New Harvest, 2013.

Silva, Daniella. "Study Finds 43 Percent of Harvard's White Students Are Legacy, Athletes, Related to Donors or Staff." NBC News, September 13, 2019. https://www.nbcnews.com/news/us-news/study-harvard-finds-43-percent-white-students-are-legacy-athletes-n1060361.

Simmons, Ruth J. "Slavery and Justice at Brown: A Personal Reflection." In Harris, Campbell, and Brophy, *Slavery and the University*, 215–23.

Skidmore College. "College Launches Restorative Justice Project." August 24, 2015. https://www.skidmore.edu/news/2015/0824-new-restorative-justice-program-launched.php.

Slaughter, Sheila, and Gary Rhoades. *Academic Capitalism and the New Economy: Markets, State, and Higher Education*. Baltimore: Johns Hopkins University Press, 2009.

Smith, Mitch, and Julie Bosman. "Congress Told Colleges to Return Native Remains. What's Taking So Long?" *New York Times*, September 15, 2022. https://www.nytimes.com/2022/09/15/us/native-american-remains-university-of-north-dakota.html.

Spitalniak, Lauren. "Colleges Seek Better Ways to Rename Buildings." Higher Ed Dive, March 22, 2022. https://www.highereddive.com/news/colleges-seek-better-ways-to-rename-buildings/620725/.

Staples, Andrew. "Ancestral Land in Butte Creek Canyon Returned to the Mechoopda Tribe." Chico State Today, September 23, 2022. https://today.csuchico.edu/bcep-transfered-to-mechoopda-tribe/.

Stein, Sharon. *Unsettling the University: Confronting the Colonial Foundations of US Higher Education*. Critical University Studies. Baltimore: Johns Hopkins University Press, 2022.

Stephens, Nicole M., Stephanie A. Fryberg, Hazel Rose Markus, Camille S. Johnson, and Rebecca Covarrubias. "Unseen Disadvantage: How American Universities' Focus on Independence Undermines the Academic Performance of First-Generation College Students." *Journal of Personality and Social Psychology* 102, no. 6 (2012): 1178–97. https://doi.org/10.1037/a0027143.

Sto. Domingo, Mariano R., Starlette Sharp, Amy Freeman, Thomas Freeman, Keith Harmon, Mitsue Wiggs, Viji Sathy, et al. "Replicating Meyerhoff for Inclusive Excellence in STEM." *Science* 364, no. 6438 (April 26, 2019): 335–37.

Stokas, Ariana González. *Reparative Universities: Why Diversity Alone Won't Solve Racism in Higher Ed.* Baltimore: Johns Hopkins University Press, 2023.

Stommel, Jesse. "Ungrading: A Bibliography." *Jesse Stommel* (blog), March 3, 2020. https://www.jessestommel.com/ungrading-a-bibliography/.

Stovall, Tyler. *White Freedom: The Racial History of an Idea.* Princeton, NJ: Princeton University Press, 2021.

Subbaraman, Nidhi. "How #BlackInTheIvory Put a Spotlight on Racism in Academia." *Nature* 582, no. 7812 (June 11, 2020): 327.

Supiano, Beckie. "The Redefinition of Rigor." *Chronicle of Higher Education*, March 29, 2022. https://www.chronicle.com/article/the-redefinition-of-rigor.

Suran, Melissa. "Keeping Black Students in STEM." *Proceedings of the National Academy of Sciences* 118, no. 23 (June 8, 2021). https://doi.org/10.1073/pnas.2108401118.

Swarns, Rachel L. "The Seminary Flourished on Slave Labor. Now It's Planning to Pay Reparations." *New York Times*, September 12, 2019. https://www.nytimes.com/2019/09/12/us/virginia-seminary-reparations.html.

Swarthmore College Black Cultural Center. "Our History: Formation of the Center." July 8, 2014. https://www.swarthmore.edu/black-cultural-center/our-history-formation-center.

Taylor, Keeanga-Yamahtta. "The End of Black Politics." *New York Times*, June 13, 2020. https://www.nytimes.com/2020/06/13/opinion/sunday/black-politicians-george-floyd-protests.html.

Texas State University. "History, Student Initiatives, Institutional Inclusive Excellence." January 8, 2016. https://www.sdi.txstate.edu/About/History.html (page discontinued).

Thelin, John R. *A History of American Higher Education.* 2nd ed. Baltimore: Johns Hopkins University Press, 2011.

Thomas, James M. *Diversity Regimes: Why Talk Is Not Enough to Fix Racial Inequality at Universities.* New Brunswick, NJ: Rutgers University Press, 2020.

Thomas, Zoe. "The Hidden Links between Slavery and Wall Street." BBC News, August 28, 2019. https://www.bbc.com/news/business-49476247.

Tryens-Fernandes, Savannah. "University of Alabama Has More Than 10,000 Native American Remains, Largest Number Cataloged by Park Service." AL.com, September 8, 2022. https://www.al.com/news/2022/09/university-of-alabama-has-more-than-10000-native-american-remains-largest-number-cataloged-by-park-service.html.

Tuck, Eve, and K. Wayne Yang. "Decolonization Is Not a Metaphor." *Decolonization: Indigeneity, Education & Society* 1, no. 1 (2012): 1–40.

——. "Introduction: Born under the Rising Sign of Social Justice." In Tuck and Wang, *Toward What Justice?*, 1–17.

——, eds. *Toward What Justice? Describing Diverse Dreams of Justice in Education.* New York: Routledge, 2018.

University of Illinois Urbana-Champaign, Bruce D. Nesbitt African American Cultural Center. "History." Accessed June 27, 2021. https://oiir.illinois.edu/bnaacc/about-bnaacc/history.

University of Kansas, Office of Multicultural Affairs. "Our Story." February 20, 2013. https://oma.ku.edu/our-story.

University of Michigan Center for Social Solutions. "The History of Diversity in Higher Education, ALI Series Part I." Accessed June 26, 2021. https://lsa.umich.edu/social-solutions/news-events/news/insights-and-solutions/infographics/ali-series-part-i---the-history-of-diversity-in-higher-education.html (page discontinued).

University of San Diego. "Center for Restorative Justice." Accessed July 12, 2022. https://www.sandiego.edu/soles/restorative-justice/.

University of Southern California, La CASA. "Nuestra Historia & Our Name." Accessed August 23, 2021. https://lacasa.usc.edu/about/history/.

University of Tennessee, Knoxville, Multicultural Student Life. "History of the Black Cultural Center." Accessed June 27, 2021. https://studentlife.utk.edu/multicultural/history/history-of-the-black-cultural-center/.

University of Virginia. "President's Commission on Slavery and the University." Accessed July 12, 2022. https://slavery.virginia.edu/.

University of Wisconsin–Madison, Multicultural Student Center. "Black Cultural Center." Accessed June 27, 2021. https://msc.wisc.edu/identity-centers/black-cultural-center/.

US Census Bureau. "2014 National Population Projections Tables." 2014. https://www.census.gov/data/tables/2014/demo/popproj/2014-summary-tables.html.

US Department of Education. "50th Anniversary of the Federal TRIO Programs: Celebrating 50 Years of Providing Hope and Opportunity for Success." 2014. https://www2.ed.gov/about/offices/list/ope/trio/trio50anniv-factsheet.pdf.

——. "Percent of Undergraduate Students Receiving Pell Grants." National Center for Education Statistics: Trend Generator. Accessed March 23, 2021. https://nces.ed.gov/ipeds/TrendGenerator/app/answer/8/35.

US Department of the Interior, Indian Affairs. "Gover Apologizes For BIA's Misdeeds." September 8, 2000. https://www.bia.gov/as-ia/opa/online-press-release/gover-apologizes-bias-misdeeds.

Valenti, Denise. "University Dedicates Marker Addressing the Complex Legacy of Woodrow Wilson." Princeton University News, October 10, 2019. https://www.princeton.edu/news/2019/10/10/university-dedicates-marker-addressing-complex-legacy-woodrow-wilson.

Vassar College. "The History of Africana Studies at Vassar College—150 Years, Vassar's Sesquicentennial." Accessed August 23, 2021. https://150.vassar.edu/histories/africana-studies/index.html.

Wake Forest University Intercultural Center. "Diversity @ Wake." Accessed August 6, 2021. https://interculturalcenter.wfu.edu/diversity-wake/.

Whitley, Sarah E., Grace Benson, and Alexis Wesaw. *A Landscape Analysis of Programs and Services at Four Year Institutions*. Washington, DC: Center for First-Generation Student Success/NASPA, 2018.

Wilder, Craig Steven. *Ebony & Ivy: Race, Slavery, and the Troubled History of America's Universities*. New York: Bloomsbury, 2013.

——. "'Sons from the Southward & Some from the West Indies': The Academy and Slavery in Revolutionary America." In Harris, Campbell, and Brophy, *Slavery and the University*, 21–45.

Williams, R. Owen. "Forgetting Slavery at Yale and Transylvania." In Harris, Campbell, and Brophy, *Slavery and the University*, 315–37.

Winograd, Greta, Jay Verkuilen, Alison Weingarten, and Lucy Walker. "Educational Opportunity Program (EOP) at a Selective Public University: Initial Findings from a Longitudinal Evaluation Study." *Learning Assistance Review* 23, no. 1 (2018): 61–93.

Wolfe, Patrick. "Settler Colonialism and the Elimination of the Native." *Journal of Genocide Research* 8, no. 4 (2006): 387–409.

Wolf-Wendel, Lisa. *Reflecting Back, Looking Forward: Civil Rights and Student Affairs*. Washington, DC: NASPA, 2004.

Wright, Will. "Seminary Built on Slavery and Jim Crow Labor Has Begun Paying Reparations." *New York Times*, May 31, 2021. https://www.nytimes.com/2021/05/31/us/reparations-virginia-theological-seminary.html.

Yale University, Afro-American Cultural Center. "History." Accessed August 6, 2021. https://afam.yalecollege.yale.edu/about-house/history.

Yale University, La Casa Cultural: Latino Cultural Center. "History." Accessed August 6, 2021. https://lacasa.yalecollege.yale.edu/about-us/history.

YaleNews. "Yale to Change Calhoun College's Name to Honor Grace Murray Hopper." February 11, 2017. https://news.yale.edu/2017/02/11/yale-change-calhoun-college-s-name-honor-grace-murray-hopper-0.

Yamane, David. *Student Movements for Multiculturalism: Challenging the Curricular Color Line in Higher Education*. Baltimore: Johns Hopkins University Press, 2001.

Young, Jeffrey R. "We Know How to Diversify STEM Fields. The Challenge Is Spreading What Works." EdSurge, July 27, 2021. https://www.edsurge.com/news/2021-07-27-we-know-how-to-diversify-stem-fields-the-challenge-is-spreading-what-works.

Zamudio-Suarez, Fernanda. "Colleges Are Waiving Tuition for Native Students. Is Your Institution Next?" *Chronicle of Higher Education*, June 21, 2022. https://www.chronicle.com/newsletter/race-on-campus/2022-06-21.

——. "5 Colleges You Might Not Know Are Tied to Slaveholders." *Chronicle of Higher Education*, December 15, 2020. https://www.chronicle.com/newsletter/race-on-campus/2020-12-15.

Zehr, Howard. *The Little Book of Restorative Justice*. Revised and updated ed. The Little Books of Justice & Peacebuilding. New York: Good Books, 2015.

Index

ableism, 105
abolitionism, 4, 26–27, 162, 175–76
Abrams, Stacey, 122
academic freedom, 100–104
academic rigor, 104–8
academic social contract, 101
achievement gap, 120, 124
Addison, Kathitha, 55*f*
admissions, 36–38, 48, 51, 58, 123, 127, 128, 130, 170. *See also* affirmative action
affirmative action, 72–74, 76, 80, 170
African Americans
  and civil rights movement, 57–61
  and desegregation, 49–51
  excluded from higher education, 29–30, 33–35, 42–47
  and GI Bill, 49
  See also Black women
African American studies departments, 63–64
African resettlement, 26–27
Agricultural College Act (Morrill Act, 1862), 15–19, 44, 157
Ahmed, Sarah, 54, 82, 94, 95, 102, 103, 112
Ahtone, Tristan, 16, 18–19
allyship, 88–89
American Association of University Professors (AAUP), 101
American Colonization Society (ACS), 26–27
American Indian Chicago Conference (1961), 54, 55*f*
American Indian Movement, 54
Angel, Thomas, 138–39
antiracist pedagogy, 111, 114, 117, 118
Ashburn, Virginia, 162–63
Asian American Political Alliance, 62*f*
Asimov, Isaac, 37

Assata's Daughters, 166
assimilation, of Native Americans, 30, 39–41

Bacone College, 40
Bacow, Lawrence, 155
Bakke, Allan, 72, 74
Bakke v. Regents of California (1978), 72–74, 76
Baldwin, Davarian, 174, 175
Banks, James A., 110
Barnard College, 34
Batwai, Sam, 145*f*
Beckert, Sven, 143
Berlin, Isaiah, 101
Bernstein, Elizabeth, 165
bias reporting systems, 161–62
Bird-Pollan, Jennifer, 171
Black colleges, 43. *See also* HBCUs (historically black colleges and universities)
Black Greek Letter Organizations (BGLOs), 45–46
#BlackInTheIvory, 93
Black student unions, 53, 59, 60, 66–67
Black women
  excluded from higher education, 33–35, 44–45
  and retributive justice for sexual assault, 165
  and student activism, 65–67
  as underrepresented in faculty, 93
Bloom, Allan, 78
boarding school system, 40–41, 42, 56
Bonilla-Silva, Eduardo, 73–74
Boostrom, Robert, 113
Brigham, Carl, 37
Brophy, Alfred F., 26, 141–42
Brown, Mary Elizabeth, 95
Brown University, 142–43
Brown v. Board of Education (1954), 49–51, 57, 80